JN032851

鳥取県の教員採用試験過去問シリーズ❺

2025年度版

鳥取県の 英語科

過去問

協同教育研究会 編

協同出版

本書には，鳥取県の教員採用試験の過去問題を
収録しています。各問題ごとに，以下のように5段
階表記で，難易度，頻出度を示しています。

難 易 度

非常に難しい ☆☆☆☆☆
やや難しい ☆☆☆☆
普通の難易度 ☆☆☆
やや易しい ☆☆
非常に易しい ☆

頻 出 度

◎ ほとんど出題されない
◎◎ あまり出題されない
◎◎◎ 普通の頻出度
◎◎◎◎ よく出題される
◎◎◎◎◎ 非常によく出題される

※本書の過去問題における資料，法令文等の取り扱いについて
　本書の過去問題で使用されている資料や法令文の表記や基準は，出題さ
れた当時の内容に準拠しているため，解答・解説も当時のものを使用して
います。ご了承ください。

はじめに〜「過去問」シリーズ利用に際して〜

　教育を取り巻く環境は変化しつつあり，日本の公教育そのものも，教員免許更新制の廃止やGIGAスクール構想の実現などの改革が進められています。また，現行の学習指導要領では「主体的・対話的で深い学び」を実現するため，指導方法や指導体制の工夫改善により，「個に応じた指導」の充実を図るとともに，コンピュータや情報通信ネットワーク等の情報手段を活用するために必要な環境を整えることが示されています。

　一方で，いじめや体罰，不登校，暴力行為など，教育現場の問題もあいかわらず取り沙汰されており，教員に求められるスキルは，今後さらに高いものになっていくことが予想されます。

　本書の基本構成としては，出題傾向と対策，過去5年間の出題傾向分析表，過去問題，解答および解説を掲載しています。各自治体や教科によって掲載年数をはじめ，「チェックテスト」や「問題演習」を掲載するなど，内容が異なります。

　また原則的には一般受験を対象としております。特別選考等については対応していない場合があります。なお，実際に配布された問題の順番や構成を，編集の都合上，変更している場合があります。あらかじめご了承ください。

　最後に，この「過去問」シリーズは，「参考書」シリーズとの併用を前提に編集されております。参考書で要点整理を行い，過去問で実力試しを行う，セットでの活用をおすすめいたします。

　みなさまが，この書籍を徹底的に活用し，教員採用試験の合格を勝ち取って，教壇に立っていただければ，それはわたくしたちにとって最上の喜びです。

協同教育研究会

C O N T E N T S

第1部 鳥取県の英語科
　　　　出題傾向分析 ……………3

第2部 鳥取県の
　　　　教員採用試験実施問題 ……………9

第1部

鳥取県の
英語科
出題傾向分析

鳥取県の英語科　傾向と対策

【中学校】

　2024年度は，法令・学習指導要領関係1題，文法・語法1題，語順整序1題，読解2題，英語教育関係の英作文1題の合計6題であった。大問数は2020年度が8題，2021・2022年度が7題，そして2023年度からが6題であり，やや減少傾向にある。配点は大問1から順に，20点(教職の法令関係8点・英語の学習指導要領関係12点)，30点，30点，25点，30点，45点である。

　2019年度から，教育に関係する法令および学習指導要領に関する出題が継続している。選択式の問題が多いが，適語を書かせる問題なども見られる。教員公務員特例法，教育基本法，中央教育審議会で取りまとめられた答申など，出題は幅広い。日ごろから教育に関する最新情報に対してアンテナを張っておく必要があるだろう。

　文法・語法問題は，空所補充形式で出題されている。基本的な単語やイディオムなどが問われる基礎的な内容であり，小問数は10とほどよい数なので，過去問で解けない問題が多いようであれば，単語集や，大学受験レベルの四択問題集を一通り学習しておく必要がある。

　整序問題も基本的な内容を問われている問題が多い。与えられた文の一部を手がかりに，時制，文型，仮定法，前置詞などに注意して，一緒に使う語句のかたまりを作っていけば解ける問題である。無生物主語の構文が代表であるが，「なぜ彼女はそうしたか。」ではなく，「何が彼女をそうさせたか。」と表現する英語の特徴をつかんでおくことが重要である。整序問題に特化した問題集で，多様な文の構成を覚えることも役立つ。

　読解問題は，語句の補充・タイトル選択・日本語による記述問題からなる。英文量は少なめである。いろいろな話題に対応して内容をつかみ，情報を素早く処理する力が求められている。

　配点が最も高いのが，英語教育関係の英作文問題である。実際の授業を想定し，モデル文を完成させる問題が中心である。対象となる学年が指定されていることから，対象生徒のレベルを考慮した英文を書くこと

が求められていることに留意する。これらの問題に対する対策としては，普段から現行の教科書に目を通すこと，英語教育関係の雑誌や専門書などを読むことで，実際の授業をどう行っていくかをイメージしておくことが大切である。

【高等学校】

　2024年度の出題は，リスニング1題，教育に関する法令関係および学習指導要領関係1題，英作文1題，読解5題の合計8題である。ここ数年間，英作文問題や文法・語法問題の出題数が流動的である。配点は大問1から順に，20点，20点(教職の法令関係8点・英語の学習指導要領関係12点)，20点，40点，25点，35点，20点，20点である。

　リスニング問題は，英文とそれに関する質問を聞いて適切な答えを選択する問題であり，問題数は多くない。出題形式も年度によって若干の変更があるので，2024年度の形式にとらわれることなく，様々なリスニング問題を多くこなしておくことが有効である。自分で無理なく聞き取れるレベルから徐々にレベルを上げていくことが大事である。

　学習指導要領の空所補充問題については，暗記したことを使いながらも，普通の読解問題と同様に空所の前後を丁寧に読み，慌てず冷静に答えたい。また学習指導要領に関しては，ただ闇雲に読んで記憶するだけでなく，それを踏まえて実際の授業をどのように運営していくかなどをイメージしながら読んでいくと，様々な問題に対応しやすくなる。大問8は読解問題に絡めつつも，与えられた題材で言語活動をどのように展開していくかを書かせる問題となっている。

　整序作文については，上記【中学校】を参照のこと。和文英訳問題は，文が長くてかたい日本語である。そのまま英訳しようとせず，日本語自体を近似の意味に変えたり，文の構成を変えたりして書きやすくする必要がある。似たような過去問で，いろいろな表現をストックしておこう。

　読解問題については，中学校とは異なり，様々な記述式の問題が出題されていることに留意したい。記述式の内容理解問題は，問題の解答と対応する箇所の英文を和訳すれば正答できる問題が多いが，対応する箇所を特定する必要がある。小問数も多く，かつ小問も複数の設問から構

成されている問題や内容を整理して記述することが求められる問題があるため，速読力が必要である。全体的には大学入試レベルの英文が多く，複雑な文もなく，読み易いものが多く出題されているが，内容がやや抽象的な英文もある。対策としては，大学入試の読解問題集を何冊か仕上げ，様々なトピックに触れておくことが挙げられる。さらに分野別に必要とされる単語やイディオムなどを整理しておくのも対策となるだろう。

過去5年間の出題傾向分析

中学＝● 高校＝▲ 中高共通＝◎

分類	設問形式	2020年度	2021年度	2022年度	2023年度	2024年度
リスニング	内容把握		◎	◎	▲	▲
発音・アクセント	発音					
	アクセント					
	文強勢					
文法・語法	空所補充	●▲	●▲	●▲	●▲	●
	正誤判断					
	一致語句					
	連立完成					
	その他	●			▲	
会話文	短文会話					
	長文会話					
文章読解	空所補充	●▲	●▲	●▲	●▲	●▲
	内容一致文	▲	●▲	●	●	
	内容一致語句	●▲	●	●	●▲	
	内容記述	●▲	▲	▲	●▲	●▲
	英文和訳	●	●	●	●▲	▲
	英問英答			▲		
	その他	●▲	●▲	●▲	▲	●▲
英作文	整序	●		●	●	●
	和文英訳	●▲	▲	●▲	▲	▲
	自由英作	●	●	●	●	●▲
	その他		●▲	●▲	●▲	●
学習指導要領		●▲	●▲	●▲	●▲	●▲

第2部

鳥取県の
教員採用試験
実施問題

2024年度　実施問題

【中学校】

【1】次の各問いに答えなさい。

(1) 次の文は，地方公務員法に規定される服務に関する条文である。①～⑥の中で，誤っているものをすべて選び，記号で答えなさい。

---

① すべて職員は，全体の奉仕者として児童・生徒の利益のために勤務し，且つ，職務の遂行に当つては，全力を挙げてこれに専念しなければならない。

② 職員は，その職務を遂行するに当つて，法令，条例，地方公共団体の規則及び地方公共団体の機関の定める規程に従い，且つ，校長の職務上の命令に忠実に従わなければならない。

③ 職員は，その職の信用を傷つけ，又は職員の職全体の不名誉となるような行為をしてはならない。

④ 職員は，職務上知り得た秘密を漏らしてはならない。その職を退いた後は，その限りではない。

⑤ 職員は，法律又は条例に特別の定がある場合を除く外，その勤務時間及び職務上の注意力のすべてをその職責遂行のために用い，当該地方公共団体がなすべき責を有する職務にのみ従事しなければならない。

⑥ 職員は，政党その他の政治的団体の結成に関与し，若しくはこれらの団体の役員となつてはならず，又はこれらの団体の構成員となるように，若しくはならないように勧誘運動をしてはならない。

---

(2) 次の文章は，令和3年1月に中央教育審議会で取りまとめられた「『令和の日本型学校教育』の構築を目指して～全ての子供たちの可能性を引き出す，個別最適な学びと，協働的な学びの実現～(答申)」

における「第Ⅰ部　総論」の「3. 2020年代を通じて実現すべき『令和の日本型学校教育』の姿」に記載された内容の一部である。（　①　）～（　③　）にあてはまる最も適切な語句を答えなさい。

第Ⅰ部　総論

3. 2020年代を通じて実現すべき「令和の日本型学校教育」の姿

---

(1)　子供の学び

○　新型コロナウイルス感染症の感染拡大による臨時休業の長期化により，多様な子供一人一人が自立した学習者として学び続けていけるようになっているか，という点が改めて焦点化されたところであり，これからの学校教育においては，子供が(　①　)も活用しながら自ら学習を調整しながら学んでいくことができるよう，「個に応じた指導」を充実することが必要である。この「個に応じた指導」の在り方を，より具体的に示すと以下のとおりである。

○　全ての子供に基礎的・基本的な知識・技能を確実に習得させ，思考力・判断力・表現力等や，自ら学習を調整しながら粘り強く学習に取り組む態度等を育成するためには，教師が支援の必要な子供により重点的な指導を行うことなどで効果的な指導を実現することや，子供一人一人の特性や学習進度，学習到達度等に応じ，指導方法・教材や学習時間等の柔軟な提供・設定を行うことなどの「指導の(　②　)」が必要である。

○　基礎的・基本的な知識・技能等や，言語能力，情報活用能力，問題発見・解決能力等の学習の基盤となる資質・能力等を土台として，幼児期からの様々な場を通じての体験活動から得た子供の興味・関心・キャリア形成の方向性等に応じ，探究において課題の設定，情報の収集，整理・分析，まとめ・表現を行う等，教師が子供一人一人に応じた

11

　　　学習活動や学習課題に取り組む機会を提供することで，子
　　供自身が学習が最適となるよう調整する「学習の(③)」
　　も必要である。
　○　以上の「指導の(②)」と「学習の(③)」を教師視
　　点から整理した概念が「個に応じた指導」であり，この
　　「個に応じた指導」を学習者視点から整理した概念が「個別
　　最適な学び」である。

(3)　次の文は，「中学校学習指導要領(平成29年3月告示)」第2章　第9
　　節　外国語　第1　目標の一部である。(①)，(②)に入る最
　　も適切な語句を書きなさい。

　　　　外国語によるコミュニケーションにおける見方・考え方を
　　　働かせ，外国語による聞くこと，読むこと，話すこと，書く
　　　ことの(①)を通して，簡単な(②)や考えなどを理解し
　　　たり表現したり伝え合ったりするコミュニケーションを図る
　　　資質・能力を次のとおり育成することを目指す。

(4)　次の文章は，「中学校学習指導要領(平成29年3月告示)」第2章　第
　　9節　外国語　第2　各言語の目標及び内容等のうち，3　指導計画
　　の作成と内容の取扱いの一部である。(①)～(④)に入る最
　　も適切な語句を，以下の(a)～(j)からそれぞれ一つずつ選び，記号で
　　答えなさい。

　　　文法事項の指導に当たっては，次の事項に留意すること。
　　　(ア)　英語の(①)を理解させるために，関連のある文法
　　　　事項はまとめて整理するなど，効果的な指導ができるよ
　　　　う工夫すること。
　　　(イ)　文法は(②)を支えるものであることを踏まえ，
　　　　(②)の目的を達成する上での必要性や有用性を実感
　　　　させた上でその知識を活用させたり，繰り返し使用する

12

> ことで当該文法事項の規則性や構造などについて気付き
> を促したりするなど，言語活動と効果的に関連付けて指
> 導すること。
> (ウ) 用語や用法の区別などの指導が中心とならないよう配
> 慮し，実際に活用できるようにするとともに，(③)
> や修飾関係などにおける(④)との違いに留意して指
> 導すること。

(a) 意味　　(b) 語順　　(c) 使用場面　　(d) 言語内容

(e) 発音　　(f) 日本語　　(g) 言語材料　　(h) 特質

(i) 文構造　　(j) コミュニケーション

(☆☆☆○○○○)

【2】次の(1)～(10)の英文の(　)に入る最も適切な単語または語句を(ア)～(エ)からそれぞれ一つずつ選び，記号で答えなさい。

(1) John thinks that it is more important to form the (　) of children's future learning than to provide them with specialized knowledge at elementary school.

(ア) classification　　(イ) foundation　　(ウ) delegation

(エ) transportation

(2) The number of students is decreasing in this school. The (　) to this problem should be sought not only by the teachers but also by everyone involved in this town.

(ア) illusion　　(イ) objection　　(ウ) relation　　(エ) solution

(3) Children learn adult behavior by (　) their parents. For instance, my daughter watches me feed her baby sister, then she feeds her dolls in the same way.

(ア) mimicking　　(イ) inciting　　(ウ) fabricating

(エ) producing

(4) Firefighters come to the nursery school in a fire engine and (　) a fire

drill three times a year.

（ア）　conduct　　　（イ）　represent　　　（ウ）　imitate

（エ）　summarize

(5)　Naomi (　　　) about her grades so much she cannot sleep well at night. She feels she must get perfect scores and is upset if she ever receives less than 100 percent.

（ア）　imparts　　　（イ）　transmits　　　（ウ）　obsesses

（エ）　reminisces

(6)　Tom was very good at (　　　) children. He sang songs well and taught us fun games, and he always told us interesting stories before going to sleep.

（ア）　donating　　　（イ）　entertaining　　　（ウ）　interpreting

（エ）　upsetting

(7)　The cafe is not a good place to go if you're on a diet because the desserts are (　　　).

（ア）　relevant　　　（イ）　complaisant　　　（ウ）　irresistible

（エ）　superficial

(8)　Sara was admitted to three universities, but she is (　　　) about which one to choose because she really likes all three of them.

（ア）　illicit　　　（イ）　irreverent　　　（ウ）　indiscriminate

（エ）　indecisive

(9)　Tomoki is a very popular instructor at the dancing school because his instructions are always clear and (　　　).

（ア）　to the point　　　（イ）　along the way　　　（ウ）　in use

（エ）　on the average

(10)　Phillip just (　　　) the full report because he did not have time to read it before the meeting.

（ア）　handed down　　　（イ）　flipped through　　　（ウ）　poured over

（エ）　indulged in

(☆☆☆○○○○)

【3】 次の(1)～(5)の〔　　〕内の単語または語句を並べ替えてそれぞれ正しい英文を作るとき，（　①　），（　②　）に入る単語または語句を(ア)～(オ)からそれぞれ一つずつ選び，記号で答えなさい。ただし，英文のはじめにくる単語または語句の頭文字も小文字にしてある。

(1) The camera my father gave me was (　　) (　①　) (　　) (　②　) (　　). I had to consider the light and the distance from the object and carefully adjust the lens to take a good picture.

〔 (ア) easy　　(イ) but　　(ウ) use　　(エ) to
(オ) anything 〕

(2) Lisa didn't like (　　) (　①　) (　　) (　②　) (　　). The other day she said to her mother that she knew what she should do.

〔 (ア) to　　(イ) do　　(ウ) being　　(エ) what
(オ) told 〕

(3) Cathy received an email from her boss(　　) (　①　) (　　) (　②　) (　　) put off until next Friday.

〔 (ア) been　　(イ) saying　　(ウ) had　　(エ) that
(オ) the sales meeting 〕

(4) (　　) (　①　) (　　) (　②　) (　　) time to play baseball, Shohei did quite well even though he didn't get any hits.

〔 (ア) first　　(イ) it　　(ウ) was　　(エ) his
(オ) considering 〕

(5) When Takeshi entered the restaurant, he (　　) (　①　) (　　) (　②　) (　　). While eating a pizza, he realized that his mother had taken him there when he was a small boy.

〔 (ア) having　　(イ) before　　(ウ) there　　(エ) been
(オ) remembered 〕

(☆☆☆◎◎◎)

15

【４】次の□の中に書かれているアメリカのニュース番組CNNで流れた4つのニュースについて，各問いに答えなさい。

(1) 次のニュースの(①)，(②)に入る最も適切な語を，それぞれ以下の(ア)～(エ)から一つずつ選び，記号で答えなさい。

Japanese Cherry Trees in Washington

Decades before the war, the (①) between the Japanese and American people was demonstrated in mutual gifts of trees. In 1912, Japan sent more than 3,000 cherry trees across the Pacific. The Japanese gift bloomed into an (②) highlight on Washington, D.C.'s Tidal Basin. Every year, in late March and early April, visitors walk through a springtime wonderland of white and pink flowers.

(April 7, 2021)

---

① (ア) difference (イ) argument (ウ) confrontation
(エ) friendship

② (ア) amiable (イ) intense (ウ) annual
(エ) overwhelming

(2) 次の③，④のニュースのタイトルとして最もふさわしいものを，それぞれ以下の(ア)～(エ)から一つずつ選び，記号で答えなさい。また，それぞれの下線部を日本語に訳しなさい。

---

③ Barack Obama's hands may be memorable to some people, but to eight sheep in England, it's his face that's unforgettable. Scientists from the University of Cambridge found they could train the animals to recognize human faces from photos. The sheep were shown images of specific celebrities, including the former president. Then the celebrity's face was shown next to an unknown person. It turns out that the sheep could identify the familiar face about four times out of five.

(November 9, 2017)

---

③のタイトル

16

(ア)　Barack Obama Identified the Sheep

(イ)　Sheep Learn to Recognize Faces

(ウ)　Celebrities Purchased Specific Sheep

(エ)　Scientists in Cambridge Didn't Forget the Sheep

---

④　One group of pigeons is taking to the skies to tell Londoners just how bad their air pollution has gotten. They're called Pigeon Air Patrol. It's a flock of 10 brave birds, all equipped with tiny, backpack sensors and assisted by Plume Labs. <u>They've been flying over the city this week, tracking the toxic air and then tweeting back their readings</u>. London has some of the world's dirtiest air.

(March 17, 2016)

---

④のタイトル

(ア)　Pigeons Monitor Air Pollution

(イ)　Air Pollution is Getting Worse

(ウ)　Brave Pigeons Died from Dirty Air

(エ)　Londoners Love Pigeons Flying Over their City

(3)　次のニュースについて下線部⑤は具体的にどうなることを意味しているのか，下線部中のthatの内容を明らかにして日本語で答えなさい。

AI News Anchor Unveiled in China

No, that's not a real person. It's a lifelike example of how artificial intelligence is developing in China. Xinhua News Agency reports that this news caster can work uninterrupted. That means no coffee breaks, no bathroom breaks, no coughing; just constant updates typed into its software. Cheap and efficient? Maybe. Missing a little personality? You bet. But, hey, ⑤<u>that is what's to come</u>.

(November 12, 2018)

(☆☆☆◎◎◎)

【5】次の資料は，[「県立夜間中学」のパンフレットの一部]である。あとの[メモ]は，[「県立夜間中学」のパンフレットの一部]の内容について簡単に日本語でまとめたものである。（　①　）～（　⑩　）の（　　）に入る最も適切な日本語を書きなさい。なお，（　①　），（　②　），（　⑤　），（　⑥　），（　⑦　）には数字を入れること。

[「県立夜間中学」のパンフレットの一部]

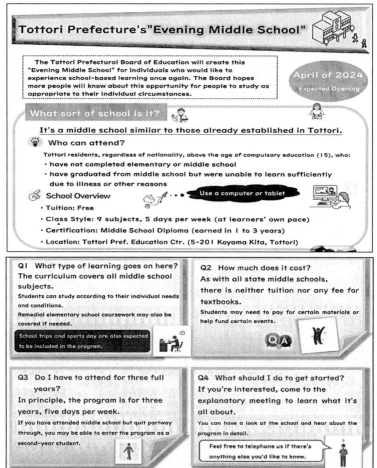

[メモ]

○開校予定	：(①)年(②)月
○入学対象者	：鳥取在住で国籍は(③)。なお，義務教育の年齢15歳以上の方で
	・小学校や中学校を卒業していない方
	・中学校を卒業したが，病気やその他の理由で十分に学べていない方
○取得できる資格	：(④)
○学校の場所	：鳥取市湖山町北5－201
○授業について	：・基本的に週(⑤)日，(⑥)年間通うことが基本
	・授業料：無料
	・(⑦)教科の授業が行われるが，必要があれば(⑧)も学べる
	・学校行事：(⑨)，(⑩)など

(☆☆☆◎◎◎)

【6】次の各問いに答えなさい。なお，それぞれの問いは，中学校の英語の授業での活動を想定している。

(1) 第2学年の授業で，自分の町のお気に入りの場所とその理由についてペアで対話する活動をさせるために，活動の導入として，英語教師と外国語指導助手(ALT)がモデルとなる会話を行いたい。次の2つ(条件)を踏まえ，(①)，(②)に適する英文を書き，二人の対話文を完成させなさい。

(条件)

・( )内にアルファベットが書いてある場合は，その文字が先頭に来る単語から始まる文を書くこと。

・一文～二文の英文で書くこと。(語数は問わない。)

英語教師	外国語指導助手（ALT）
(① W　　　)?	
	The park near my house.
Why do you like that park?	
	Because I can walk my dog there and play with him. I can also see my friends who have dogs too.
That's nice!	
	How about you? Tell me about your favorite place and why you like it.
OK. (　　②　　).	

(2)　第3学年の授業で，ディベートをさせるにあたり，モデルとして生徒に提示する(英語のメモ)を作成する。論題に対して賛成側，反対側の立場を一つ選び，(英語のメモ)内のどちらかの(　　)に〇を書き入れなさい。また，「主張」にその理由を英語で書きなさい。その際，次の3つ(条件)を踏まえること。

(条件)

・理由を二つ書くこと。

・理由には接続詞のifを用いた文を一文入れること。

・一文〜二文の英文で書くこと。(語数は問わない。)

(英語のメモ)

論題	Boxed lunches are better than school lunches.
立場	(　　) I agree.　　　　(　　) I disagree.
主張	

(3)　第3学年の授業で，将来なりたいものについて，理由やその職業でしたいことを入れてスピーチをさせる際，関係代名詞を用いた文を使わせたい。モデルとして提示する文章を英語で書きなさい。その際，次の2つ(条件)を踏まえること。

(条件)

・45語程度の英語で書くこと。文の数は問わない。

・I'mのような短縮形は1語として数え，符号(，や．など)は(例)のよ

うに書き，語数に含めないこととする。

(例) 符号をつける場合の書き方：～ a boy , Tom .

(☆☆☆☆◎◎◎◎)

【高等学校】

【1】放送を聞いて，次の(1)～(5)の各問いの答えとして最も適切なもの
を，それぞれ①～④から一つずつ選び，番号で答えなさい。

なお，英文は1回のみ放送します。

(1) What did the city intend to do when it was founded?

① To build the town's department store.

② To keep an area open for a certain purpose.

③ To forget everything they knew.

④ To use some of the land for a school.

(2) What was the zoo originally designed for?

① The preservation of endangered animals.

② Scientific research.

③ A place for children to go to.

④ The city's building.

(3) Which section will the students visit first?

① The monkey enclosure.

② The nursery.

③ The education block.

④ The DVD shop.

(4) Which is NOT TRUE about the Petting Zoo?

① The animals are friendly.

② The students are allowed to go close to the animals.

③ It's in the east side of the zoo.

④ The students can visit it only one time during the tour.

(5) Where will the students be meeting their teacher after their free time?

① The education block.

  ② The entrance.

  ③ The African savannah.

  ④ The bus.

(☆☆☆◎◎◎◎)

【２】次の各問いに答えなさい。

(1) 次の文は，地方公務員法に規定される服務に関する条文である。①～⑥の中で，誤っているものをすべて選び，記号で答えなさい。

---

  ① すべて職員は，全体の奉仕者として児童・生徒の利益のために勤務し，且つ，職務の遂行に当つては，全力を挙げてこれに専念しなければならない。

  ② 職員は，その職務を遂行するに当つて，法令，条例，地方公共団体の規則及び地方公共団体の機関の定める規程に従い，且つ，校長の職務上の命令に忠実に従わなければならない。

  ③ 職員は，その職の信用を傷つけ，又は職員の職全体の不名誉となるような行為をしてはならない。

  ④ 職員は，職務上知り得た秘密を漏らしてはならない。その職を退いた後は，その限りではない。

  ⑤ 職員は，法律又は条例に特別の定がある場合を除く外，その勤務時間及び職務上の注意力のすべてをその職責遂行のために用い，当該地方公共団体がなすべき責を有する職務にのみ従事しなければならない。

  ⑥ 職員は，政党その他の政治的団体の結成に関与し，若しくはこれらの団体の役員となつてはならず，又はこれらの団体の構成員となるように，若しくはならないように勧誘運動をしてはならない。

---

(2) 次の文章は，令和3年1月に中央教育審議会で取りまとめられた「『令和の日本型学校教育』の構築を目指して～全ての子供たちの可

22

能性を引き出す，個別最適な学びと，協働的な学びの実現〜(答申)」
における「第Ⅰ部　総論」の「3. 2020年代を通じて実現すべき
『令和の日本型学校教育』の姿」に記載された内容の一部である。
(①)〜(③)にあてはまる最も適切な語句を答えなさい。

第Ⅰ部　総論

3. 2020年代を通じて実現すべき「令和の日本型学校教育」
の姿

(1)　子供の学び

○　新型コロナウイルス感染症の感染拡大による臨時休業の
長期化により，多様な子供一人一人が自立した学習者とし
て学び続けていけるようになっているか，という点が改め
て焦点化されたところであり，これからの学校教育におい
ては，子供が(①)も活用しながら自ら学習を調整しなが
ら学んでいくことができるよう，「個に応じた指導」を充実
することが必要である。この「個に応じた指導」の在り方
を，より具体的に示すと以下のとおりである。

○　全ての子供に基礎的・基本的な知識・技能を確実に習得
させ，思考力・判断力・表現力等や，自ら学習を調整しな
がら粘り強く学習に取り組む態度等を育成するためには，
教師が支援の必要な子供により重点的な指導を行うことな
どで効果的な指導を実現することや，子供一人一人の特性
や学習進度，学習到達度等に応じ，指導方法・教材や学習
時間等の柔軟な提供・設定を行うことなどの「指導の
(②)」が必要である。

○　基礎的・基本的な知識・技能等や，言語能力，情報活用
能力，問題発見・解決能力等の学習の基盤となる資質・能
力等を土台として，幼児期からの様々な場を通じての体験
活動から得た子供の興味・関心・キャリア形成の方向性等
に応じ，探究において課題の設定，情報の収集，整理・分

析，まとめ・表現を行う等，教師が子供一人一人に応じた学習活動や学習課題に取り組む機会を提供することで，子供自身が学習が最適となるよう調整する「学習の（　③　）」も必要である。

○　以上の「指導の（　②　）」と「学習の（　③　）」を教師視点から整理した概念が「個に応じた指導」であり，この「個に応じた指導」を学習者視点から整理した概念が「個別最適な学び」である。

(3)　『高等学校学習指導要領』(平成30年3月告示)で示されている教科「外国語」に関する各問いに答えなさい。

第1款　目標

外国語によるコミュニケーションにおける見方・考え方を働かせ，外国語による聞くこと，読むこと，話すこと，書くことの（　1　）及びこれらを結び付けた（　2　）な（　1　）を通して，情報や考えなどを的確に理解したり適切に表現したり伝え合ったりするコミュニケーションを図る資質・能力を次のとおり育成することを目指す。

(1)　外国語の音声や語彙，表現，文法，言語の働きなどの理解を深めるとともに，これらの知識を，聞くこと，読むこと，話すこと，書くことによる実際のコミュニケーションにおいて，目的や（　3　），状況などに応じて適切に活用できる技能を身に付けるようにする。

(以下省略)

(ア)　上の目標の空欄（　1　）～（　3　）に入る適切な語句をそれぞれ答えなさい。なお，同じ番号の（　　）には，同じ語句が入るものとする。

(イ)　次の①～③について，『高等学校学習指導要領』(平成30年3月告示)に示されていることと一致すれば「○」を，そうでなけれ

ば「×」をそれぞれ書きなさい。

① 「英語コミュニケーション」では五つの領域別に，「論理・表現」では三つの領域別に設定する目標の実現を目指す。

② 「英語コミュニケーションⅠ」から「英語コミュニケーションⅢ」になるにつれて，扱う内容がより高度になるため支援の量も増やしていくことになる。

③ より早い段階から発展的内容に触れるため，生徒の習熟度を判断して「英語コミュニケーションⅠ」を履修せずに，「英語コミュニケーションⅢ」を履修することも推奨している。

(☆☆☆○○○)

【3】次の英文を読み，各問いに答えなさい。

When a movie like *One Hundred and One *Dalmatians* comes out, people rush to the pet store buy a puppy like the ones on the screen.

If you find yourself wanting a pet pig or a dog you saw on TV or in a magazine, you stop and do some thinking. Many people who have jumped into owning a pet without enough knowledge on the animal has made themselves and their pet unhappy. For example, when you live in an apartment, a Dalmatian is probably not for you if you are a long distance runner. Dalmatians were born to run long distances, not to be house pets. Lovely little baby pigs grow to weigh 125 pounds, and they are enough smart to learn how to open refrigerators.

Before deciding on a pet, think (1) your own life. How long are you at school or work? If you cannot stay home (2) the day, is there someone who can come to feed and exercise your pet? If not, you may want to consider an animal that can be (3) its own for 8 hours a day. Do you want an animal that will give you lots of attention or would you be happier (4) a pet that is fine whether you play with it or not?

When you have answered these questions and still want to own a pet, you can get information on the pet you are considering and find a good match

25

(　5　) you and your lifestyle before you go to the pet store.

　　注　＊Dalmatian(s)：ダルメシアン(猟犬の一種)

　　　　(実教出版　平成28年度版　全国商業高等学校協会主催　英語
　　　　検定試験問題集　を参照)

(1)　1〜6文目には，明らかな誤りが全部で5か所ある。【例】の答え方
　　にならって，文全体の流れを考えながら，その誤りを正しなさい。

　　【例】2文目　is → am

(2)　空欄(　1　)〜(　5　)に入る適切な語を，次の①〜⑤から一つず
　　つ選び，番号で答えなさい。なお，一つの語は1度しか使用しては
　　いけない。

　　①　during　　②　for　　③　with　　④　on　　⑤　about
　　　　　　　　　　　　　　　　　　　　　　　　　(☆☆☆◎◎◎)

【4】次の各問いに答えなさい。

(1)　次の問いにおいて，それぞれの(　　)の語句を並べかえて意味の
　　通る英文を完成させなさい。

①　Over the last few decades, the negative effects on the environment of
　burning fossil fuels have become increasingly obvious. As a result, (
　trying hard / the amount of energy / governments / get / they use / reduce
　/ people / have been / to / to).

②　Deer are now (keep / they / be hunted / have to / the national park /
　abundant in / to / down / so / their numbers).

③　A : Professor, what do you think about the prospects for world peace
　　　in our lifetimes?

　　B : I'm always hopeful, Wendy, but (unlikely / conflicts / could / it /
　　　that soon / that / solved / seems / be / all the world's).

④　Because many young workers choose to put their families before their
　jobs, (their work / often accuses / being dedicated / the older generation
　/ them / not / of / to).

　　(旺文社　2013年度版　英検準1級・2級過去6回全問題集　を参照)

(2) 次の会話は，家族とともにアメリカから東京に引っ越しをしてきたばかりのLisaと，近所に住むTeruとのやりとりです。自然な流れになるように，空欄に20語以上の英語を記入しなさい。ただし，英文の数は問わない。

Lisa : Who's there?

Teru : It's Teru Matsumoto from next door. I'm sorry to bother you.

Lisa : Oh! It's no trouble. Please come in.

Teru : Thank you. What a lovely home! So much light!

Lisa : Thank you, I'm sorry it's such a mess in here.

Teru : It's difficult when you are raising children, isn't it? I seem to be cleaning every hour of the day. Particularly since my daughter was born.

Lisa : (   )

Teru : Me neither. Sometimes I just give up cleaning the whole house. By the way …(以下省略)

(Xam　2022英語 より抜粋)

(3) 次の文章を英訳しなさい。

　　昨今，地球環境への意識が高まり，『サステナビリティ』がキーワードとして定着している中，人類の持続的な発展には今まで以上に科学の力が必要不可欠だと感じております。その科学および人類の発展を手助けするのが宇宙に眠る無限の科学知識です。

(株式会社ALE (エール) / ALE Co.,Ltd.　HP より抜粋)

(☆☆☆○○○)

【5】次の英文を読み，各問いに答えなさい。

　　Birds do not have propellers any more than human beings move around on wheels. Wings and 　　ア　　 are different but fulfill the same flight function; legs and wheels are different but fulfill the same movement function.

　　Interest in the behavior of computers as information-processing systems has aroused interest in the behavior of the brain itself as an information-processing system. It is probable that without the (　1　) interest there would be much less interest in the possibility of treating the (　2　) in this way. Many useful ideas have originated in the computer field and proved useful in understanding the function of the brain. But there may be very fundamental differences in behavior between computer systems and the brain system. (3) In some ways the dominance of computer ideas may actually lead away from a better understanding of brain function.

Laughter is a fundamental characteristic of the brain system but not of the computer system. And with laughter goes creativity. It will be a sinister day when computers start to laugh, because that will mean they are capable of a lot of other things as well.

It is perfectly possible that a computer could be deliberately programmed to imitate the functions of the brain system, probably even to the extent of ☐　イ　☐ and ☐　ウ　☐. But this would not mean that the two systems were functioning in a similar manner except on the final level, that is to say the outcome level. It is quite easy to tell someone to draw a square, but much more cumbersome to give him the mathematical definition of a square, though (4) the outcome would be the same. A similarity of outcome does not imply a similarity of ☐　エ　☐

　　　　　　　（旺文社　1999年度版　全国大学入試問題正解　を参照）

(1) 空欄 ☐　ア　☐ ～ ☐　ウ　☐ に，それぞれ適切な英単語一語を本文中より抜き出して書きなさい。

(2) 空欄(　1　), (　2　)に，computerかbrainのいずれか適当なものを選択して書きなさい。

(3) 下線部(3)を和訳しなさい。

(4) 下線部(4)とは具体的にはどういうことか，日本語で説明しなさい。

(5) 空欄 ☐　エ　☐ に適切な英単語一語を書きなさい。

（☆☆☆☆○○○）

【6】次の英文を読み，各問いに答えなさい。

There is one episode from the history of medicine that illustrates particularly well how (ア)an evidence-based approach forces the medical establishment to accept the conclusions that emerge when medicine is put to the test. Florence Nightingale, today a well-known figure, was a woman with very little reputation, (1) she still managed to win a bitter argument against the male-dominated medical establishment by arming herself with solid, unquestionable data. (2), she can be seen as one of the earliest advocates of evidence-based medicine, and she successfully used it to transform Victorian healthcare.

Florence and her sister were born during an extended and very productive two-year-long Italian honeymoon taken by their parents William and Frances Nightingale. Florence's older sister was born in 1819 and named Parthenope after the city of her birth — Parthenope being the Greek name for Naples. Then Florence was born in the spring of 1820, and she too was named after the city of her birth. It was expected that Florence Nightingale would grow up to live the life of a privileged English Victorian lady, but as a teenager she regularly claimed to hear God's voice guiding her. Hence, it seems that her desire to become a nurse was the result of a "divine calling." (3)This distressed her parents, because nurses were generally viewed as being poorly educated, indecent and often drunk, but these were exactly (4).

The prospect of Florence nursing in Britain was already shocking enough, so her parents would have been doubly terrified by her subsequent decision to work in the hospitals of *the Crimean War. Florence had read scandalous reports in newspapers such as *The Times, which highlighted the large number of soldiers who were dying of cholera and malaria. She volunteered her services, and by November 1854 Florence was running the Scutari Hospital in Turkey, which was notorious for its filthy wards, dirty beds, blocked sewers and rotten food. It soon became clear to her that the main cause of death was not the wounds suffered by the soldiers, but rather the

(5) that were widespread under such filthy conditions. As one official report admitted, "The wind blew sewer air up the pipes of numerous outdoor toilets into the corridors and wards where the sick were lying."

Nightingale set about transforming the hospital by providing decent food, clean linen, clearing out the drains and opening the windows to let in fresh air. In just one week she removed 215 handcarts of filth, flushed the sewers nineteen times and buried the carcasses of two horses, a cow and four dogs which had been found in the hospital grounds. The officers and doctors who had previously run the institution felt that these changes were an insult to their professionalism and fought her every step of the way, but she pushed ahead regardless. The results seemed to validate her methods: in February 1855 the death rate for all admitted soldiers was 43 per cent, but after her reforms it fell dramatically to just 2 per cent in June 1855. When she returned to Britain in the summer of 1856, Nightingale was greeted as a (h 6).

(旺文社　2016年度版　全国大学入試問題正解　を参照)

注

*the Crimean War：クリミア戦争(1853 － 56年；ロシアがトルコ・フランス・英国・サルディニアを相手に主にクリミア半島で戦った)

*The Times：『タイムズ』(1785年創刊の英国の新聞)

(1)　空欄(1)と(2)に入る英語として適切な組み合わせを次の(A)〜(D)から一つ選び，記号で答えなさい。

	(A)	(B)	(C)	(D)
1	so	so	but	but
2	Nonetheless	Indeed	Nonetheless	Indeed

(2)　下線部(3)の内容を日本語で説明しなさい。

(3)　空欄(4)に入る適切な英語を次の(ア)〜(エ)から一つ選び，記号で答えなさい。

(ア)　the prejudices that Florence was determined to crush

(イ)　the conclusions that Florence was determined to object to

(ウ)　the opinions that Florence was determined to agree to

(エ)　the biases that Florence was determined to accept

(4)　空欄(5)に入る適切な英単語一語で書きなさい。

(5)　下線部(ア)について，ナイチンゲールにおける例を示しながら日本語で説明しなさい。

(6)　本文の内容から判断して，空欄(6)にあてはまる英語を，与えられたアルファベットで始まる英単語一語で書きなさい。

(☆☆☆☆◎◎◎)

【7】次の英文は，『リスニングとスピーキングの理論と実践』というタイトルの本からの要約である。英文を読み，各問いに答えなさい。

Section 1

"What is English Speaking?"

It is essential to obtain a clearer understanding of ①the characteristics of speaking skills and the mechanism of speech production. The L2 speaking skill should be developed in a language classroom with a deep understanding about the characteristics of speaking; otherwise speaking could be regarded as too difficult by learners, though it is the skill many of them would like to learn most.

Section 2

"Influential Factors for Speaking"

This section focuses on major factors that influence speaking processes and outcomes. First, we provide basic information concerning the effects of the cognitive complexity of tasks on speaking, showing various kinds of speaking tasks. Second, we discuss ②factors that make speaking difficult from the viewpoint of learner factors (e.g., motivation, proficiency), code complexity (e.g., topic familiarity, task familiarity), cognitive complexity (e.g., the amount and clarity of information), and communicative stress(e.g., time pressure, speaking speed). Finally, the section illustrates major characteristics of facilitating factors for successful speaking, demonstrating the effects of borrowing and repetition by referring to numerous previous studies.

Section 3

"Teaching English Speaking"

This section deals with a variety of activities to develop speaking skills. Oral communication ability is closely related to listening, reading and writing. Proper and sufficient input is indispensable for meaningful oral output. Creating an encouraging atmosphere is essential in the classroom setting. Therefore, this section begins with "Classroom English". Tourism dialogues that provide practical situations for English use are introduced next. Advanced activities, such as public speaking and ③debate, are also discussed with teaching tips. Lastly, creating dramas and drama techniques are exemplified as a promising method to develop oral communication skills with group dynamics.

　　　（大修館書店　リスニングとスピーキングの理論と実践　より抜粋)
(1)　下線部①について，次の図を見て，図の中央部にある左右方向の
　　矢印が意味していることはどういうことか，日本語で説明しなさい。

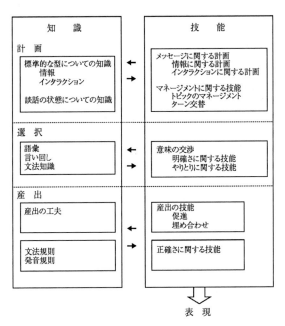

図：Bygate(1987)によるスピーキング技能の概観

(2) 下線部②について，その要因の一つに様々なスピーキング活動の
タスクの複雑性と条件を理解していないことが考えられる。次の表
を見て，それぞれのスピーキング活動の特徴を考え，空欄(1)～
(4)に当てはまるものを，以下の①～④から一つずつ選び，番号
で答えなさい。

表：スピーキングの種類例

タスクの条件		タスクの複雑さ	
方向性	タイプ	プランあり・先行知識あり	プランなし・先行知識なし
一方向	オープン	(1)	即興のスピーチ
	クローズド	自宅までの道順を説明	(2)
双方向	オープン	ディベートの一部	(3)
	クローズド	問題解決タスク	(4)

① インフォメーション・ギャップゲーム

② 即興スキット

③ 絵の描写

④ Show & Tell

(3) "Classroom English" の意義について，Section 3に書いてあることから判断し，日本語で説明しなさい。

(4) 下線部③について，授業の帯活動として，授業の最初に毎時間異なる論題でミニディベートをする場合，どのような論題が適するか，あなたが考える論題を一つ英語で書きなさい。

(☆☆☆☆☆○○○)

【8】国の「GIGA スクール構想」により，鳥取県立高等学校全日制課程では，令和4年度入学生から年次進行で，指定する端末(Chromebook)を生徒が1人1台ずつ購入し，授業などで活用しています。英語の学力を高めるために，英語の授業，及び英語の授業外で，タブレット端末をどのように活用していくか考えていくことが必要となります。次の英文を読み，各問いに答えなさい。

　　From a small start - just a simple e-mail requesting used book donations - Room to Read, an organization pursuing quality education for all children around the world, has grown into a well-known nonprofit organization. It has established over 14,000 libraries, distributed over eleven million books, and built more than 1,500 schools, improving the lives of over six million children in Asia and Africa. These figures are updated regularly and show what a big difference those involved are actually making. The successful growth and sound management of this nonprofit project has been greatly supported by the lesson John Wood, who is the founder of Room to Read and used to be the executive at Microsoft, learned in the competitive business world. Room to Read is still growing in the strong belief that education is crucial in breaking the cycle of poverty and taking control of one's life.

　　(東京書籍　*PROMINENCE English Communication Ⅲ*　を参照)

(1)　この英文を題材として，書くことや話すことの言語活動をどのように行うか，日本語で書きなさい。

(2)　(1)で述べた言語活動を行うにあたって，Chromebookなどの端末の活用方法について，日本語で説明しなさい。その際，学び合いや協働学習の視点も述べること。

(3)　(2)で述べた活用方法に対して，どのような効果が得られるか，日本語で説明しなさい。

(☆☆☆☆◎◎◎◎)

解答・解説

【中学校】

【 1 】(1)　①，②，④　　(2)　①　ICT　　②　個別化　　③　個性化
(3)　①　言語活動　　②　情報　　(4)　①　(h)　　②　(j)
③　(b)　　④　(f)

〈解説〉(1)　公立学校の教員には地方公務員法が適用され，同法第6節でその服務について定められている。①は同法第30条で「すべて職員は，全体の奉仕者として公共の利益のために勤務し，且つ，職務の遂行に当つては，全力を挙げてこれに専念しなければならない」，②は同法第32条で「職員は，その職務を遂行するに当つて，法令，条例，地方公共団体の規則及び地方公共団体の機関の定める規程に従い，且つ，上司の職務上の命令に忠実に従わなければならない」，④は同法第34条第1項で「職員は，職務上知り得た秘密を漏らしてはならない。その職を退いた後も，また，同様とする」とされている。　(2)　「『令和の日本型学校教育』の構築を目指して～全ての子供たちの可能性を引き出す，個別最適な学びと，協働的な学びの実現～(答申)」は，中央教育審議会が2021年1月26日答申したもので，「各学校においては，教科等の特質に応じ，地域・学校や児童生徒の実情を踏まえながら，授

業の中で『個別最適な学び』の成果を『協働的な学び』に生かし，更にその成果を『個別最適な学び』に還元するなど，『個別最適な学び』と『協働的な学び』を一体的に充実し，『主体的・対話的で深い学び』の実現に向けた授業改善につなげていくことが必要である」としている。この答申を踏まえて2022年12月に出された中央教育審議会答申「『令和の日本型学校教育』を担う教師の養成・採用・研修等の在り方について～『新たな教師の学びの姿』の実現と，多様な専門性を有する質の高い教職員集団の形成～(答申)」も学習しておきたい。

(3)　「見方・考え方」，「表現したり伝え合ったり」，「資質・能力」等は，現行の中学校学習指導要領のキーワードである。出題の「外国語科」の目標と併せて「英語」の目標も押さえておくこと。　(4)　現行の中学校学習指導要領では，従来の学習指導要領より，一層英語によるコミュニケーション能力の育成が重視されるようになった。文法事項は知識として学ぶだけではなく，学んだことを実際のコミュニケーションに活用することで，児童生徒に定着させることが求められるようになった。「文法事項の指導に当たっての配慮事項」は，他自治体でも頻出箇所であるので，学習指導要領の内容については同解説外国語編を参照しながら，よく確認しておくこと。

【２】(1)　(イ)　　(2)　(エ)　　(3)　(ア)　　(4)　(ア)　　(5)　(ウ)　　(6)　(イ)　　(7)　(ウ)　　(8)　(エ)　　(9)　(ア)　　(10)　(イ)

〈解説〉(1)　「ジョンは，小学校で専門的な知識を教えるよりも子供たちの将来の学習の基礎を形成することの方が重要だと考えている」。foundation「基礎」。　(2)　「この学校では生徒数が減少している。この問題の解決は，教師だけでなく，この町に関わるすべての人に模索されるべきである」。solution「解決」。　(3)　「子どもは親の真似をして大人の行動を学ぶ」。mimic「真似る」。現在分詞はmimickingとなる。(4)　「消防士が消防車で保育園に来て，年に3回消防訓練をする」。conduct「実施する」。　(5)　「ナオミは成績にこだわって，夜もよく眠れない」。obsess about～「～を心配する」。　(6)　「トムは子供たちを

36

楽しませるのがとても上手だった」。entertain「楽しませる」。
(7) 「そのカフェはデザートがたまらなく美味しいので，ダイエット中の人は行かない方がいい」。irresistible「抑えられない」。 (8) 「サラは3つの大学に合格したが，3つともとても気に入っているからどの大学にするか迷っている」。indecisive「優柔不断の，決定的でない」。
(9) 「トモキはダンススクールの人気インストラクターである，というのも彼の指示はいつも明確で，的を得ているからだ」。to the point「的確で」。 (10) 「フィリップは会議の前に報告書を読む時間がなかったので，パラパラと目を通しただけだった」。flip through「ざっと読む」。

【3】(1) ① (イ) ② (エ) (2) ① (オ) ② (ア)
(3) ① (エ) ② (ウ) (4) ① (イ) ② (エ)
(5) ① (ア) ② (ウ)

〈解説〉(1) 「父からもらったカメラは使いやすいものではなかった」。anything but〜「決して〜でない」。整序すると，anything but easy to useとなる。 (2) 「リサは指図されるのが嫌いだった」。整序すると，being told what to doとなる。 (3) 「キャシーは上司から，営業会議は来週の金曜日に延期されたというメールを受け取った」。整序すると，saying that the sales meeting had beenとなる。 (4) 「初めての野球だったことを考えれば，ショウヘイはヒットを打てなかったものの，とてもよくやった」。整序すると，Considering it was his firstとなる。
(5) 「タケシはレストランに入ると，以前にも来たことがあることを思い出した」。整序すると，remembered having been there beforeとなる。

【4】(1) ① (エ) ② (ウ) (2) ③ タイトル…(イ) 訳…羊は約8割(5回中4回くらい)の割合で見覚えのある顔を認識することがわかった。 ④ タイトル…(ア) 訳…ハトたちは今週ロンドン上空を飛び回り，大気中の有害物質を記録し，その結果をツイッター上

に送っている。　　(3)　人間の仕事が人工知能技術(AI)に取って代わられる時代が来るということ。

〈解説〉(1)　「戦前の数十年間は，日米両国民の友好関係が樹木の贈り合いで示されていた」。「日本からの贈り物は咲き誇り，ワシントンD.C.のタイダルベイスンで例年のハイライトとなった」。

(2)　③　2文目および5文目より，タイトルは「羊は顔を認識するようになる」が適切。It turns out〜「〜と判明する」。four times out of five「5回中4回」。　④　1文目および4文目より，タイトルは「ハトが大気汚染を監視する」が適切。track the toxic air「有毒な大気を追跡する」。tweet back「ツイートを返す」。readings「読取り値」。　(3)　that is what's to come.「それがこれから起きることである」。AIニュース・キャスターを例に，人間の仕事がAIに取って代わられることを指している。

【5】①　2024(令和6)　②　4　③　問わない　④　中学校卒業資格　⑤　5　⑥　3　⑦　9　⑧　小学校の内容　⑨　修学旅行　⑩　運動会(体育祭，スポーツの日)

〈解説〉①・②　パンフレットのタイトルの右下に日付がある。April of 2024 Expected Opening「2024年4月オープン予定」。　③　リード文の下のWhat sort of school is it？のWho can attend？の項の冒頭文。Tottori residents, regardless of nationality「鳥取在住，国籍は問わない」。

④　同じく，What sort of school is it？のSchool Overviewの項の3文目 Certificationに，Middle School Diploma「中学校卒業資格」とある。

⑤・⑥　Q3 Do I have to attend for three full years?の項の1文目。In principle, the program is for three years, five days per week.「原則として，プログラムは3年間，週5日」。　⑦　School Overviewの項の2文目。9 subjects「9教科」。　⑧　Q1 What type of learning goes on here？の項の3文目。Remedial elementary school coursework may also be covered if needed.「必要に応じて，小学校の補習授業も行われる」。

⑨・⑩　Q1の項の下にある囲み文。School trips and sports day are also

expected to be included in the program. 「修学旅行や運動会もプログラム
に含まれる予定である」。

【6】(1) ① Where(What) is your favorite place (in your town)?
② My favorite place is the library because I like reading books. So I often
go there and borrow many books. (2) (I agree.) First, if you bring a
boxed lunch, you don't have to eat foods that you don't like. Second, you don't
have to serve school lunches, so you can save time and have a longer lunch
break. (36語) (3) I want to be a tour guide and visit many countries in
the world. I have wanted to go abroad since I started learning English. I think
I can see many people, so I want to talk with them in English. It will be
interesting. (45語)

〈解説〉(1) 第2学年の活動であることを踏まえ, 第2学年の文法事項や
語彙を意識して, ①には「お気に入りの場所をたずねる英文」, ②に
は「お気に入りの場所を理由とともに答える英文」を書く。 (2) 同
じく, 第3学年の活動であることを踏まえ, 第3学年の文法事項や語彙
を意識して書く。解答例では, 論題「学校給食より弁当のほうがよい」
に賛成(I agree.)の立場で意見を述べている。反対(I disagree.)の立場で
は「給食のほうが栄養バランスがよい」,「温かいものが提供される」,
「親の作る手間が省ける」等が理由として挙げられる。 (3) 45語程
度とあるので, 3~4文くらいを目安とする。

【高等学校】

【1】(1) ② (2) ③ (3) ③ (4) ④ (5) ①
〈解説〉スクリプトは非公開。英文を聞いて, 印刷されている選択肢から
正しいものを選ぶ形式。放送は一度のみ。質問は「市は創立時に何を
意図したのか」,「動物園はもともと何のために設計されたのか」,「生
徒たちは最初にどのセクションを見学するのか」,「ふれあい動物園に
ついて正しくないものはどれか」,「生徒たちは自由時間の後, 先生と
どこで待ち合わせるか」。きわめて一般的な形式であり, 日常的な内

容のアナウンスだと推測できる。設問には必ず目を通し，聞くポイントを明確にしてから臨むこと。

【２】(1)　①，②，④　　(2)　①　ICT　　②　個別化　　③　個性化
(3)　(ア)　1　言語活動　　2　統合的　　3　場面　　(イ)　①　○
②　×　　③　×
〈解説〉(1)　公立学校の教員には地方公務員法が適用され，同法第6節でその服務について定められている。　①は同法第30条で「すべて職員は，全体の奉仕者として公共の利益のために勤務し，且つ，職務の遂行に当つては，全力を挙げてこれに専念しなければならない」，②は同法第32条で「職員は，その職務を遂行するに当つて，法令，条例，地方公共団体の規則及び地方公共団体の機関の定める規程に従い，且つ，上司の職務上の命令に忠実に従わなければならない」，④は同法第34条第1項で「職員は，職務上知り得た秘密を漏らしてはならない。その職を退いた後も，また，同様とする」とされている。　(2)「『令和の日本型学校教育』の構築を目指して～全ての子供たちの可能性を引き出す，個別最適な学びと，協働的な学びの実現～(答申)」は，中央教育審議会が2021年1月26日答申したもので，「各学校においては，教科等の特質に応じ，地域・学校や児童生徒の実情を踏まえながら，授業の中で『個別最適な学び』の成果を『協働的な学び』に生かし，更にその成果を『個別最適な学び』に還元するなど，『個別最適な学び』と『協働的な学び』を一体的に充実し，『主体的・対話的で深い学び』の実現に向けた授業改善につなげていくことが必要である」としている。この答申を踏まえて2022年12月に出された中央教育審議会答申「『令和の日本型学校教育』を担う教師の養成・採用・研修等の在り方について～『新たな教師の学びの姿』の実現と，多様な専門性を有する質の高い教職員集団の形成～(答申)」も学習しておきたい。(3)　(ア)「外国語科の目標」については特に，どこが空所になっても文言の再生ができるようしておくことが求められる。出題の(1)の項は，外国語科における「知識及び技能」の習得に関わる目標として掲げら

れたもの。中学校の外国語科では，「実際のコミュニケーションにおいて活用できる技能」の習得を目標とするが，高等学校においては，これを発展させ，「実際のコミュニケーションにおいて，目的や場面，状況などに応じて適切に活用できる技能」を身に付けることが目標とされている。 (イ) ② 例えば，英語コミュニケーションⅡでは，より自律した英語学習者の育成を目指し，英語コミュニケーションⅠの多くの支援を活用する段階から，必要に応じて一定の支援を活用する段階へと移行するので，誤り。 ③ 英語コミュニケーションⅡは，原則として英語コミュニケーションⅠを履修した後に，また英語コミュニケーションⅢは，原則として英語コミュニケーションⅡを履修した後に，更に英語の履修を希望する生徒の能力・適性などに応じて選択履修させる科目として創設されているので，誤り。

【3】(1) ・1文目 buy → to buy / buying / and buy(rush→who rushでも可) ・2文目 you stop → stop / you should stop ・3文目 has → have ・4文目 if → unless(are → are notでも可) ・6文目 enough smart → smart enough から5つ (2) 1 ⑤ 2 ① 3 ④ 4 ③ 5 ②

〈解説〉(1) 1文目「…人々はスクリーンに出てくるような子犬を買うためペットショップに殺到する」。目的を表す不定詞にする。 2文目「テレビや雑誌で見たブタや犬を飼いたいと思ったら，ちょっと立ち止まって考えてみよう」。主語は不要。またはyou should stop等にする。3文目「その動物に関する十分な知識を持たずにペットを飼い始めた人の多くが，自分自身とペットを不幸にしている」。主語はMany peopleなのでhaveにする。 4文目「アパート住まいの場合，ダルメシアンは向かないだろう」と「あなたが長距離ランナーである」をつなぐ接続詞はunless～「もし～でなければ」。次の文でダルメシアンが長距離走る犬種であることが述べられている。 6文目「可愛い子豚は冷蔵庫の開け方を覚えるほど賢い」。〈形容詞＋enough to～〉「～するほど…，とても…なので～する」。 (2) 1 think about～「～につい

て考える」。　2　during the day「日中」。　3　on one's own「ひとりで，自分で」。　4　happy with〜「〜に満足して」。　5　a match for〜「〜に見合うもの」。

【4】(1)　①　governments have been trying hard to get people to reduce the amount of energy they use　②　so abundant in the national park they have to be hunted to keep their numbers down(abundant in the national park so they have to be hunted to keep their numbers down)　③　it seems unlikely that all the world's conflicts could be solved that soon(it seems that all the world's conflicts could unlikely be solved that soon)　④　the older generation often accuses them of not being dedicated to their work　(2)　I don't have the energy to keep the house. My kids seem to make a mess right after I clean it up anyway. (23 words)　(3)　With the growing awareness of the global environment and the topic of "sustainability" becoming more common in recent years, I believe the power of science is vital more than ever now for the sustainable development of humankind. The infinite scientific knowledge, which are yet to be found in the universe, will help the development of science and humankind.

〈解説〉(1)　①「ここ数十年の間に，化石燃料の燃焼が環境に及ぼす悪影響はますます明らかになってきた。その結果，政府は人々が使用するエネルギーの量を減らすよう懸命に努力している」。get＋O＋to do「Oに〜させる」。　②「国立公園ではシカが大量に生息するようになり，その数を減らすために捕獲が必要になっている」。so that構文のthatが省略された形で表す。あるいは接続詞soで2文をつなぐ。
③　A：「教授は，私たちが生きている間に世界平和が実現する可能性についてどうお考えですか」。B：「ウェンディ，私はいつも希望を抱いているんだが，世界中の全紛争がそんなに早く解決されるとは思えないね」。It's unlikely that〜「〜する可能性は低い」。　④「多くの若い労働者は仕事よりも家庭を優先させるので，年配の世代からは仕事に熱心でないと非難されることが多い」。accuse A of B「AをBのこと

で非難する」。 (2) Teruの「僕は四六時中掃除をしているようだ。娘が生まれてからは特に」と「僕もない。家中を掃除するのをあきらめることもある」の間のLisaのセリフ。Me, neither.にうまく続く文を考える。解答例は「家を片付ける気力がないわ。私が片付けた直後に子供たちが散らかすから」。 (3) 「～している中」は，付帯状況を表すwithを使って表すことができる。2文目は解答例の他にも，強調構文でも表せる。

【5】(1) ア propellers イ laughter ウ creativity
(2) 1 computer 2 brain (3) いくつかの点では，コンピュータの概念ばかりに考えが縛られると，脳の機能をもっと理解することには実はかえって邪魔になることもあるかもしれない。 (4) 正方形ができること。 (5) process(procedure)

〈解説〉(1) ア 「翼とプロペラは異なるが同じ飛行機能を果たし…」となる。文の後半で脚と車輪を対比させていることから判断する。イ・ウ 第3段落の「笑いは脳システムの基本的な特徴であるが，コンピューターシステムにはない。そして笑いには創造性が伴う」を受けて，「コンピュータが脳システムの機能，おそらく笑いや創造性までを模倣するようプログラムされる…」となる。 (2) 第2段落の1文目「情報処理システムとしてのコンピュータの動作に興味を持ったことで，情報処理システムとしての脳そのものの動作に興味を持つようになった」を「コンピュータへの関心がなければ，このように脳を扱う可能性への関心はもっと低かっただろう」と言い換えている。よって，1はcomputer, 2はbrain。 (3) dominance「優勢，優越」。lead away from～「～から遠ざかる」。 (4) 「誰かに正方形を描くように指示するのは簡単だが，正方形の数学的定義を与えるのは，結果は同じでもずっと面倒だ」。結果は「正方形ができること」を指す。
(5) 「結果が同じであることはプロセス，または手順が同じであることを意味しない」となる。

【6】(1)　(D)　　(2)　看護師になりたいというナイチンゲールの願望
(3)　(ア)　　(4)　diseases(illnesses, sicknesses)　　(5)　食事内容を改良
し，清潔な寝具を提供するなど病院を改革することで(環境衛生の徹底，
下水の清掃など病院を改革することで)全兵士の死亡率を43パーセント
から2パーセントに減少させたデータに基づく取り組み。

(6)　hero(heroine)

〈解説〉(1)　「今日ではよく知られた人物であるナイチンゲールは，ほと
んど名声のない女性であった」と「彼女は…男性優位の医学界に対抗
して辛辣な論争を勝ち抜くことに成功した」は逆説の関係。「実際，
彼女はエビデンスに基づく医療の最も初期の提唱者の一人と見ること
ができ，ヴィクトリア朝の医療を一変させることに成功した」と続く。
(2)　ナイチンゲールの両親を悩ませた内容を答える。her desire to
become a nurse「看護師になりたいという願望」。　(3)　空所前は「看
護婦は一般的に教養が低く，不品行で，しばしば酒に溺れるものと見
られていた」という内容。しかし，これらはまさに「フローレンスが
打ち砕こうと決意した偏見」だったと続ける。　(4)　the main cause of
death was not～but rather…「死因の主なものは～ではなく，むしろ…だ
った」。…にあてはまる英単語として，「(このような不潔な環境下で蔓
延していた)病気」が適切。　(5)　下線部の意味は「エビデンスに基
づくアプローチ」。最終段落から，彼女がすすめた病院の改革とその
結果のデータに触れてまとめる。　(6)　「ナイチンゲールは英雄とし
て迎えられた」等が考えられる。

【7】(1)　・スピーキングを行うためには知識があるだけでは行えない
こと。　　・実際にスピーキングを行うことで，必要な知識を高めて
いくこと。　から1つ　　(2)　1　④　　2　③　　3　②　　4　①
(3)　スピーキングの力を身に付けさせるには，授業の中で教師ができ
るだけ英語で話し，生徒もできるだけ英語で話すという雰囲気をつく
ることが大切だから。　　(4)　We should wear school uniforms.

〈解説〉(1)　インプット(知識の習得)とアウトプット(実践練習)の両方が

必要だという観点からまとめる。　(2)　①　異なる情報を持つ者が，コミュニケーションを通してお互いの情報の差を埋めていく活動。「双方向」で特定の答えを見つけ出す活動なので「クローズド」。
②　即興スキットは「双方向」で「オープン」。　③　絵の描写は「一方向」で「クローズド」。　④　自分の持ち物等について示しながら，それについて話す活動。「一方向」で「オープン」。
(3)　Section3には「意味のある口頭でのアウトプットのためには，適切で十分なインプットが不可欠」，「教室では，励まし合える雰囲気づくりが不可欠」とある。これらと関連付け，まとめる。　(4)　ミニディベートの論題として高校生のアルバイト，レジ袋の有償化など生徒に身近な問題から，消費税率や週休3日制導入の是非など社会問題にも発展させられる。

【8】〈解答例1〉…(1)　John Wood になりきって，Room to Read について英語でプレゼンテーションする活動。　(2)　それぞれが考えたプレゼンテーションを自分で録画し，ドライブ上に保存し共有させ，感想をドライブ上で述べる。　(3)　授業で行うプレゼンテーションでは1度しか他人のものが見れないが，ドライブ上に保存することで何度も繰り返し視聴できる。　〈解答例2〉…(1)　教育に困難がある国の現状を調べ，自分たちに何ができるかのポスターを英語で作成する。(2)　オンラインでRoom to Read の職員に発表する機会を作り，作成したポスターについて発表する。　(3)　遠隔地の人であっても，自分が考えたことを英語で伝える機会を持つことができる。また，そこで撮影した動画を学校のホームページに載せることで，他生徒も端末を使ってそれを視聴できる。
〈解説〉ここでは，(1)〜(3)について2種類の解答例が挙げられている。
(1)　題材となっている英文は，世界中のすべての子どもたちに質の高い教育を提供することを目指す団体，Room to Readの活動紹介と「貧困の連鎖を断ち切り，自分の人生をコントロールするためには教育が不可欠だ」とする創設者John Woodの信念に触れている。解答例の他

にも，団体や創設者についてさらに詳しく調べた内容を発表する等が考えられる。　(2)　他の生徒の活動をいつでも共有できるなど，Chromebookの特長を生かした活用方法を解答する。　(3)　メールツールやビデオ会議ツールなどにより，活動の幅が広がり，それにより得られる効果も大きい。解答例は「何度も視聴できる」，「遠隔地の人と交流できる」等を挙げている。

2023年度　実施問題

【中学校】

【1】次の各問いに答えなさい。

(1) 次の文は，教育基本法第2条の条文である。条文中の(①)～(④)にあてはまる語句の組み合わせとして最も適切なものを，以下の(ア)～(カ)から一つ選び，記号で答えなさい。

> 第2条　教育は，その目的を実現するため，(①)を尊重しつつ，次に掲げる目標を達成するよう行われるものとする。
>
> 1　幅広い知識と教養を身に付け，真理を求める態度を養い，豊かな情操と(②)を培うとともに，健やかな身体を養うこと。
>
> 2　個人の価値を尊重して，その能力を伸ばし，(③)を培い，自主及び自律の精神を養うとともに，職業及び生活との関連を重視し，勤労を重んずる態度を養うこと。
>
> 3　正義と責任，男女の平等，自他の敬愛と協力を重んずるとともに，公共の精神に基づき，主体的に社会の形成に参画し，その発展に寄与する態度を養うこと。
>
> 4　生命を尊び，自然を大切にし，環境の保全に寄与する態度を養うこと。
>
> 5　伝統と文化を尊重し，それらをはぐくんできた我が国と郷土を愛するとともに，他国を尊重し，(④)の平和と発展に寄与する態度を養うこと。

	①	②	③	④
（ア）	学問の自由	道徳心	創造性	自国
（イ）	表現の自由	道徳心	社会性	自国
（ウ）	学問の自由	道徳心	創造性	国際社会
（エ）	表現の自由	奉仕の心	社会性	国際社会
（オ）	学問の自由	奉仕の心	社会性	自国
（カ）	表現の自由	奉仕の心	創造性	国際社会

(2)　次の文章は，令和元年10月25日付けの文部科学省初等中等教育局長通知である「不登校児童生徒への支援の在り方について」の一部である。（　①　）・（　②　）にあてはまる最も適切な語句を答えなさい。なお，同じ番号の(　　)には，同じ語句が入るものとする。

> 1　不登校児童生徒への支援に対する基本的な考え方
> 　(1)　支援の視点
> 　　　不登校児童生徒への支援は，「学校に登校する」という結果のみを目標にするのではなく，児童生徒が自らの進路を主体的に捉えて，（　①　）的に自立することを目指す必要があること。また，児童生徒によっては，不登校の時期が休養や自分を見つめ直す等の（　②　）的な意味を持つことがある一方で，学業の遅れや進路選択上の不利益や（　①　）的自立へのリスクが存在することに留意すること。

(3)　次の文は，「中学校学習指導要領(平成29年3月告示)」第2章　第9節　外国語　第1　目標の一部である。空欄（　①　），（　②　）に入る最も適切な語句を書きなさい。

> 　　コミュニケーションを行う目的や場面，状況などに応じて，日常的な話題や(　①　)な話題について，外国語で簡単な情報や考えなどを理解したり，これらを活用して(　②　)したり伝え合ったりすることができる力を養う。

(4)　次の文章は，「中学校学習指導要領(平成29年3月告示)」第2章　第

48

9節　外国語　第2　各言語の目標及び内容等に示された内容〔知識及び技能〕の一部である。空欄（　①　）～（　④　）に入る最も適切な語句を，以下の(a)～(j)からそれぞれ一つずつ選び，記号で答えなさい。なお，同じ番号の(　)には，同じ語句が入るものとする。

---

(1)　英語の特徴やきまりに関する事項

　　実際に英語を用いた言語活動を通して，小学校学習指導要領第2章第10節外国語第2の2の(1)及び次に示す（　①　）のうち，1に示す五つの領域別の目標を達成するのにふさわしいものについて理解するとともに，（　①　）と言語活動とを効果的に関連付け，実際のコミュニケーションにおいて活用できる技能を身に付けることができるよう指導する。

ア　音声

　　次に示す事項について取り扱うこと。

　(ア)　現代の標準的な発音

　(イ)　語と語の（　②　）による音の変化

　(ウ)　語や句，文における基本的な（　③　）

　(エ)　文における基本的なイントネーション

　(オ)　文における基本的な区切り

イ　(省略)

ウ　(省略)

エ　文，文構造及び文法事項

　　小学校学習指導要領第2章第10節外国語第2の2の(1)のエ及び次に示す事項について，意味のある（　④　）でのコミュニケーションの中で繰り返し触れることを通して活用すること。

(a)　関係　　(b)　能力　　(c)　場面　　(d)　言語材料

(e)　強勢　　(f)　文脈　　(g)　言語内容　　(h)　強調

(i)　目的　　(j)　連結

(☆☆☆◎◎◎)

【2】 次の(1)～(10)の英文の(　　)に入る最も適切な単語または語句を
(ア)～(エ)からそれぞれ一つずつ選び，記号で答えなさい。

(1)　When I read his biography, I was very moved to learn that Beethoven
(　　) Symphony No.9 despite his hearing disability.
(ア)　deserted　　(イ)　composed　　(ウ)　deposited
(エ)　obtained

(2)　John did not have enough money to pay for a new house all at once, so
he decided to take out a loan and pay for it in (　　).
(ア)　installments　　(イ)　impediments　　(ウ)　impairments
(エ)　persuasions

(3)　The group of scientists carried out (　　) on rats to see the effectiveness
of a newly developed medicine against a disease for which there is
currently no cure.
(ア)　amusements　　(イ)　statements　　(ウ)　judgments
(エ)　experiments

(4)　Sara's grandfather gave her his old watch, thinking it was still useful.
However, it was (　　).
(ア)　faultless　　(イ)　obsolete　　(ウ)　somber
(エ)　ambiguous

(5)　At the event's entrance, staffs were checking the (　　) of the guest's
bags. They didn't want the live performance recorded.
(ア)　payments　　(イ)　targets　　(ウ)　contents　　(エ)　receipts

(6)　The hotel was exceptional in every way. It had many first-class (　　),
including a golf course, a spa, and an indoor pool.
(ア)　incentives　　(イ)　delicacies　　(ウ)　amenities
(エ)　inclinations

(7)　Anna's a genius at math. She (　　) the homework assignment in less
than 20 minutes, while it took everyone else at least an hour.
(ア)　drove out　　(イ)　sailed through　　(ウ)　powered up
(エ)　believed in

(8)　A doctor and some nurses were standing (　　) during the triathlon to take care of any runners who got injured or sick.

(ア)　by　　(イ)　down　　(ウ)　aside　　(エ)　in

(9)　The new employee neither had the skills she said she had nor the correct attitude. In short, she did not (　　) to the job, so she was fired.

(ア)　cover for　　(イ)　count down　　(ウ)　hammer out

(エ)　measure up

(10)　We talked for hours but did not (　　) any good ideas. We decided that each of us would consider the problem and meet again the next Saturday.

(ア)　make light of　　(イ)　do away with　　(ウ)　come up with

(エ)　take away from

(☆☆☆○○○○)

【3】次の(1)～(5)の〔　　〕内の単語または語句を並べ替えてそれぞれ正しい英文を作るとき，(　①　)・(　②　)に入る単語または語句をそれぞれ一つずつ選び，記号で答えなさい。

(1)　〔(ア)　tail　　(イ)　until　　(ウ)　with　　(エ)　her

(オ)　wagging〕

The dog stood on the platform (　　)(　①　)(　　)(　②　)(　　) the train was completely out of sight.

(2)　〔(ア)　transferred　　(イ)　to　　(ウ)　the marketing　　(エ)　be

(オ)　department〕

Mr. Osaki suggested that Jane (　　)(　①　)(　　)(　②　)(　　). He said her technical knowledge would be helpful in making advertisements.

(3)　〔(ア)　buy　　(イ)　than　　(ウ)　could　　(エ)　more

(オ)　no〕

The toilet rolls were very cheap in the advertisement, but at the store I found that each shopper (　　)(　①　)(　　)(　②　)(　　) one pack of them.

(4)　〔(ア)　giving　　(イ)　spoiling　　(ウ)　their　　(エ)　by

(オ)　children〕

Some people are (　　)(　①　)(　　)(　②　)(　　) them everything they ask for. It's very important for children to learn the value of money by working for it.

(5)　〔(ア)　difficulty　　(イ)　balance　　(ウ)　keeping

(エ)　having　　(オ)　her〕

Lisa is very good at sports. She's (　　)(　①　)(　　)(　②　)(　　) on the ice now, but I'm sure she will learn to skate well before long.

(☆☆☆○○○○)

【4】次の英文は，2020年11月7日(現地時間)に，アメリカ合衆国副大統領のカマラ・ハリス氏がデラウェア州「チェイスセンター」で行った演説の一部である。この英文を読み，以下の(1)〜(4)の各問いに答えなさい。

(前略)

And so, ①I am thinking about my mother and about the generations of women－black women, Asian, white, Latina, Native American women－who, throughout our nation's history, have paved the way for this moment tonight; women who fought and sacrificed so much for equality and liberty and justice for all; including the black women who are often－too often－overlooked but so often prove that they are the backbone of our democracy; all the women who have worked to secure and protect the right to vote for over a century; 100 years ago with the 19th Amendment, 55 years ago with the Voting Rights Act, and now, in 2020, with a new generation of women in our country who cast their ballots and continue the fight for their fundamental right to vote and be heard.

Tonight, I reflect on their struggle, their determination and the strength of their vision to see what can be unburdened by what has been. And I stand on their shoulders.

And what a testament it is to Joe's character that he had the audacity to break one of the most substantial barriers that exists in our country and select a woman as his vice president.

But while I may be the first woman in this office, I will not be the (②), because every little girl watching tonight sees that this is a country of possibilities.

And to the children of our country: regardless of your gender, our country has sent you a clear message: ③Dream with ambition, lead with conviction and see yourselves in a way that others may not simply because they've never seen it before, but know that we will applaud you every step of the way.

And to the American people: No matter who you voted for, I will strive to be a vice president like Joe was to President Obama—loyal, honest and prepared, waking up every day thinking of you and your family.

Because now is when ④the real work begins—the hard work, the necessary work, the good work, the essential work, to save lives and beat this epidemic; to rebuild our economy so it works for working people; to root out systemic racism in our justice system and society; to combat the climate crisis; to unite our country and heal the soul of our nation.

(「バイデン＆ハリス勝利宣言The Victory Speeches of Joe Biden and Kamala Harris」朝日出版社より一部改)

(1)　下線部①の英文を日本語にしなさい。
(2)　本文の内容を踏まえて，(②)に入る最も適切な語を，次の(ア)〜(エ)から一つ選び，記号で答えなさい。
　　(ア)　right　　(イ)　middle　　(ウ)　beginning　　(エ)　last
(3)　下線部③の英文を日本語にしなさい。
(4)　下線部④の内容について，後の本文中にあげられている具体的な例の中から三つを選び，日本語で答えなさい。

(☆☆☆◎◎◎◎)

【5】次の英文を読み，以下の(1)〜(5)の各問いに答えなさい。

　　We come to the job with our personalities already formed, but there are abilities and attitudes which can be learnt and worked on. ①<u>As a teacher of young children it helps a lot if you have a sense of humour, you're open-minded, adaptable, patient, etc., but even if you're the silent, reserved type, you can work on your attitudes and abilities.</u>

Abilities

We may not all be brilliant music teachers like Susan's Mr. Jolly, but most of us can learn to sing or even play a musical instrument. All music teachers would agree in any case that everyone can sing, although perhaps not always in tune!

We can all learn to mime, to act and to draw very simple drawings. We can all learn to organise our worksheets so that they are planned and pleasing to look at. And we can certainly all learn to have our chalk handy!

Attitudes

Respect your pupils and be realistic about what they can manage at an individual level, then your expectations will be realistic too.

As a teacher you have to appear to like all your pupils equally. Although at times this will certainly include the ability to act, the children should not be aware of it. Children learning a foreign language or any other subject need to know that the teacher likes them. Young children have a very keen sense of (②).

It will make all the difference in the world if you yourself feel secure in what you are doing. Knowing where you are going and what you are doing is essential. You can build up your own security by planning, reading, assessing and talking to others.

(③)

Once children feel secure and content in the classroom, they can be encouraged to become independent and adventurous in the learning of the language. Security is not an attitude or an ability, but it is essential if we want our pupils to get the maximum out of the language lessons.

Here are some of the things which will help to create a secure class atmosphere:

● As we said above, know what you're doing. Pupils need to know what is happening, and they need to feel that you are in charge.

● Respect your pupils. In the school twelve-year-old Gerd would like, "People and teachers would be friends and they could speak to each other like friends."

● Whenever a pupil is trying to tell you something, accept whatever he or she says─mistakes as well. Constant, direct correction is not effective and it does not help to create a good class atmosphere. Correction has its place when you are working on guided language exercises, but not when you are using the language for communication.

● Just as Terry's ideal teacher is one 'who doesn't mind children getting things wrong, sometimes', ideal pupils shouldn't laugh at others' mistakes, and this has to be one of the rules of the class. Children of all ages are sometimes unkind to each other without meaning to be and are sometimes unkind to each other deliberately. Pupils have to be told that everyone makes mistakes when they are learning a new language, and that it is all right.

(中略)

● Avoid organised competition. Although it can be great fun and usually leads to a great deal of involvement, there is almost always a winner and a loser, or a winning team and a losing team. Language learning is a situation where everyone can win. Children compete naturally with each other─to see who's finished first etc., but this is something different.

● Avoid giving physical rewards or prizes. It tells others that they have not 'won' and it does not help learning to take place. It is far better to tell the pupil that you like his or her work, or put it up on the display board, or read the story aloud for others or do whatever seems appropriate. ④<u>This gives the pupil a sense of achievement which doesn't exclude the other pupils</u>. Include, don't exclude.

（「Teaching English to Children / Wendy A. Scott and Lisbeth H. Ytreberg」Longmanより一部省略)

(1)　下線部①の英文を日本語にしなさい。

(2)　本文の内容を踏まえて，（　②　)に入る最も適切な語を，次の(ア)～(エ)から一つ選び，記号で答えなさい。

　(ア)　humour　　(イ)　shame　　(ウ)　responsibility

　(エ)　fairness

(3)　（　③　)には，この後に続く段落全体のタイトルが入る。そのタイトルとして最もふさわしいものを，次の(ア)～(エ)から一つ選び，記号で答えなさい。

　(ア)　Having get the children to know each other

　(イ)　Helping the children to feel secure

　(ウ)　Avoiding giving the children a sense of security

　(エ)　Giving the children plans to think individually in the classroom

(4)　下線部④の英文を，Thisが示している内容を具体的に明らかにして，日本語にしなさい。

(5)　本文の内容に合っているものを，次の(ア)～(エ)から一つ選び，記号で答えなさい。

　(ア)　教師は，自分が立てた授業計画に基づき，何をしようとしているかを子どもたちに示さずに授業をすることで，子どもたちの興味や関心を引き出すことができる。

　(イ)　子どもたちがコミュニケーションのためにことばを使っている場合でも，正確性を高めるためには，発話の間違いをその場で訂正してやったほうがよい。

　(ウ)　どんな年代の子どもであっても，時に他の子どもに対して不親切や意地悪になることがあるため，他の子どもの間違いを笑わないということを教室のルールのひとつにすべきである。

　(エ)　言語を扱う学習では，活動の中で子どもたちが自然と競い合うような場面を教師が仕組み，常に競争を意識させながら学習に

取り組ませることが大切である。

(☆☆☆◎◎◎◎)

【6】次の(1)～(3)の各問いに答えなさい。

(1) 中学校第2学年の英語の授業で，これまでに自分が経験したことの中で相手が驚くようなことについて友だちと対話する活動をさせる。次の(条件)を踏まえて(①)・(②)に適する英文を一つずつ書き，モデルとして示す対話文を完成させなさい。

(条件)

・( )内にアルファベットが書いてある場合は，その文字が先頭に来る単語から始まる文を書くこと。(語数は問わない。)

・一～二文の英文で書くこと。(語数は問わない。)

生徒A	生徒B
(① H) ?	
	Yes. I've seen a professional basketball player, Michael Johnson at Osaka Station. He was so tall and big! I took a picture of him.
Oh, you were lucky! I've never seen a famous person.	
	Tell me about your unusual experience.
OK. (②).	
	Wow! You were lucky too!

(2) 中学校第2学年の英語の授業で，クラスメートへの(インタビュー結果)をもとに，クラスで「好きな季節」についてレポートを書かせる。その際，比較表現を使わせたい。次の(インタビュー結果)の表をもとに，モデルとして提示する比較級を用いた文と最上級を用いた文を，それぞれ一文ずつ書きなさい。(語数は問わない。)

(インタビュー結果)

Q: What's your favorite season?	Spring	Summer	Fall	Winter
	8	13	4	10

(3) 中学校第3学年の英語の授業で，外国人観光客に日本文化を紹介する記事を英語で書く活動をさせる。その際，関係代名詞もしくは分詞の後置修飾を用いた文を使わせたい。モデルとして提示する文章を45語程度で書きなさい。(文の数は問わない。)

(☆☆☆◎◎◎)

【高等学校】

【１】放送される指示に従って答えなさい。

(Part 1)

Are you satisfied with your own society?

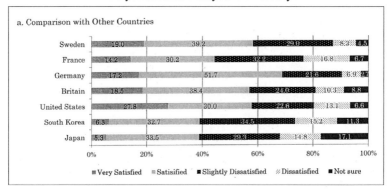

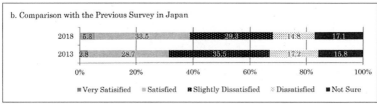

（内閣府『我が国と諸外国の若者の意識に関する調査（平成30年度）』を参照）

(Part 2)

No.1

Airport Guide

Shops & Restaurants	Third Level
Baggage Claim	Second Level
International Arrivals	First Level
Public Transportation	Basement Level

No.2

(Part 3)

1.

　(A)　To restore a violinist's abilities to play

(B) To remove a brain tumor

(C) To establish a new operation procedure

(D) To study how the brain controls the hands

2.

(A) The violinist didn't survive.

(B) The operation was stopped because the violinist started moving.

(C) The violinist couldn't move her hands.

(D) The violinist's hands still work normally.

(☆☆☆○○○○○)

【2】次の各問いに答えなさい。

(1) 次の文は，学校教育法において「第6章 高等学校」にある条文の一部である。(出題の都合上，途中，省略した部分がある。)各条文中の(①)～(④)にあてはまる語句の組み合わせとして，最も適切なものを以下の(ア)～(ク)から一つ選び，記号で答えなさい。なお，同じ番号の( )には，同じ語句が入るものとする。

> 第50条 高等学校は，中学校における教育の基礎の上に，心身の発達及び(①)に応じて，高度な普通教育及び専門教育を施すことを目的とする。
> 第51条 高等学校における教育は，前条に規定する目的を実現するため，次に掲げる目標を達成するよう行われるものとする。
> 1 義務教育として行われる普通教育の成果を更に発展拡充させて，豊かな人間性，(②)及び健やかな身体を養い，国家及び社会の形成者として必要な資質を養うこと。
> 2 社会において果たさなければならない使命の自覚に基づき，個性に応じて将来の(①)を決定させ，一般的な教養を高め，専門的な知識，技術及び技能を習得させること。
> 3 個性の確立に努めるとともに，社会について，広く深い理

解と健全な(　③　)を養い，社会の発展に寄与する態度を養うこと。

第52条　高等学校の学科及び教育課程に関する事項は，(中略)，(　④　)が定める。

	①	②	③	④
(ア)	学力	自立性	批判力	文部科学大臣
(イ)	進路	創造性	批判力	教育長
(ウ)	学力	創造性	貢献力	文部科学大臣
(エ)	進路	自立性	貢献力	地方公共団体の長
(オ)	学力	自立性	貢献力	教育長
(カ)	進路	自立性	貢献力	文部科学大臣
(キ)	学力	創造性	批判力	地方公共団体の長
(ク)	進路	創造性	批判力	文部科学大臣

(2)　次の文章は，「高等学校学習指導要領(平成30年3月告示)」において「第1章　総則」に記載された，道徳教育に関する内容の一部である。(出題の都合上，途中，省略した部分がある。)(　①　)～(　③　)にあてはまる，最も適切な語句を答えなさい。なお，同じ番号の(　)には，同じ語句が入るものとする。

第1款　高等学校教育の基本と教育課程の役割

　道徳教育や体験活動，多様な表現や鑑賞の活動等を通して，豊かな心や創造性の涵養を目指した教育の充実に努めること。

　学校における道徳教育は，(　①　)に関する教育を学校の教育活動全体を通じて行うことによりその充実を図るものとし，各教科に属する科目(以下「各教科・科目等」という。)，総合的な探究の時間及び特別活動(以下「各教科・科目等」という。)のそれぞれの特質に応じて，適切な指導を行うこと。

　道徳教育は，教育基本法及び学校教育法に定められた教育の根本精神に基づき，生徒が自己探求と自己実現に努め国家・社会の一員としての自覚に基づき行為しうる発達の段階

にあることを考慮し，(　①　)を考え，主体的な判断の下に行
動し，自立した人間として他者と共によりよく生きるための
基盤となる道徳性を養うことを目標とすること。

第7款　道徳教育に関する配慮事項
　道徳教育を進めるに当たっては，道徳教育の特質を踏まえ，
第6款までに示す事項に加え，次の事項に配慮するものとする。
1　各学校においては，(中略)道徳教育の目標を踏まえ，道徳
　教育の全体計画を作成し，校長の方針の下に，道徳教育の
　推進を主に担当する教師(「(　②　)」という。)を中心に，
　全教師が協力して道徳教育を展開すること。なお，道徳教
　育の全体計画の作成に当たっては，生徒や学校の実態に応
　じ，指導の方針や重点を明らかにして，各教科・科目等と
　の関係を明らかにすること。その際，公民科の「公共」及
　び「倫理」並びに(　③　)が，(　①　)に関する中核的な指
　導の場面であることに配慮すること。

(3)　『高等学校学習指導要領　外国語』(平成30年3月告示)に関する各
　問いに答えなさい。

第2款　各科目
第4　論理・表現Ⅰ
　2　内容
　　(省略)
　(3)　言語活動及び言語の働きに関する事項
　　①　言語活動に関する事項
　　　(2)に示す事項については，(1)に示す事項を活用し
　　て，例えば，次のような三つの領域別の言語活動及
　　び複数の領域を結び付けた統合的な言語活動を通し
　　て指導する。

　　　ア　話すこと[やり取り]
　　　(ア)　関心のある事柄や学校生活などの日常的な話題
　　　　　について，使用する語句や文，やり取りの具体的
　　　　　な進め方が(　１　)状況で，(　２　)や考え，気持
　　　　　ちなどを話して伝え合ったり，やり取りを通して
　　　　　必要な(　２　)を得たりする活動。また，やり取り
　　　　　した内容を整理して発表したり，文章を書いたり
　　　　　する活動。
　　　(イ)　日常的な話題や(　３　)的な話題に関して聞いた
　　　　　り読んだりした内容について，使用する語句や文，
　　　　　やり取りの具体的な進め方が(　１　)状況で，優
　　　　　れている点や改善すべき点を話して伝え合った
　　　　　り，意見や主張などを適切な理由や根拠とともに
　　　　　伝え合ったりするディベートや(　４　)をする活
　　　　　動。また，やり取りした内容を踏まえて，自分自
　　　　　身の考えなどを整理して発表したり，文章を書い
　　　　　たりする活動。
　(以下省略)

第3款　英語に関する各科目にわたる指導計画の作成と内容の
　　取扱い
１　指導計画の作成に当たっては，小学校や中学校における
　　指導との接続に留意しながら，次の事項に配慮するもの
　　とする。
　(省略)
　(5)　実際に英語を使用して自分自身の考えを伝え合うな
　　　どの言語活動を行う際は，既習の語句や文構造，文法
　　　事項などの学習内容を(　Ｘ　)指導し定着を図ること。
　(6)　生徒が英語に触れる機会を充実させるとともに，授

62

業を実際の(Y)の場面とするため，授業は英語で行
うことを基本とする。その際，生徒の理解の程度に応
じた英語を用いるようにすること。

(以下省略)

(あ) (1)〜(4)に入る語句を，①〜④の中からそれぞれ一つ
ずつ選び，番号で答えなさい。なお，同じ番号の( )には，同
じ語句が入るものとする。

(1) ① 示されない   ② わずかに示される
　　　　③ 示される   ④ 十分に示される
(2) ① 情報   ② 事実
　　　　③ 仮説   ④ 常識
(3) ① 社会   ② 時事
　　　　③ 一般   ④ 国際
(4) ① プレゼンテーション ② ディスカッション
　　　　③ スピーチ   ④ ペア・ワーク

(い) (X)，(Y)に入る適切な語句をそれぞれ答えなさい。

(☆☆☆○○○)

【3】次の(1)〜(6)の英文の( )に入る最も適切な語または語句を，①〜
④の中からそれぞれ一つずつ選び，番号で答えなさい。

(1) The paper I have given you should be kept strictly( ).
　　① conferenced   ② confidential   ③ confronted
　　④ confiscated

(2) ( )you need any help, just let me know.
　　① Do   ② Had   ③ Should   ④ Like

(3) People prefer to pay more money for safer food.But still,the high price
　　of organic food is an ( )for a majority of people.
　　① objection   ② obligation   ③ problem   ④ obstacle

(4) The continuing decline in the economy will probably ( )to an

increase in unemployment.

  ① accumulate   ② cause   ③ lead   ④ direct

(5) Please remain (   )until the aircraft comes to a complete stop.

  ① seated   ② be seated   ③ having seated   ④ seating

(6) (   )wishes to join our club will be welcome.

  ① Anyone   ② No matter who   ③ All that   ④ Whoever

(☆☆☆○○○○○)

【4】【例】にならって，各語または語句の説明に合うように，それぞれ
の(   )にあてはまる最も適切な語を英語一語で答えなさい。

  【例】doctor

     a person whose profession is to attend to and treat (sick) people

(1) opinion

    what a person thinks about something, based on personal judgement rather
    than actual(   )

(2) human rights

    the non-political rights of freedom, equality,etc., which belong to any
    person (   )regard to race, religion, color, sex, etc.

(3) sympathy

    (   )to and understanding of the sufferings of other people, often
    expressed in a willingness to give help

(☆☆☆○○○)

【5】次の各問いに答えなさい。

(1) 次の2人の会話の下線部を英語にしなさい。

> A：Oh, no! I have two meetings scheduled tomorrow at two, and ( ).
>
> B：Then you'll just have to cancel one of them.
>
> A：どうしよう！明日2時に2つ会議が予定されていて，どっちももう変えられない。
>
> B：それならそのうちどちらかを欠席するしかないでしょう。

(旺文社2021年度版　英検準1級過去6回全問題集を参照)

(2) 次の文章を英語にしなさい。

> オーストラリアで最も愛されている動物の1つが，さらに絶滅寸前の状態に陥っています。政府当局者は，オーストラリア東海岸全域においてのコアラを絶滅危惧種であると宣言しました。当局者は，主に気候変動が責めを負うべきであると述べています。

(NHKゴガク　ニュースで英語術より抜粋)

(3) 次の健(Ken)さんと真由(Mayu)さんによるディベートの対話の流れに合うように空所に適切な英文を書きなさい。ただし，文の数は問わない。

> Moderator(司会者)：Hi, today we will have a debate. The topic is "Schools should have strict rules for students about their appearances." Ken, what do you think?
>
> Ken(肯定側)：I agree with this statement. In my opinion, the most important thing in school is to study. Without rules on hair styles and clothing, students would dress in strange ways that would distract themselves from their studies.

| Moderator | : Mayu, what is your counter argument, and why do you think so? |
| Mayu (否定側) | : (　　). |

(KINSEIDO　*Viewpoints : For and Against*を参照)

(☆☆☆○○○)

【6】次の英文を読み，各問いに答えなさい。

When it comes to influencing others, delivering the right number of messages to support your proposal or proposition is going to be crucial. Too (　①　), and your attempt might come across as halfhearted,indifferent or plain weak. But too many messages can hurt you too. Like adding too much spice to the dish, your influence attempt could become overpowering－one that even the dog will turn his nose up at. So when it comes to successfully persuading others, what is the optimal number of claims that you should employ to produce the most positive impression?

One potential answer to this question comes from a brand new study conducted by researchers Suzanne Shu from UCLA's Anderson School of Business and Kurt Carlson from the marketing department at Georgetown University. In their studies, participants were assigned to one of six groups and asked to read descriptions of five different target objects－a breakfast cereal, a restaurant, a shampoo, an ice cream store, and a politician.

As an example, the shampoo advertisement was introduced as follows: *"Imagine that you are reading one of your favorite magazines and an ad for a new brand of shampoo catches your attention. You decide to read the ad carefully to see if it is worth switching to this new product. The ad says that this new shampoo does the following:*

＜BLANK SPACE＞

The blank space was then filled with one,two,three,four,five or six positive claims about the shampoo object. For example participants who were shown all six claims read *"Makes hair cleaner, stroger, healthier, softer, shinier, and fuller."*

In the advertisement for the politician, participants who were shown all six claims read that he was "honest, had ②integrity,experience, intelligence, interpersonal skills, and a desire to serve."

After seeing the ads the attitudes of each participant toward the target objects were measured along with how positive or negative their impressions for each were. The researchers also measured levels of skepticism in an attempt to identify (③) people started to think that the claims on the ads were just a dishonest attempt to persuade them.

The results clearly demonstrated that those who had read *three* claims rated all the items (regardless of whether they were shampoos or politicians)significantly more positively than participants who had read adverts with one, two, four, five, or six claims. So it would appear that adding additional positive claims to a persuasive appeal increases the effectiveness of that appeal but only until the third claim is reached. But beyond three, further persuasion attempts increase skepticism which,in turn, can heighten resistance to the overall persuasion appeal.

This squares with another recent study, this time conducted by Daniel Feiler. Leigh Tost and Adam Grant, for the Make-A-Wish Foundation. Participants were randomly assigned to receive a request to donate to the charity that had either two egoistic reasons to give, two altruistic reasons or all four reasons combined. Giving intentions were much lower in the group who were provided with four reasons to donate with post study surveys revealing a simple reason ④why. People could see the persuasion attempt for what it was—an attempt to influence them. More evidence shows that there comes a point at which adding additional arguments and justifications to your proposal only serves to heighten resistance which, in turn, can reduce its impact.

So the answer to the question "What is the optimal number of claims that should be used to produce the most positive impression?" seems to be three.

Or, as Shu and Carlson write, "(⑤)*charms but* (⑥)*alarms.*"

(INFLUENCE AT WORK *Two, Four or Six? When Persuading, What Numbers of Claims is Most Effective?* より抜粋，一部改編)

(1) 空所①に入る最も適切な語を，(ア)～(エ)の中から一つ選び，記号で答えなさい。

　(ア) few　　(イ) little　　(ウ) many　　(エ) much

(2) 下線部②の語の意味に最も近いものを，(ア)～(エ)の中から一つ選び，記号で答えなさい。

　(ア) attention　　(イ) consideration　　(ウ) praise

　(エ) trustworthiness

(3) 本文の内容に合うように空所③に適切な英語一語を書きなさい。

(4) 下線部④が表す内容として最も適切なものを，(ア)～(エ)の中から一つ選び，記号で答えなさい。

　(ア) why participants who received egoistic reasons were less likely to make donations compared to those who received altruistic reasons

　(イ) why all the participants tended to donate a lot

　(ウ) why participants were asked to donate to the charity

　(エ) why it was likely that participants provided with four reasons donated less

(5) 本文全体の内容を踏まえ，空所⑤と⑥に入る適切な数字をそれぞれ英語で書きなさい。

(☆☆☆○○○○○)

【7】次の英文を読み，各問いに答えなさい。

The truths of science are verifiable, and the progress of science can be measured in many fields from heart-transplant surgery to nuclear fission. From its earliest days, Western science has restricted itself to answerable questions, and has scrupulously observed rules of proof and evidence, as the arts have not.(①) 'scientific truth' means something definite, whereas 'artistic truth' is a nebulous concept. It is true to say, for example, that the earth goes around the sun, whereas to claim that Pollock is a better painter than Alma-Tadema, or vice versa, is not a verifiable proposition but an opinion, and ②this would be so even if it were an opinion that very many people, or possibly all living people shared.

Does this mean that the arts have no access to truth? Art-lovers have often strenuously denied such an imputation. Schopenhauer maintained that art was a form of knowledge, giving intuitive, direct access to metaphysical truths, 'the permanent, essential forms of the world and all its phenomena'. The philosopher Hans-Georg Gadamer has called art 'a transformation into the true' ; the painter Piet Mondrian contended that abstract art revealed 'the true content of reality' and 'the great hidden laws of nature' ; Jeanette Winterson refers to 'the huge truth of a Picasso', and so on. What are we to make of such claims? Obviously they are different from the claims to truth that science makes, since they are not verifiable, and it is unfortunate that the way they are phrased sometimes obscures this difference. It would be impossible to prove that a Picasso was any more 'true' than, say, a washing machine or a packet of crisps. 'The permanent, essential forms of the world and all its phenomena', as an atomic physicist would understand the phrase, would bear no relation to what Schopenhauer meant by it, and what Schopenhauer meant by it would seem to most people nowadays merely fanciful. Claims about the 'truth' of art are statements of personal belief, and since they are not subject to verification or falsification they cannot have the same kind of authority as claims that are.

(③), a more serious objection to claims that art is 'true' is that they are restrictive and limiting. Though their aim seems to be to aggrandize art, they in fact diminish it. Science's concentration on truth is reductive, in that every true answer displaces innumerable false ones. Science's progress is at the expense of its past mistakes, which cease to have any scientific interest, and become merely part of the history of science. Art does not operate in this way. There are no false answers in art, because there are no true answers, and ④the past matters because the present does not displace it. Since art must accommodate all personal tastes and choices, it is as illimitable as humanity, and as extensive as the imagination. The aim of science, by contrast, is to find solutions that are unaffected by taste or choice, and which consequently climinate the human element altogether. In this respect, ⑤art is infinite, whereas science is bounded. But art is infinite only because, and so long as, it does not allow truth-claims. Once truth-claims are admitted—the claim, for instance, that Picasso is more 'true' than some other painter—the terrain of what can be counted as 'real' art shrinks, and is subjected to ⑥policing, instead of being as lawless and inventive as human intelligence.

(旺文社　*2010年度版　全国大学入試問題正解*　を参照)

(1) この英文全体で対比されている2つのものは何か。日本語で端的に答えなさい。

(2) 空所①と③に入る最も適切な語または語句を，(ア)～(エ)の中からそれぞれ一つずつ選び，記号で答えなさい。

  (ア)　Consequently　　(イ)　For example　　(ウ)　Meanwhile

  (エ)　However

(3) 下線部②について，"this would be so" の内容を明確にして，下線部全体を和訳しなさい。ただし固有名詞は英語表記のままでかまわない。

(4) 下線部④の内容と対照的な内容を述べている一文を本文中から抜き出し，その文の最初と最後の3単語(ピリオド除く)をそれぞれ書きなさい。

(5) 下線部⑤のように言える理由を30字以内(句読点含む)の日本語で答えなさい。

(6) 下線部⑥と同じ意味を表す語句を本文中から抜き出し，書きなさい。

(☆☆☆◎◎◎◎◎)

【8】英語学習について書かれた次の[A], [B], [C]の英文を読み，各問いに答えなさい。

A

One thing that can drive teachers wild is when their students are apparently unwilling to use English in the classroom, especially during communicative activities. This is often seen as an example of student/teacher failure. After all,if students are not using English everyone is wasting their time. However, there are many understandable reasons why students revert to their own language in certain activities.

A principal cause of this L1 use is the language required by the activity. If we ask beginners to have a free and fluent discussion about global warming, for example, we are asking them to do something which they are linguistically incapable of. Their only possible course of action, if they really want to say anything about the topic, is to use their own language. In other words the choice of task has made the use of L1 almost inevitable: students can hardly be blamed for this.

Another reason why students use their own language in the classroom is because it is an entirely natural thing to do; when we learn a foreign language we use translation almost without thinking about it, particularly at elementary and intermediate levels. This is because we try to make sense of a new linguistic (and conceptual)world through the linguistic world we are already familiar with. Code-switching between L1 and L2 is naturally developmental, and not some example of misguided behavior.

Students use their L1 when performing pedagogical tasks, especially when one student is explaining something to another. This is a habit that in most cases will occur without encouragement from the teacher.

Another cause of mother tongue use can be teachers themselves. If, they frequently use the students'language (whether or not they themselves are native speakers of that language), then the students will feel comfortable doing it too. Teachers need,therefore,to be aware of the kind of example they themselves are providing.

Finally, it is worth pointing out that the amount of LI use by particular students may well have a lot to do with differing learner styles and abilities. Some use mostly English from the very beginning, whereas others seem to nccd to use their L1 more frequently.

B

The idea that all use of the mother tongue in the language classroom should be avoided stems from the advent of the Direct Method at the beginning of the twentieth century (where the language itself was talked and taught rather than being talked about in the students' L1), and from the training of native-English speaker teachers who either had to deal with multilingual classes and/or teach in countries before they were themselves competent in the language of their students.

More recently, however, attitudes to the use of the students' mother tongue have undergone a significant change. David Atkinson argued that it is not difficult to think of several general advantages of judicious use of the mother tongue, suggesting that such activities as grammar explanations, checking comprehension, giving instructions, discussing classroom methodology and checking for sense fell into this category. If teachers can use the students' language, he claims, these tasks will be expedited more efficiently.

(中略)

Two issues seem to arise here. In the first place, since students are likely to use their L1 anyway, there is little point in trying to stamp it out completely. Such an approach will not work, and may only discourage the students who feel the need for it at some stages. However, a lot will depend on when students use their L1. If they are working in pairs studying a reading text, for example, the use of their L1 may be quite acceptable since they are using it to further their understanding of English. If, on the other hand, they are doing an oral fluency activity, the use of a language other than English makes the activity essentially pointless. Furthermore, as teachers we will want to promote as much English use as possible. So we will try and insist on the use of English in language study and oral production activities, but be more relaxed about it in other pedagogic situations, though we will continue to encourage students to try to use it as often as possible.

As for teachers, they are a principal source of comprehensible input; teacher-talking time (TTT)has an important part to play in language acquisition. It therefore makes sense for us to speak English as much as possible in the class, especially since if we do not, students will not see the need to speak too much English either. However, there are times, especially at lower levels, where the use of LI may help both teacher and students such as in an e xplanation or discussion of methodology, or the giving of announcements which would be impossibly difficult in English.

C

During communicative activities, however, it is generally felt that teachers should not interrupt students in mid-flow to point out a grammatical, lexical, or pronunciation error, since to do so interrupts the communication and drags an activity back to the study of language form or precise meaning. Indeed, according to one view of teaching and learning, speaking activities in the classroom, especially activities at the extreme communicative end of our continuum, act as a switch to help learners transfer 'learnt' language to the 'acquired' store or a trigger, forcing students to think carefully about how best to express the meanings they wish to convey. Part of the value of such activities lies in the various attempts that students have to make to get their meanings across; processing language for communication is, in this view, the best way of processing language for acquisition. Teacher intervention in such circumstances can raise stress levels and stop the acquisition process in its tracks.

If that is the case, the methodologist Tony Lynch argues, then students have a lot to gain from coming up against communication problems. Provided that they have some of the words and phrases necessary to help them negotiate a way out of their communicative impasses, they will learn a lot from so doing. When teachers intervene, not only to correct but also to supply alternative modes of expression to help students, they remove that need to negotiate meaning, and thus they may deny students a learning opportunity. In such situations teacher intervention may sometimes be necessary, but it is nevertheless unfortunate－even when we are using gentle correction.In Tony Lynch's words, '…the best answer to the question of when to intervene in learner talk is: as late as possible.'

(Jeremy Harmer, *The Practice of English Language Teaching*より抜粋，一部改編)

(1) 英文Ａについて表1のようにまとめるとき，(ア)～(ウ)にあてはまる内容を日本語で答えなさい。

表1

トピック：生徒が授業中に英語を話さない原因	
一つ目の原因	(ア)
二つ目の原因	(イ)
三つ目の原因	(ウ)
四つ目の原因	学習スタイルや能力における個人差があり，初めから英語を話そうとする者もいれば，そうでない者もいる。

(2) 英文Ｂについて，下線部のDavid Atkinson氏の主張を日本語で説明しなさい。

(3) 英文Ｂについて，英語の授業を英語で行うことの必要性を本文に即して日本語で説明しなさい。

(4) 英文Ｃの内容を踏まえて，英語コミュニケーションⅠの授業の初めにスモールトーク(ペアなどで日常的な話題等について話す活動)を行う際の指導上の留意点について表2のようにまとめるとき，(ア)～(ウ)にあてはまる内容を日本語で答えなさい。

表2

活動内容	日常的な話題について，ペアを変えて，スモールトークを2回行う。
活動によって身につけさせたい力や姿勢	（ア）
教師の指導または支援の内容例	（イ）
（イ）の指導または支援を行うタイミング	（ウ）

（☆☆☆☆☆◎◎◎◎◎）

解答・解説

【中学校】

【1】(1) （ウ）　(2) ① 社会　② 積極　(3) ① 社会的　② 表現　(4) ① (d)　② (j)　③ (e)　④ (f)

〈解説〉(1) 教育基本法第2条は，「教育の目標」について規定したもの。教育基本法第1条で規定されている「教育の目的」の実現のためにどのようにすればよいか，5つの教育目標を挙げている。　(2) 従前は，不登校児童生徒への支援はあくまでも「学校への復帰」であると解釈されることが多く，フリースクールやインターネットによる学習を出席日数と見なすかどうかは，学校によって見解が分かれていた。本通知は，支援に関する共通理解を図るために，不登校児童生徒への支援は「学校に復帰すること」ではなくて，「児童生徒が将来，社会的に自立すること」であることを明示したもの。　(3) 出題は，外国語科の「思考力，判断力，表現力等」に関する目標である。平成29(2017)年の学習指導要領改訂によって，校種間の接続が一層重視されるようになっている。よって，中学校の外国語科の目標は，小学校の外国語科の目標から発展したものになっていることに留意したい。例えば，空欄①については，小学校(第5学年及び第6学年)の外国語科では「身近で簡単な事柄」となっているが，中学校では「日常的な話題や社会

75

的な話題」を扱うようになる。空欄②については，小学校の外国語科では「自分の考えや気持ちなどを伝え合うことができる基礎的な力」となっているが，中学校では「表現したり伝え合ったりすることができる力」になっている。　(4)　空欄①については，2つ目の空欄に着目する。現行の学習指導要領において言語材料は言語活動を通して指導することが求められている。次に，空欄②と③については，音声に関する内容であることを踏まえれば使用できる選択肢は限られる。特に③については，その直後にある「イントネーション」がヒントになるだろう。最後に④については，言語活動の目的や場面，状況等のことであり，小学校の外国語科の学習指導要領においても同じ記述がある。

【２】(1)　(イ)　　(2)　(ア)　　(3)　(エ)　　(4)　(イ)　　(5)　(ウ)
(6)　(ウ)　　(7)　(イ)　　(8)　(ア)　　(9)　(エ)　　(10)　(ウ)
〈解説〉(1)　空欄を含んだ節は「ベートーベンが聴覚に障害を持ちながらも交響曲第9番を作曲したことを知って私はとても感動した」の意である。composedは「作曲した」の意味である。　(2)　空欄を含んだ節は「なので，彼はローンを組んで家の代金を分割で支払うことに決めた」の意である。in installmentsは「分割払いで」の意味である。
(3)　空欄を含んだ文は「その科学者のグループは，現在治療法のない病気に対して新しく開発された薬の有効性を確かめるために，ネズミを使った実験を行った」の意である。experimentsは「実験」の意味である。　(4)　与えられた2文は「サラの祖父はまだ使えると思って，サラに古い時計をあげた。しかしそれは時代遅れのものであった」の意である。obsoleteは「時代遅れの」の意味である。　(5)　空欄を含んだ文は「そのイベントの入場口で，スタッフは観客の鞄の中身を確認していた」の意である。次の文に，その理由としてライブ音楽を録音されたくなかったと述べられている。contentsは「中身」の意味である。　(6)　空欄を含んだ文は「そのホテルはゴルフ場，スパ，屋内プールなど多くの一流の快適な設備を有していた」の意である。amenitiesは「快適な設備(施設)」の意味である。　(7)　空欄を含んだ

節は「彼女は20分もかからないうちに，その宿題をなんなくこなした」の意である。sail throughは「楽にこなす，容易にやり遂げる」の意味である。　(8)　空欄を含んだ文は「けがをしたり具合を悪くしたりした走者を看病するために，医者と看護師たちはトライアスロン競技中に待機していた」の意である。stand byは「待機する(スタンバイする)」の意味である。　(9)　与えられた2文は「新しい社員は，自身が言っていた技術も有していなければ，仕事に良い姿勢で取り組んでもいなかった。つまり，彼女はその仕事の基準に達していなかったので，解雇された」の意である。measure upは「基準などに達する(かなう)」の意味である。　(10)　空欄を含んだ文は「私たちは何時間も話をしたが，何も良いアイデアが全く思いつかなかった」の意である。come up withは「思いつく」の意味である。

【3】(1)　①　(エ)　　②　(オ)　　(2)　①　(ア)　　②　(ウ)
(3)　①　(ア)　　②　(エ)　　(4)　①　(ウ)　　②　(エ)
(5)　①　(ア)　　②　(オ)

〈解説〉(1)　完成した英文はThe dog stood on the platform with her tail wagging until the train was completely out of sight.であり，「電車が完全に見えなくなるまで，その犬は尻尾を振りながらホームに立っていた」の意である。　(2)　完成した英文はMr. Osaki suggested that Jane be transferred to the marketing department.であり，「Osaki氏はJaneをマーケティング部に異動させることを提案した」の意である。　(3)　完成した節はbut at the store I found that each shopper could buy no more than one pack of them.であり，「しかし，お店では客1人につき1パックしかトイレットペーパーを買えなかった」の意である。　(4)　完成した英文はSome people are spoiling their children by giving them everything they ask for.であり，「子どもが求めるものを全て与えることで，甘やかしてしまう人もいる」の意である。　(5)　完成した節はShe's having difficulty keeping her balance on the ice now,であり，「今，彼女は氷上でバランスをとることが困難である」の意である。

【４】(1)　私は考えています，母のことや，いろんな世代の女性たち－黒人女性，アジア系，白人，ラテン系，ネイティブアメリカンの女性たち－のことを。彼女たちが，我が国の歴史全体にわたって，今夜のこの瞬間に至る道を切り開いてきたのです。　　(2)　(エ)　　(3)　大志を抱いて夢見てください。自信を持って先陣を切り，単に前例がないからという理由で他の人がやらないような道にも進んでみてください。　　(4)　・命を救ってこの伝染病を打ち負かす　　・経済を立て直して労働者を益するようにする　　・我が国の司法制度や社会から構造的人種差別を一掃する　　・気候危機と戦う　　・国をまとめて国家の魂を癒す　から3つ

〈解説〉(1)　まず，about my motherとabout the generations of womenがandで並列されてthinkに後続する前置詞句を構成している。そして，generations of womenの例としてAsian, white, Latina, Native American womenがあり，それらを関係代名詞節が修飾している。関係代名詞節はthroughout our nation's historyが挿入された形になっていることに留意したい。　　(2)　空欄の前後に着目すると，空欄の直前には「しかしながら，私はこの職場では最初の女性かもしれないが，（　　）ではないだろう」とあり，空欄の直後には「なぜなら，今夜これを見ている全ての少女は，ここが可能性のある国であるとわかっているからである」とある。したがって，「私は最後の女性ではないだろう」を意味する(エ)が正解。　　(3)　まず，Dream with ambition, lead with convictionそしてsee yourselves in a way…がandで並列されている。次に，see yourselvesを修飾するin a way以下であるが，others may notの後にはseeが省略されていることに留意し，後続するsimply because以下の内容がothers may notの理由であることに着目すればよいだろう。　　(4)　下線部の直後に具体例が5つ述べられており，セミコロンで列挙されている。これらの中から日本語で答えやすい3つを選んで解答すればよいだろう。

【5】(1) 子どもを教える教師にはユーモアのセンス，心の広さ，適応力，我慢強さが大いに役立つが，たとえ無口で内気なタイプであっても，努力によって必要な能力と態度を身につけることができる。
(2) （エ）　(3) （イ）　(4)「先生はあなたの作品を好きだと思うよ」と言ってやるとか，掲示板に貼ってやるとか，クラスのみんなに読んで聞かせるとか，ごほうびや賞を与える以外の適当な方法でほめるようにすれば，他の子どもを除外することなく，その子どもに達成感を与えることができる。　(5) （ウ）

〈解説〉(1) まず，As a teacher of young childrenで前置詞句が区切られていることに留意しつつ，it helps a lotのitが後続するif節の内容であることに着目する。このif節はyou have…etc.,までである。次に，but even ifのif節であるが，ここはyou're the silent, reserved type「だったとしても」の意であることに留意して，主節you can work on…を訳せばよい。
(2) 空欄を含んだ文のあるパラグラフの1文目に「教師として，全ての子どもたちを平等に好きであるように見えないといけない」と述べていることから，空欄を含んだ文は「幼い子どもたちは，公平性に非常に敏感な感覚を持っている」の意となるのが適切。　(3) 空欄直後の2文に着目すると，安心感が言語学習における自立と冒険を促すこと，そして，語学の授業から最大限のことを得るために安心感が不可欠だと述べられている。さらに，その直後の文に述べられているが，箇条書きされている内容は，安心感のあるクラスの雰囲気作りの方法のことである。したがって，「子どもたちに安心感を与える」を意味する(イ)が正解。　(4) Thisが指す内容は下線部の直前の文であり，直前の内容と併せて和訳をするように解答すればよい。　(5) 4番目の箇条書きの1文目と2文目に対応する記述がある。

【6】(1) ① Have you ever had an unusual experience?　② I've caught an eel in the river near my house.　(2) 比較級…Winter is more popular than spring in our class.　最上級…Thirteen of our classmates like summer the best.　(3) A *furoshiki* is a piece of cloth that is used to wrap and carry things. It is wide and square, but you can fold it up and keep it in your pocket. *Furoshiki* are not only convenient, but good for the environment. If you use *furoshiki* instead of plastic bags, you won't waste resources. (54語)

〈解説〉(1)　いずれの空欄についても前後の発話に着目しながら解答を作成すればよい。まず，①については，生徒Bは1つ目の発話I've seen a professional basketball player.と答えており，2つ目の発話でTell me about your unusual experienceと聞き返していることに着目すると，解答例にあるように「珍しい経験をしたことがありますか」という質問が自然である。次に，②については，生徒Bの3つ目の発話でYou were lucky too!とあることから，貴重な経験の例を答えればよい。　(2)　比較級と最上級を用いた例文を書く問題である。解答例の他にも，比較級を用いた文であればSpring is more popular than Fall in our class.最上級を用いた文であればSummer is the most popular in our class.なども可能であろう。　(3)　関係代名詞または分詞の後置修飾を用いて日本文化について説明する英文を書くことが求められている。制限語数が45語程度であるため，解答例にあるふろしきのように，日本文化を代表するものを1つ挙げて紹介するのが書きやすいだろう。

【高等学校】

【1】Part1　C　　　Part2　No.1　D　　　No.2　D　　　Part3　(1)　B
　(2)　D

〈解説〉スクリプトは非公開である。全て多肢選択式の問題であるが，いずれの問題も問題用紙に質問文が印刷されていない点に留意したい。
Part 1　グラフが与えられているが，選択肢も音声で流される問題である。グラフから読み取れる内容についての問題であると推測できる。
Part 2　No.1は表が与えられているが，No.2は全く情報がない。No.1の表からは，空港の案内に関する問題であると推測できる。
Part 3　選択肢が印刷されているが，視覚情報などは与えられていない。与えられた選択肢からは，脳に異常のあるバイオリニストに関する問題であると推測できる。

【２】(1)　(ク)　　(2)　①　人間としての在り方生き方　　②　道徳教育
推進教師　　③　特別活動　　(3)　(あ)　1　④　　2　①
3　①　　4　②　　(い)　X　繰り返し　　Y　コミュニケーション
〈解説〉(1)　学校教育法第50条は高等学校の目的，第51条は同目標を定
めたもの。第52条は教育課程についての規定であるが，学校教育法施
行規則第84条に「高等学校の教育課程については，この章に定めるも
ののほか，教育課程の基準として文部科学大臣が別に公示する高等学
校学習指導要領によるものとする」とあることに注意したい。
(2)　①「人間としての在り方生き方」という記述は，平成元(1989)年
度の学習指導要領改訂時に，学校における道徳教育に関して初めて導
入され，その後も引き継がれてきた。平成30(2018)年度改訂の高等学
校学習指導要領では，道徳教育においては「人間としての在り方生き
方に関する『教育を行う』」，公民では「同『自覚を育てる』」，総合的
な探究の時間では「同『考えることができるようにする』」，特別活動
では「同『自覚を深める』」ことが求められていることに留意する。
②　道徳教育推進教師の役割として，全体計画の作成の他に，道徳の
授業における各教師の相談役，授業研修や授業公開の実施による情報
提供など，授業を実施しやすい環境づくり，各種資料・図書・掲示物
の整備など，全体をコーディネートすることなどが求められている。
③　特別活動の目標には「人間としての在り方生き方」が掲げられて
いることから，公民科の「公共」及び「倫理」とともに，人間として
の在り方生き方に関する中核的な指導の場面として重視する必要があ
る。　(3)　(あ)　高等学校学習指導要領の「論理・表現Ⅰ」の内容に
おける「言語活動及び言語の働きに関する事項」について適語を選択
する問題である。　1　やり取りを継続させるための具体的なモデル
を提示する必要があることを踏まえればよい。　2　インフォメーシ
ョン・ギャップがある状況において，情報を伝え合ったり，やり取り
を通して情報を得たりする活動が求められていることに着目する。
3　小学校外国語科では「身近で簡単な事柄」となっていたが，中学
校，高校と校種が上がるにつれて発展した形である。　4　現行の学

習指導要領から導入された「論理・表現」はディベートやディスカッションが主要な言語活動である。　(い)　X　1つの単元だけで言語材料を完璧に定着させるのではなく，既習の言語材料についても言語活動を通して定着を図ることが求められている。　Y　英語の授業を英語で行う理由について述べられている。言語活動によるコミュニケーションが授業の中心であることを踏まえ，授業をコミュニケーションの場面とすることが求められている。

【3】(1) ②　　(2) ③　　(3) ④　　(4) ③　　(5) ①　　(6) ④
〈解説〉(1)　空欄を含んだ文は「私があなたに渡した書類は極秘に保管すること」の意である。confidentialは「秘密の」の意味である。
(2)　空欄を含んだ文は「もし助けが必要でしたら，教えてください」の意である。今回のshouldはIfと同じ意味で用いられている。
(3)　空欄を含んだ文は「しかし依然として，高価な自然食品を買うのは大多数の人にとっては差しさわりがある」の意である。obstacleは「(何らかの進行を妨げる)障害」の意味である。③のproblemも意味上は問題ないが，空欄前に不定冠詞anがあることから，obstacleが正解と判断できる。　(4)　空欄を含んだ文は「経済の継続的な衰退は失業者の増加につながるだろう」の意である。lead toは「～につながる」の意味である。　(5)　空欄を含んだ文は「飛行機が完全に停止するまで座席に座っていてください」の意である。remainは「～のままである」を意味して状態を示す用法があり，seatは動詞で「座らせる」の意味がある。「座らせられたままにしておく」という意味になるよう過去分詞を選ぶ。　(6)　空欄を含んだ文は「当クラブへの入会希望者は誰でも歓迎します」の意である。Whoeverは「～する人は誰でも」を意味する代名詞である。

【4】(1) fact(s)　　(2) without　　(3) sensitivity
〈解説〉(1)　opinionは「意見」という意味であり，与えられた定義は「事実よりも個人的な判断に基づいて個人が考えたこと」の意である。

(2) human rightsは「人権」という意味であり，与えられた定義は「人種，宗教，肌の色，性別などを問わず，あらゆる人が持っている非政治的な自由や平等の権利のこと」の意である。without regard to～で「～を問わず，～に関わらず」の意味になる。 (3) sympathyは「共感」という意味であり，与えられた定義は「他人の苦しみに対する感受性と理解のことであり，助けようとする意思によって表現されることがある」の意である。

【5】 (1) it's too late to change either of them. (2) One of the most beloved animals in Australia is falling closer to extinction. Government officials have declared the koala an endangered species across the country's east coast. They say climate change is largely to blame. (3) Your idea sounds good, but I don't think it's true. In my opinion, appearance has no effect on academic achievement. For example, I know a school in which students can choose their hair styles freely and many students pass the entrance exams for difficult national universities.

〈解説〉(1) 日本語に引きずられてnot bothの形にしてしまうと，「どちらも変更できないわけではない」という部分否定になるので注意したい。(2) 英語にしたときに主語(主部)と動詞の関係がわかりやすい日本語であるため，素直に直訳をしていけばよいだろう。解答例にはやや難しい語彙も含まれているが，文構造はできるだけ活かして，別の語彙で置き換えられないかを考えたい。 (3) 学校が生徒の身だしなみについて厳しい校則を設けるべきか，というトピックのディベートにおける対話の中で，肯定側の立論に対して理由を添えて否定側の反駁を行う場面である。肯定側の主張としては，身だしなみに関する校則がないと，勉強に集中できないということを述べているため，その主張に対する反論と理由を述べればよい。

【6】(1)　(ア)　　(2)　(エ)　　(3)　when　　(4)　(エ)　　(5)　⑤　three
⑥　four
〈解説〉(1)　空欄のある次の文にBut too manyとあることに着目すればよ
い。対比される内容であることがわかるので，fewが正解。　　(2)　下
線部は，政治家に関する広告として6つ全ての肯定的な主張が与えら
れた場合の例である。integrityとは「高潔さ」のことであり，「信頼」
を意味するエが最も近い意味である。　　(3)　空欄の前後に節があり，
直前の節は「研究者たちは(　　)を特定するために懐疑心の段階も測
定した」，そして直後の節は「広告の主張は，単に自分たちを説得す
るような不誠実なものだと人々が考え始めた」の意である。直後の節
は，直前の節にある「(　　)を特定する」の目的語であることから，
名詞句であることに着目すると，「いつ〜するか」を意味する疑問詞
のwhenが正解である。　　(4)　下線部の直前には，4つの理由が与えら
れた実験参加者グループは寄付に対する意思が非常に低かったことが
述べられており，下線部の直後にはそれらの理由として，自分たちを
説得しようとする意図を理解できたから，と述べられている。このこ
とから，下線部は「4つの理由を与えられた実験参加者は寄付が少な
かった理由」であることがわかる。　　(5)　空欄部の前にあるパラグラ
フで，最も好意的な印象を与えるために効果的なのは主張を3つにす
ることであると述べられている。この点を踏まえると，「3つは魅力的
であるが，4つは警告になる」という意味になるようにする。

【7】(1)　科学(的真理)と芸術(的真理)　　(2)　①　(ア)　　③　(エ)
(3)　極めて多くの人が，またはひょっとすると，全ての生きている人
が共有する意見であったとしても，PollockはAlma-Tademaより優れた
画家である，またはその逆であると主張することは，検証可能な説で
はなく，1つの意見である。　　(4)　Science's progress is〜history of
science　　(5)　芸術は全ての人の嗜好や選択を許容しなければいけな
いから(芸術は真理の主張を認めないから)。
(6)　verification or falsification

〈解説〉(1) scientific truthとartistic truthは，第1パラグラフの3文目や本文中の様々なところで対比されていることがわかる。 (2) ① 空欄の直前で，西洋科学は解答可能な問題に限定し，証明と証拠の規則を厳密に守ってきたが，芸術はそうではなかったと述べられており，空欄の直後で，「科学的な真実」は明確なものである一方で，「芸術的な真実」は漠然とした概念であると述べられている。つまり，空欄の直前の内容がまとめた形で述べられているため，Consequentlyが正解。③ 空欄の直前で，芸術の真偽に関する主張は個人の信条の表明であり，また，芸術は検証や改ざんの対象ではないため，主張と同じような権威は持てないと述べられており，空欄の直後で，芸術が真実という主張に対する深刻な反論は，それが制限的かつ限定的であると述べられている。これらが逆接的な関係にあるためにHoweverが正解。

(3) this would be soの内容は，下線部の直前にあるto claim that Pollock is a better painter…but an opinionを指している。また，this would be so以降の下線部については，いわゆる仮定法過去の形になっている点に注意したい。 (4) 下線部は，「芸術においては現在が過去にとって代わることがないため，過去が重要である」という意味である。前述のように，この英文では科学と芸術が対比されていることに着目すると，科学に関して過去の扱いを述べている箇所を探せばよいことがわかる。よって，科学の発展には過去を犠牲にしているという第3パラグラフの4文目が正解。 (5) 下線部の直前にあるIn this respectに着目すると，下線部より前で芸術について述べられている箇所に着目すればよい。すると，第3パラグラフの7文目に該当箇所がある。なお，下線部の直後の文にBut art is infinite only because…とあることに着目すると，その直後に述べられている内容が別解である。 (6) 下線部は「治安維持」の意であり，芸術はそれに関する主張が認められると治安維持の対象になる，すなわち検証の対象になるということである。従って，第2パラグラフの最後の文にあるverification or falsificationが正解である。

【8】(1)　(ア)　話題や活動が生徒のレベルにあっていないので，活動のために必要な表現力がない。　　　(イ)　特に初級，中級のレベルでは，ほとんど無意識に訳を活用する。　　　(ウ)　教師自身が母国語を使い，それを見て，生徒も母国語を使う。　　　(2)　文法の説明，理解の確認，指示を出したり，教室で指導法について話し合ったり，意味を確認したりする活動は，母語を使うことで効率よく行うことができる。(3)　流暢に話す活動や，口頭発表は実際に英語で行わなければ意味がなくなってしまう。また，教師は主たるインプットの提供者であり，理解可能なインプットがより生徒の言語習得を促したり，生徒のモデルとなり，生徒が英語を使う必要性を高める。　　　(4)　(ア)　既習の表現を用いて，即興的に話して相手と情報，考えまたは思いなどをやり取りできる力(既習の表現を活用し，情報，考えまたは思いなどを相手に伝える力や，伝えようとする態度を育てる，でも可)。　　　(イ)　誤りを訂正することや，わからない語句等を教えること。　　　(ウ)　生徒が活動中は行わず，活動後に行う(1回目の活動後と2回目の活動後に行う，でも可)。

〈解説〉(1)　生徒が授業中に英語を話さない原因を3つ，日本語で答える問題である。それぞれ第2パラグラフ，第3パラグラフそして第5パラグラフの内容を簡潔に整理して記述すればよい。　　　(2)　下線部の直後にarguedとあることから，それ以降の内容をほぼ直訳するだけでよい。(3)　第3パラグラフの後半と第4パラグラフの前半に着目する。まず，第3パラグラフの後半では，流暢に話す活動は英語以外で行うと意味がなくなってしまうことなどが述べられている。また，第4パラグラフの前半では，教師が英語のインプット源であることや，生徒の英語の必要感を高めることなどが述べられている。　　　(4)　英文に書かれている内容と，与えられた表にある活動内容を踏まえて考える必要があることに留意したい。　　　(ア)　第1パラグラフの2文目の後半および3文目に述べられている内容をまとめればよい。　　　(イ)　第2パラグラフの2文目と3文目の前半で述べられているが，教師の介入としては，生徒がコミュニケーションを行うために必要な語句を教えたり，生徒の発

話を修正したりすることだけに留める必要がある。　（ウ）　第1パラグラフの1文目にあるように，途中で中断すべきではないということ，また，第2パラグラフの最後の文にある「学習者の会話にいつ介入するべきかという質問への答えは，遅ければ遅いほどよい，である」という内容を踏まえると，教師の介入は活動後に行うことがよいことがわかる。

2022年度　実施問題

【中高共通】

【１】放送される指示に従って答えなさい。

(Part 1)

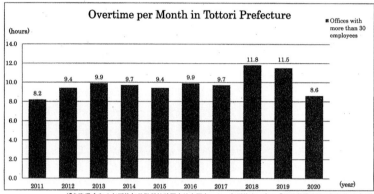

(『鳥取県令和２年平均毎月勤労統計調査地方調査　３．年平均表　表２「月間労働時間の推移」』を参照)

(Part 2)

No.1

No.2

(Part 3)

1

   (A)　A professional photo studio

   (B)　A food processing company

   (C)　A fitness center

   (D)　A sporting goods store

2

   (A)　Arrive early to an event

   (B)　Try to get a free coupon

   (C)　Check the event schedule online

(D)　Enter a contest

(☆☆☆◎◎◎)

【中学校】

【1】次の各問いに答えなさい。

(1)　次の文は，教育基本法第4条の条文である。条文中の[　]に入る共通の語句として適切なものを以下の(ア)～(オ)から一つ選び，記号で答えなさい。

> 第4条　すべて国民は，ひとしく，その能力に応じた教育を受ける機会を与えられなければならず，人種，信条，性別，社会的身分，経済的地位又は門地によって，教育上差別されない。
>
> 2　[　]は，障害のある者が，その障害の状態に応じ，十分な教育を受けられるよう，教育上必要な支援を講じなければならない。
>
> 3　[　]は，能力があるにもかかわらず，経済的理由によって修学が困難な者に対して，奨学の措置を講じなければならない。

(ア)　国民　　　　　　　　　(イ)　教育委員会
(ウ)　国及び地方公共団体　　(エ)　父母その他の保護者
(オ)　教育長

(2)　次の文章が説明する制度の名称として，最も適切なものを答えなさい。

> 平成16年に法制化され，その後，平成29年の法改正により，その設置が教育委員会の努力義務となっている。学校と地域住民等が力を合わせて学校の運営に取り組むことが可能となる「地域とともにある学校」への転換を図るための有効な仕組みである。
> 学校運営に地域の声を積極的に生かし，地域と一体となっ

　　て特色ある学校づくりを進めていくことができる。

　　　なお，法律に基づいて教育委員会が学校に設置するこの制
　　度に関する機関には，主な役割として以下の3つがある。
　　○校長が作成する学校運営の基本方針を承認する。
　　○学校運営に関する意見を教育委員会又は校長に述べること
　　　ができる。
　　○教職員の任用に関して，教育委員会規則に定める事項につ
　　　いて，教育委員会に意見を述べることができる。

(3)　次の文章は，令和3年1月26日に中央教育審議会で取りまとめられ
　　た「『令和の日本型学校教育』の構築を目指して～全ての子供たち
　　の可能性を引き出す，個別最適な学びと，協働的な学びの実現～
　　(答申)」における「第Ⅱ部　各論」の「6．遠隔・オンライン教育を
　　含むICTを活用した学びの在り方について」に記載された内容の一
　　部である。(①)～(④)にあてはまる，最も適切な語句の組
　　合せを以下の(ア)～(ク)から一つ選び，記号で答えなさい。

　　　第Ⅱ部　各論

　　　6．遠隔・オンライン教育を含むICTを活用した学びの在
　　　　り方について

　　(1)　基本的な考え方
　　○　これからの学校教育を支える基盤的なツールとして，ICT
　　　は必要不可欠なものであり，1人1台の端末環境を生かし，
　　　端末を日常的に活用していく必要がある。また，ICTを利用
　　　して　(①)制約を緩和することによって，他の学校・地
　　　域や海外との交流なども含め，今までできなかった学習活
　　　動が可能となる。
　　○　学校教育におけるICTの活用に当たっては，新学習指導要
　　　領の趣旨を踏まえ，各教科等において育成するべき資質・
　　　能力等を把握し，心身に及ぼす影響にも留意しつつ，まず

はICTを日常的に活用できる環境を整え，児童生徒が「（ ② ）」として活用できるようにし，「主体的・対話的で深い学び」の実現に向けた（ ③ ）に生かしていくことが重要である。

○ また，AI技術が高度に発達するSociety5.0時代にこそ，教師による（ ④ ）や児童生徒同士による学び合い，地域社会での多様な学習体験の重要性がより一層高まっていくものである。もとより，学校教育においては，教師が児童生徒一人一人の日々の様子，体調や授業の理解度を直接に確認・判断することで，児童生徒の理解を深めたり，生徒指導を行ったりすることが重要であり，あわせて，児童生徒の怪我や病気，災害の発生等の不測のリスクに対する安全管理への対応にも万全を期す必要がある。

	①	②	③	④
（ア）	集団的・画一的	文房具	環境構築	オンライン授業
（イ）	集団的・画一的	教科書	環境構築	オンライン授業
（ウ）	集団的・画一的	文房具	環境構築	対面指導
（エ）	集団的・画一的	教科書	授業改善	対面指導
（オ）	空間的・時間的	文房具	授業改善	対面指導
（カ）	空間的・時間的	教科書	授業改善	対面指導
（キ）	空間的・時間的	文房具	授業改善	オンライン授業
（ク）	空間的・時間的	教科書	環境構築	オンライン授業

(4) 次の文は，「中学校学習指導要領(平成29年3月告示)」第2章に示された，外国語の目標の一部である。空欄（ ① ），（ ② ）に入る最も適切な語句を書きなさい。

外国語の背景にある文化に対する理解を深め，聞き手，読み手，話し手，書き手に（ ① ）しながら，主体的に外国語を用いてコミュニケーションを図ろうとする（ ② ）を養う。

(5) 次の文章は，「中学校学習指導要領(平成29年3月告示)」第2章　第

9節　外国語　第2　各言語の目標及び内容等に示された内容〔思考力，判断力，表現力等〕の一部である。空欄(　①　)～(　④　)に入る最も適切な語句を，以下の(a)～(j)からそれぞれ一つずつ選び，記号で答えなさい。

　情報を整理しながら考えなどを形成し，英語で表現したり，伝え合ったりすることに関する事項

　具体的な課題等を設定し，コミュニケーションを行う(　①　)や場面，状況などに応じて，情報を整理しながら考えなどを形成し，これらを論理的に表現することを通して，次の事項を身に付けることができるよう指導する。

　ア　日常的な話題や社会的な話題について，英語を聞いたり読んだりして(　②　)や考えなどを捉えること。

　イ　日常的な話題や社会的な話題について，英語を聞いたり読んだりして得られた情報や表現を，選択したり抽出したりするなどして(　③　)し，話したり書いたりして事実や自分の考え，気持ちなどを表現すること。

　ウ　日常的な話題や社会的な話題について，(　④　)を整理し，英語で話したり書いたりして互いに事実や自分の考え，気持ちなどを伝え合うこと。

(a)　必要な情報　　　(b)　話し手の意向　　　(c)　概要

(d)　要点　　　　　　(e)　意義　　　　　　　(f)　伝える内容

(g)　知識　　　　　　(h)　目的　　　　　　　(i)　活用

(j)　把握

(☆☆☆○○○)

【2】次の(1)～(10)の英文の(　　)に入る最も適切な単語または語句を(ア)～(エ)からそれぞれ一つずつ選び，記号で答えなさい。

(1)　Jason was (　　) joy when he got the news that he had been accepted into a famous university. It was the happiest day of his life.

(ア)　filled with　　(イ)　due to　　(ウ)　required of

(エ)　suffering from

(2)　The preacher said that communication was an important (　　) of marriage. He said that it is a basic part of every relationship.

(ア)　surface　　(イ)　experiment　　(ウ)　element　　(エ)　loan

(3)　Last week's winter festival was a huge success. (　　) many as 1,500 people came.

(ア)　Beyond　　(イ)　As　　(ウ)　For　　(エ)　By

(4)　Melany wanted her son to get no (　　) than 85 percent on his science test. She was proud when he got a perfect score.

(ア)　matter　　(イ)　fewest　　(ウ)　less　　(エ)　least

(5)　Makiko's parents had always thought of Uruguay as a (　　) country that they would never go to. However, when Makiko moved there, they decided to visit her.

(ア)　visible　　(イ)　various　　(ウ)　distributive　　(エ)　distant

(6)　The sports day at Aranda's school was (　　) because of heavy rain. The school will hold it next week instead.

(ア)　reproached　　(イ)　achieved　　(ウ)　postponed

(エ)　completed

(7)　The married couple loved the house but decided that the price was (　　) their reach. They looked for something cheaper instead.

(ア)　without　　(イ)　despite　　(ウ)　beyond　　(エ)　throughout

(8)　We hope the disputes between the two regions will be settled peacefully as soon as possible. We do not (　　) any violent means.

(ア)　advocate　　(イ)　maintain　　(ウ)　elaborate

(エ)　stimulate

(9)　I suggest that you check out the (　　) before deciding whether to go to a nearby high school. There are a lot of choices you can make.

(ア)　consideration　　(イ)　alternatives　　(ウ)　assumptions

(エ)　domination

(10)　Pedestrians walking by Stewart gave him a (　　) look. He was walking on the crowded street while smoking.

(ア)　reverent　　(イ)　generous　　(ウ)　scornful　　(エ)　generic

(☆☆☆○○○)

【3】次の(1)～(10)の〔　　〕内の単語または語句を並べ替えてそれぞれ正しい英文を作るとき，(　①　)と(　②　)に入る単語または語句をそれぞれ一つずつ選び，記号で答えなさい。ただし，英文のはじめにくる単語または語句の頭文字も小文字にしてある。

(1)〔(ア)　up　　(イ)　not　　(ウ)　late　　(エ)　stay
(オ)　better　〕
You had (　)(　①　)(　)(　②　)(　) every night.

(2)〔(ア)　a　　(イ)　at　　(ウ)　is　　(エ)　for　　(オ)　loss
(カ)　never　〕
The man has a wide range of interests and (　)(　①　)(　)
(　②　)(　)(　) topics of conversation.

(3)〔(ア)　for　　(イ)　her　　(ウ)　can　　(エ)　losing
(オ)　blame　〕
No one (　)(　①　)(　)(　②　)(　) the game last week.

(4)〔(ア)　a　　(イ)　of　　(ウ)　way　　(エ)　out
(オ)　figured　　(カ)　accomplishing　〕
Nancy (　)(　①　)(　)(　②　)(　)(　) the task in a better way.

(5)〔(ア)　to　　(イ)　it　　(ウ)　get　　(エ)　very
(オ)　difficult　〕
Paul found (　)(　①　)(　)(　②　)(　) a job.

(6)〔(ア)　up　　(イ)　you　　(ウ)　have　　(エ)　could
(オ)　picked　〕
If you had phoned me at home yesterday, my wife (　)(　①　)
(　)(　②　)(　).

(7) 〔 (ア) at   (イ) to   (ウ) an hour   (エ) least

(オ) driving   (カ) spend 〕

In my country, many people (   ) (①) (   ) (②) (   )

(   ) and from work.

(8) 〔 (ア) to   (イ) come   (ウ) have   (エ) the party

(オ) should 〕

You (   ) (①) (   ) (②) (   ), but you didn't.

(9) 〔 (ア) at   (イ) the   (ウ) the truck   (エ) speed

(オ) which 〕

The police estimated (   ) (①) (   ) (②) (   ) was

traveling.

(10) 〔 (ア) a   (イ) of   (ウ) has   (エ) deal

(オ) great   (カ) spent〕

John (   ) (①) (   ) (②) (   ) (   ) money on the car.

(☆☆☆☆◎◎◎)

【4】次の英文は，2009年4月5日(現地時間)に，第44代アメリカ合衆国大
統領のバラク・オバマ氏がチェコ共和国プラハ市で行った演説の一部
である。この英文を読み，(1)～(6)の各問いに答えなさい。

(前略)

We are here today because enough people ignored the voices who told
them that the world could not change.

①We're here today because of the courage of those who stood up and took
risks to say that freedom is a right for all people, no matter what side of a wall
they live on and no matter what they look like.

(中略)

Now, I know that there are ②〔 on / we / act / who / can / will / some / such
/ question / whether 〕 a broad agenda. There are those who doubt whether
true international cooperation is possible, given the inevitable differences
among nations. And there are those who hear talk of a world without nuclear

95

weapons and doubt whether it's worth setting a goal that seems impossible to achieve.

But make...make no mistake: We know where that road leads. ③When nations and peoples allow themselves to be defined by their differences, the gulf between them widens. When we fail to pursue peace, then it stays forever beyond our grasp. We know the path when we choose fear over (④). To denounce or shrug off a call for cooperation is an easy but also a cowardly thing to do. That's how wars begin. That's where human progress ends.

There is violence and injustice in our world that must be confronted. ⑤We must confront it, not by splitting apart but by standing together as free nations, as free people. I know that a call to arms can stir the souls of men and women more than a call to lay them down. But that is why the voices for peace and progress must be raised together.

(中略)

Human destiny will be what we make of it. And here, in Prague, let us honor our past by reaching for a better future. Let us bridge our divisions, build upon our hopes, accept our responsibility to leave this world more (⑥) and more peaceful than we found it. Together we can do it.

Thank you very much. Thank you, Prague.

(オバマ「核なき世界」演説　より抜粋)

(1)　下線部①の英文を日本語にしなさい。

(2)　下線部②の〔　　〕内の単語をならべかえ，意味のとおる英文にしなさい。

(3)　下線部③の英文を日本語にしなさい。

(4)　本文の内容を踏まえて，(④)，(⑥)に入る最も適切な語を次の(ア)～(エ)から一つ選び，記号で答えなさい。

　　④　(ア)　hope　　　(イ)　certainty　　(ウ)　danger
　　　　(エ)　anxiety
　　⑥　(ア)　disastrous　(イ)　contagious　(ウ)　prosperous
　　　　(エ)　erroneous

96

(5) 下線部⑤の英文を日本語にしなさい。

(6) 次の(ア), (イ)の英文の意味が表す単語一語を, 本文中からそれぞれ抜き出しなさい。

(ア) the process of improving or developing, or of getting nearer to achieving or completing something

(イ) what happens to somebody or what will happen to them in the future, especially things that they cannot change or avoid

(☆☆☆◎◎)

【5】次の英文を読み, (1)～(4)の各問いに答えなさい。

≪ ① ≫: when planning, it is vital to consider what students will be doing in the classroom; we have to consider the way they will be grouped, whether they are to move around the class, whether they will work quietly side-by-side researching on the Internet or whether they will be involved in a boisterous group-writing activity.

We should make decisions about activities almost independently of what language or skills we have to teach. Our first planning thought should centre round what kind of activity would be best for a particular group of students at a particular point in a lesson, or on a particular day. By deciding what kind of activity to offer them - in the most general sense — we have a chance to balance the exercises in our lessons in order to offer the best possible chance of engaging and motivating the class.

The best lessons offer a (A) of activities within a class period. Students may find themselves standing up and working with each other for five minutes before returning to their seats and working for a time on their own. The same lesson may end with a whole-class discussion or with pairs writing dialogues to practise a language function or grammar point.

≪ ② ≫: we need to make a decision about which language skills we wish our students to develop. This choice is sometimes determined by the

97

syllabus or the coursebook. However, we still need to plan exactly how students are going to work with the skill and what sub-skills we wish to practise.

Planning decisions about language skills and sub-skills are co-dependent with the content of the lesson and with the activities which the teachers will get students to take part in.

≪　③　≫: we need to decide what language to introduce and have the students learn, practise, research or use.

One of the dangers of planning is that where language is the main focus it is the first and only planning decision that teachers make. Once the decision has been taken to teach the present continuous, for example, it is sometimes tempting to slip back into a drill-dominated teaching session which lacks variety and which may not be the best way to achieve our aims. But language is only one area that we need to consider when planning lessons.

≪　④　≫: lesson planners have to select content which has a good chance of provoking interest and involvement. Since they know their students personally they are well placed to select appropriate content.

Even where the choice of subject and content is to some extent dependent on a coursebook, we can still judge when and if to use the coursebook's topics, or whether to replace them with something else. We can predict, with some accuracy, which topics will work and which will not.

However, the most interesting content can be made bland if the activities and tasks that go with it are unimaginative. (　B　), subjects that are not especially fascinating can be used extremely successfully if the good planner takes time to think about how students can best work with them.

When thinking about the elements we have discussed above we carry with us not only the knowledge of the students, but also our belief in the need to create an appropriate balance between variety and coherence.

　　　(THE PRACTICE OF ENGLISH LANGUAGE TEACHING /
　　　Jeremy Harmer より抜粋)

(1) ≪ ① ≫～≪ ④ ≫には，そのパラグラフの内容を簡潔に表
　　す一語が入る。その組合せとして最も適切なものを，(ア)～(エ)か
　　ら一つ選び，記号で答えなさい。

	①	②	③	④
(ア)	Language	Activities	Skills	Content
(イ)	Activities	Skills	Language	Content
(ウ)	Language	Skills	Content	Activities
(エ)	Activities	Language	Content	Skills

(2) 本文の内容を踏まえて，(A)，(B)に入る最も適切な語を
　　(ア)～(エ)から一つ選び，記号で答えなさい。

　A (ア) variety　　　(イ) uniformity　　(ウ) providence
　　(エ) background

　B (ア) Nevertheless　(イ) Repeatedly　(ウ) Suddenly
　　(エ) Similarly

(3) 下線部について，このパラグラフ内で例示されている具体的な場
　　面と内容はどのようなものか。日本語で書きなさい。

(4) 本文の内容に合っているものを(ア)～(オ)から二つ選び，記号で
　　答えなさい。

　(ア) 生徒に身につけさせたい技能や下位技能は，シラバスや教科
　　　書によって決められるので，細かく計画する必要はない。

　(イ) 題材の内容が興味を引くものであれば，学習活動や課題の良
　　　し悪しに関わらず，生徒にとって非常に興味深く，主体的に関与
　　　できる授業になるものである。

　(ウ) 生徒にどのような活動を提供するかを先に決めてしまうと，
　　　授業中の練習活動のバランスを取る機会を失うことになる。

　(エ) 題材の選択において，教科書で取り上げられている題材を使
　　　うのか，もしくは別の題材と置き換えるのか，などといったこと

は教師が判断する必要がある。

(オ)　授業計画を立てる際には，生徒についての知識だけでなく，多様性と一貫性の間で適切なバランスを保つ教師の信念が必要である。

(☆☆☆☆◎◎◎)

【6】次の(1)〜(3)の各問いに答えなさい。

(1)　中学校の英語の授業で，道案内の場面を指導する。次の(条件)を踏まえて，(　①　)〜(　③　)に適する英文を一つずつ書き，モデルとして示す観光客と生徒の対話文を完成させなさい。

(条件)

・観光客と生徒は地下鉄の駅で話をしている。

・観光客は，地下鉄を使ってイロハ空港(Iroha Airport)へ行きたい。

・観光客と生徒がいる駅から空港までは，およそ30分ほどかかる。

観光客	生徒
Excuse me.	
	Yes?
(　①　)?	
	Sure. We are at Manyo Station now. Go to Genji Station and change trains there.
OK. (　②　)?	
	Take the Heike Line. The Iroha Airport Station is the fifth station.
How long does it take to get to the airport from here?	
	(　③　).
Thank you very much.	
	You're welcome. Have a nice trip!

(2)　中学3年生の英語の授業において，ホームページで学校を紹介する原稿の作成に取り組ませようと思う。次の内容を生徒に書かせる時，モデルとして提示する文を，それぞれ英語で書きなさい。(ただし，語数，文の数は問わない。)

①　毎年11月に文化祭があり，たくさんの来客がある。

②　サッカー部は週に5日練習をしており，地元の大会で数回優勝している。

③　吹奏楽部に興味があったら，3階の音楽室に来てほしい。

(3)　中学3年生の英語の授業において，「中学校の思い出」についてスピーチをさせようと思う。その際，その中で関係代名詞を用いた文を使わせたい。モデルとして提示するスピーチ原稿を45語程度で書きなさい。(ただし，文の数は問わない。)

(☆☆◎◎◎)

【高等学校】

【1】次の各問いに答えなさい。

(1)　次の文は，教育基本法第4条の条文である。条文中の[　　]に入る共通の語句として適切なものを以下の(ア)～(オ)から一つ選び，記号で答えなさい。

> 第4条　すべて国民は，ひとしく，その能力に応じた教育を受ける機会を与えられなければならず，人種，信条，性別，社会的身分，経済的地位又は門地によって，教育上差別されない。
> 2　[　　]は，障害のある者が，その障害の状態に応じ，十分な教育を受けられるよう，教育上必要な支援を講じなければならない。
> 3　[　　]は，能力があるにもかかわらず，経済的理由によって修学が困難な者に対して，奨学の措置を講じなければならない。

(ア)　国民　　　　　　　　　(イ)　教育委員会
(ウ)　国及び地方公共団体　　(エ)　父母その他の保護者
(オ)　教育長

(2)　次の文章が説明する制度の名称として，最も適切なものを答えなさい。

> 　平成16年に法制化され，その後，平成29年の法改正により，その設置が教育委員会の努力義務となっている。学校と地域住民等が力を合わせて学校の運営に取り組むことが可能とな

101

> る「地域とともにある学校」への転換を図るための有効な仕
> 組みである。
>
> 　学校運営に地域の声を積極的に生かし，地域と一体となっ
> て特色ある学校づくりを進めていくことができる。
>
> 　なお，法律に基づいて教育委員会が学校に設置するこの制
> 度に関する機関には，主な役割として以下の3つがある。
> ○校長が作成する学校運営の基本方針を承認する。
> ○学校運営に関する意見を教育委員会又は校長に述べること
> 　ができる。
> ○教職員の任用に関して，教育委員会規則に定める事項につ
> 　いて，教育委員会に意見を述べることができる。

(3)　次の文章は，令和3年1月26日に中央教育審議会で取りまとめられた「『令和の日本型学校教育』の構築を目指して〜全ての子供たちの可能性を引き出す，個別最適な学びと，協働的な学びの実現〜(答申)」における「第Ⅱ部　各論」の「6. 遠隔・オンライン教育を含むICTを活用した学びの在り方について」に記載された内容の一部である。(　①　)〜(　④　)にあてはまる，最も適切な語句の組合せを以下の(ア)〜(ク)から一つ選び，記号で答えなさい。

> 第Ⅱ部　各論
>
> > 　6. 遠隔・オンライン教育を含むICTを活用した学びの在
> > 　り方について
>
> (1)　基本的な考え方
> ○　これからの学校教育を支える基盤的なツールとして，ICT
> 　は必要不可欠なものであり，1人1台の端末環境を生かし，
> 　端末を日常的に活用していく必要がある。また，ICTを利用
> 　して(　①　)制約を緩和することによって，他の学校・地域
> 　や海外との交流なども含め，今までできなかった学習活動

が可能となる。

○　学校教育におけるICTの活用に当たっては，新学習指導要領の趣旨を踏まえ，各教科等において育成するべき資質・能力等を把握し，心身に及ぼす影響にも留意しつつ，まずはICTを日常的に活用できる環境を整え，児童生徒が「(　②　)」として活用できるようにし，「主体的・対話的で深い学び」の実現に向けた(　③　)に生かしていくことが重要である。

○　また，AI技術が高度に発達するSociety5.0時代にこそ，教師による(　④　)や児童生徒同士による学び合い，地域社会での多様な学習体験の重要性がより一層高まっていくものである。もとより，学校教育においては，教師が児童生徒一人一人の日々の様子，体調や授業の理解度を直接に確認・判断することで，児童生徒の理解を深めたり，生徒指導を行ったりすることが重要であり，あわせて，児童生徒の怪我や病気，災害の発生等の不測のリスクに対する安全管理への対応にも万全を期す必要がある。

	①	②	③	④
(ア)	集団的・画一的	文房具	環境構築	オンライン授業
(イ)	集団的・画一的	教科書	環境構築	オンライン授業
(ウ)	集団的・画一的	文房具	環境構築	対面指導
(エ)	集団的・画一的	教科書	授業改善	対面指導
(オ)	空間的・時間的	文房具	授業改善	対面指導
(カ)	空間的・時間的	教科書	授業改善	対面指導
(キ)	空間的・時間的	文房具	授業改善	オンライン授業
(ク)	空間的・時間的	教科書	環境構築	オンライン授業

(4)　「高等学校学習指導要領(平成30年3月告示)」における教科「外国語」に関する各問いに答えなさい。

第2章　各学科に共通する各教科

第8節　外国語

第1款　目標

　外国語によるコミュニケーションにおける見方・考え方を働かせ，外国語による聞くこと，読むこと，話すこと，書くことの言語活動及びこれらを結び付けた（　1　）的な言語活動を通して，情報や考えなどを的確に理解したり適切に表現したり伝え合ったりするコミュニケーションを図る資質・能力を次のとおり育成することを目指す。

(1)　外国語の音声や語彙，表現，文法，言語の働きなどの理解を深めるとともに，これらの知識を，聞くこと，読むこと，話すこと，書くことによる実際のコミュニケーションにおいて，目的や場面，状況などに応じて適切に活用できる（　2　）を身に付けるようにする。

(2)　コミュニケーションを行う目的や場面，状況などに応じて，日常的な話題や（　3　）的な話題について，外国語で情報や考えなどの概要や要点，詳細，話し手や書き手の意図などを的確に理解したり，これらを活用して適切に表現したり伝え合ったりすることができる力を養う。

(3)　外国語の背景にある文化に対する理解を深め，聞き手，読み手，話し手，書き手に配慮しながら，（　4　）的，自律的に外国語を用いてコミュニケーションを図ろうとする態度を養う。

第2款　各科目

第1　英語コミュニケーションⅠ

　1　目標

　　英語学習の特質を踏まえ，以下に示す，聞くこと，読むこと，話すこと［　X　］，話すこと［　Y　］，書くことの

> 五つの領域(以下この節において「五つの領域」という。)別
> に設定する目標の実現を目指した指導を通して，第1款の
> (1)及び(2)に示す資質・能力を一体的に育成するとともに，
> その過程を通して，第1款の(3)に示す資質・能力を育成す
> る。
> (以下省略)

(あ) (1)~(4)に入る語句を，①~⑧の中からそれぞれ一つ
ずつ選び，番号で答えなさい。

① 社会　② 主体　③ 国際　④ 判断力　⑤ 技能
⑥ 統合　⑦ 効率　⑧ 学習

(い)　 X ， Y に入る最も適切な語句をそれぞれ答えなさ
い。

(☆☆☆☆◎◎◎)

【2】次の(1)~(6)の英文の(　　)に入る最も適切な語又は語句を，①~④
の中からそれぞれ一つずつ選び，番号で答えなさい。

(1)　The region (　　) large numbers of young entrepreneurs.

① attracting　② attracts　③ was attracted

④ has been attracted

(2)　I didn't expect (　　) work in January.

① his completing　② him complete　③ he complete

④ him to complete

(3)　Sending a person to Mars would be too big (　　) to carry out.

① project　② projects　③ a project　④ the project

(4)　All you have to do is to go and (　　) all concerned.

① apologize　② apologize to　③ apologizing

④ to apologize

(5)　Joseph was interested in automobiles and knew a lot about them, so
when his car suddenly stopped running, he was able to (　　) his

knowledge of engines and fix it.

① pull through　　② let down　　③ mark down　　④ draw on

(6) The ad claimed the medicine could relieve headache pain in just three minutes, but Evan was (　　). He did not believe a painkiller could work that quickly.

① expressive　　② inessential　　③ forceful　　④ skeptical

(☆☆☆○○○○○)

【3】【例】にならって，次の(1)，(2)における会話体の英文(a)を英文(b)のように説明するとき，それぞれの(　　)にあてはまる最も適切な語を英語一語で答えなさい。

【例】 (a) "Go straight for three blocks," Susan said. "Turn left, and go past the bank and turn right. The train station is just around the corner. You can't miss it."

(b) Susan (explained) the way to the train station.

(1) (a) "Hey, Lucy. What a fascinating flyer! This recommended plate looks nice." "Jeff, don't make me say the same thing again and again. Ordering food from a restaurant is costly for us as a big family. Also, a lot of take-out food is high in fat and salt."

(b) Lucy was (　　) to ordering food delivery in terms of health concerns and family finances.

(2) (a) "Mr. Roger. Your words have made me decide to do my best on the team. I will never give up, no matter what." "I'm glad to hear that, Mike. The other members are looking forward to playing with you again."

(b) Mr. Roger (　　) Mike into changing his mind about quitting the team.

(☆☆☆○○○)

【4】次の各問いに答えなさい。

(1) 次の会話の下線部を英語にしなさい。

Karen : So, John, do you have any plans for your family vacation?

John : Well, we usually visit my parents in Florida, but the drive is so tiring we may stay closer to home this year.

Karen : ①_____ My kids really like being free to move around, and they love the sleeping compartments.

John : That sounds appealing. ②_____

Karen : ところでジョン，家族旅行の予定はあるの？

John : うーん，いつもはフロリダにいる僕の両親のところに行くんだけれど，運転がとても疲れるから今年はもっと家の近くですますかもしれないな。

Karen : ①代わりに列車に乗っていけば？　うちの子供たちは自由に動き回れるのが本当に好きで，寝台車も大好きよ。

John : それは良さそうだ。②犬の世話をしてくれる人を探さなくてはいけないけど，そうしてみる価値はあるかも。

(旺文社　2018年度版　英検準1級過去6回全問題集　を参照)

(2) 次の「英語借用語(English loan words)」について書かれた文章を英語にしなさい。

　日本語には英語からの借用語がたくさんあります。英語のもとの意味と形を残しているものもあれば，意味や形がいろいろと変わるものもあります。後者のほうがずっと多く，それには少なくても7種のパターンが見られます。その中の一つにジャパニーズ・イングリッシュと呼ばれるものがあります。日本語は英語の語句を借りて，新しい英語らしい言葉を作ります。英語のネイティブスピーカーにわかることもあれば，わからないこともあります。

(有斐閣　日本人の考え方を英語で説明する辞典　を参照)
(☆☆☆☆☆○○○○)

【５】ある記者のリポートを起こした次の英文を読み，各問いに答えなさい。

For lifeguards in Dubai, rushing across the burning sand to reach those in trouble is no easy task. But the lifeguards you are about to meet are getting a helping hand - from cutting-edge drones.

Off the coast of Dubai, the city's newest emergency responder is put through its paces. Designed to quickly respond to crowning cases, the smart rescue drone contains a raft that automatically inflates when it touches the water. If a swimmer is seen to be in trouble, the drone is flown with a remote control to the person in (　A　). It's equipped with a voice-communication system that can speak to the victims and guide them on what to do until a lifeguard arrives.

"When the drone takes off and when there's a drowning person, it will take only 10 seconds to reach the victim, (　B　) is faster than a normal lifeguard procedure." (Ali Villacrosis, lifeguard and drone pilot)

The rescue drone is just one of a number of high-tech innovations (　C　) here at Al Mamzar Beach Park*, the region's first "smart park," right here in Dubai. Developed by the Dubai Municipality, the park is brimming with smart technologies designed to attract more visitors, providing a new way to modernize public spaces.

"The government is looking forward, to implement, like, various technologies to move towards creating a smart city. (　D　), having a smart park is one of the initiatives that Dubai Municipality is moving towards." (Fatima Sulaiman, landscape architect, Dubai Municipality)

An irrigation system uses smart technologies and sensors that detect the exact amount of water that grass and plants need. It's already reduced water usage by 25 percent.

A solar-powered system called the Smart Oasis converts humid air into drinkable fresh water. Every day, up to 90 liters of drinking water can be produced.

And if your phone runs out of battery or data, solar-powered smart benches enable visitors to charge their electronic devices and connect to a wireless Internet service.

"We are enhancing people's experience through their day in the park by finding solutions for their problems - smart solutions." (Salem Ahmed, supervisor, Al Mamzar Beach Park)

The government says it's planning on making all parks in the city smart within the next two years to effectively improve the user experience. Through sustainable technologies and these initiatives, Dubai is revolutionizing the way services are being delivered, in hopes of achieving its ambitious plan to become the smartest city in the world.

(朝日出版社　CNN ENGLISH EXPRESS 2019年5月号　を参照)

注)　Al Mamzar Beach Park　マムザール公園(ドバイにある観光スポットとしても人気の公園)

(1)　本文中の(A)～(D)に入る最も適切な単語を，①～④の中からそれぞれ一つずつ選び，番号で答えなさい。

A　① anger　　② number　　③ need
　　④ fact

B　① when　　② what　　③ who
　　④ which

C　① installed　② left　　③ fixed
　　④ improved

D　① However　② Immediately　③ So
　　④ Meanwhile

(2)　本文の内容を踏まえ，次の(あ)～(う)の問いの答えとして最も適切なものを，①～④の中からそれぞれ一つずつ選び，番号で答えなさい。

(あ)　What can the drone do?

  ①　It can carry a drowning person to the shore.

  ②　It can dive under the water.

  ③　It can fly in the sky without being controlled by a human.

  ④　It can instruct the drowning person what to do.

(い)　What is the government planning for Al Mamzar Beach Park?

  ①　To make the most amazing smart park in the world.

  ②　To create a facility to study smart technology.

  ③　To increase the number of visitors by incorporating various smart technologies.

  ④　To incorporate various smart technologies into the Dubai Municipality.

(う)　What can people do in Al Mamzar Beach Park by using smart technology?

  ①　They can learn the proper amount of water to grow grass and plants.

  ②　They can make 25 percent of the drinking water needed in the city.

  ③　They can transform humid air into dry air.

  ④　They can get new phones when their phones need to be charged.

(☆☆☆○○○○○)

【6】次の英文を読み，各問いに答えなさい。

Few people question the ubiquity of the applications of science. We are led to believe that technology is all for the good, and indeed is a measure of humankind's progress. There is a simple equation: the more technology we have the more advanced and better off we are. We are seldom encouraged to question this. Nevertheless ①this axiom should be questioned because we have reached a point where technology is beginning to define us, rather than us defining technology. Unfortunately, people who question the virtuousness of technology are often ridiculed as being technophobes or ②Luddites, in

110

reference to the group of 19th century workers who stood against the advance of technology.

Who really benefits from technologies: the consumers and users of technology, or the designers and creators? We, as consumers, are told that if we acquire a certain technology our lives will be enhanced. And yet, soon we are again being encouraged to buy the next version of the device, because yet again our lives will be enhanced. On unpacking the new product we all experience that glow of pleasure at being the owner of the latest and greatest gadget, but this excitement soon disappears. And yet, we have become addicted: an addiction that is soon sated by the purchase of the next and better model. Surely, it is not we, the consumers that benefit from this conveyor belt of endless production and consumption, is it?

We tend to think of technology as being a concrete object, something we can hold and interact with. Yet some academics also consider intangible things such as ③writing systems to be a form of technology. Writing, the ability to represent and communicate ideas in a way that can be understood by others in different times and places, has surely had a huge positive impact on the lives of humans. It has allowed both knowledge about the world and inspiring literature to be passed down the ages so that literate people can benefit from the wisdom and creativity of people who are no longer alive. In spite of that, even this technology may have done more harm than good. For example, Postman[1] in quoting from Plato, indicates that the danger of writing is that we come to rely on books rather than using our own memories. A similar criticism has also been made against the Internet. Bauerlein[2] argues that young people's use of the Internet, rather than making them smarter, has in fact made them dumber.

On the other hand, there are those who believe that computers and the Internet will have a positive impact on how we learn. Yet this absolute belief in all things shiny in the world of education has been questioned. Berry[3] (2001, p. 132) wrote: "The complicity of the arts and humanities in this conquest (of technology) is readily apparent in the enthusiasm with which the disciplines, schools, and libraries have accepted their ever-growing dependence in electronic technologies that are, in fact, as all of history shows, not necessary to learning or teaching and which have produced no perceptible improvement in either." So, the next time you are about to buy a piece of technology, ask yourself, "Who is going to benefit most from my purchase?"

References:

[1] *N. Postman. Technopoly: The Surrender of Culture to Technology. New York: Vintage Books, 1993*

[2] *M. Bauerlein. The Dumbest Generation. New York: Jeremy P Tarcher / Penguin, 2009*

[3] *W. Berry. Life Is a Miracle: An Essay Against Modern Superstition. Washington, DC: Counterpoint Press, 2001.*

(旺文社　2014年度版　全国大学入試問題正解　を参照)

(1)　下線部①とは何を指すか。日本語で簡単に説明しなさい。

(2)　下線部②とはどのような人たちのことか。最も適切なものを，(ア)～(エ)の中から一つ選び，記号で答えなさい。

　(ア)　Academics who have written about technology

　(イ)　Teachers who support the use of technology in education

　(ウ)　People who were against the introduction of technology

　(エ)　Users of the latest and greatest gadgets

(3)　下線部③のwriting systemが及ぼす人への影響についての筆者の考えを，65字以内の日本語でまとめなさい。ただし，句読点も1字と数える。

(4)　テクノロジーに対する筆者の姿勢として最も適切なものを，(ア)～(エ)の中から一つ選び，記号で答えなさい。

　(ア)　He believes that it Is almost always beneficial to humans.

　(イ)　He claims that it is a sign of our progress.

　(ウ)　He believes that it mainly benefits its creators.

(エ)　He thinks it is necessary to enhance education.

(5)　(　　)に適切な1語を入れて，この英文にふさわしい標題を完成しなさい。

　　　(　　) technology

(☆☆☆☆◎◎◎)

【7】英語学習に対する生徒の態度について書かれた次の英文を読み，各問いに答えなさい。

Attitudes to English

'It's too difficult'

'I'll never need English anyway.'

'It's stupid. I feel silly trying to speak.'

'It's boring.'

'It'll be useful for a job.'

'I like English pop music.'

'I want to go to America, so I must speak English.'

'Everyone has to speak English.'

How did *you* feel when you started to learn another language? Do you remember? Your attitude was probably more influenced by the teacher you had than by whether you actually wanted or did not want to learn English.

There is absolutely no doubt that the enthusiasm and skill of the teacher has an enormous effect on the attitudes of learners. You will want to share your own fascination with the language with your students. You may have a story to tell about how you go so involved in English. You may want to tell your class what your knowledge of English has meant to you. There may be English－speaking people in the country in which you are leaching, and talking about their achievements may arouse the interest of your class. There may be natives of the country who, through their knowledge of English, have been able to influence events in the world. There could be very practical reasons for your particular students to learn English perhaps because they live in a tourist area, perhaps because English is an important language used in secondary or tertiary education, perhaps because they are in an international school overseas.

You may have things to show your students which might spark off their interest — photos, books, magazines, music, letters and so on. ①<u>Posters and wall-chart</u> add to the atmosphere and remind students that the subject has a great deal to do with life, outside the classroom.

You could invite your students to bring anything with English words on it into class one day and use ②<u>the realia as a motivating force</u>. Or your students could produce ③<u>a list of all the English words they see in their daily lives</u>, noting where each one is：

Word	Where seen
Stop	On a road
Push	Entrance in a shop

If the list would not be ridiculously long, you could put it up on the wall in the class and help the students to add to it.

It is not only at the beginning (although first impressions *are* very important) that positive attitudes to learning English need to be fostered. After what is, we hope, the initial excitement of beginning to learn a language, there is almost always a stage when students reach a ④'<u>plateau</u>', when they begin to feel that they are not making any progress. At this point you need to find new ways of motivating your classes and making it all seem worthwhile. For example, you could use an English program from the radio, or a map of the world on which to identify all the countries where English is spoken, or a recording of an English song, or, if your school is lucky enough to have the facilities, a video or a film. Exchanging emails with friends and trips abroad also play a significant part in maintaining motivation. Where such steps are impracticable, it is even more important for the teacher to seize every opportunity to make the learning of English 'meaningful' for the students.

Whatever facilities are available, and in some situations they may be very few indeed, ⑤it is the lively, purposeful class atmosphere with plenty to do which will do most to maintain positive attitudes. It is the skill and enthusiasm of the teacher which will be the most important factor in keeping the studeuts motivated. If you ever doubt this, think back to your own favorite teacher when you were a student and consider what it was that made his or her classes so special.

(Mary Underwood. *Effective Class Management* より抜粋，一部改編)

(1) 下線部①を利用することで，教室での英語の授業にどのような影響をもたらしますか。本文の内容に即して日本語で答えなさい。

(2) 下線部②に関連して，あなたが授業でrealiaを用いる場合，何を，どのような目的で使いますか。その一例を具体的に答えなさい。

(3) 下線部③に関連して，あなたが生徒に英単語リストを作らせる際に，自分の作成した単語リストの例を提示して生徒に説明します。単語リストの例の空欄に具体例を2つ英語で答えなさい。但し，文中で述べられている例以外の内容とすること。

単語リストの例

Word	Where seen

(4) 下線部④は，どのような状態か，本文の内容に即して日本語で答えなさい。

(5) 下線部⑤について，授業中に，生徒が目的を持ち主体的に英語を用いてコミュニケーションを図ろうとする態度を育成するために，あなたはどのような指導を生徒に行いますか？　次の英文を題材として生徒に言語活動を行わせるとし，以下の空欄(A)～(C)に解答しなさい。

What is Children's Day in Japan?

It's the fifth day of the fifth month, otherwise known as Childrens Day. Formerly meant just for boys, the festival has changed its name to include both boys and girls, and in 1948, it was designated a national holiday by the Japanese government. Not only limited to Japan, the festival is also celebrated in most parts of Asia.

Families traditionally fly colorful carp-shaped flags, or "koinobori," for each child in their house. In Japanese folklore, the carp is a symbol of determination and vigor, overcoming all obstacles to swim upstream. Samurai warrior figurines and samurai "kaboto" helmets can also he displayed in homes to inspire strength and bravery.

Like any other Japanese festival, it wouldn't be complete without an assortment of event-specific fare: for Children's Da,. the little ones can feast on "kashiwa-moch" and "chimaki." Some families even take baths sprinkled with the leaves and roots of a certain plant, called "shobu" , which has the same sound as the Japanese words "prowess" and "bout," as doing so is thought to promote good health and ward off evil.

Interestingly, for many people in Japan, the May 5 celebrations still center on boys, due to the fact that girls get their own special day about two months earlier, on March 3, with a celebration known as a "hina maturi," or "doll festival."

(アルク　ENGLISH JOURNAL 2019年5月号　より抜粋)

生徒に身に付けさせたい英語表現	(A)
言語活動の目的・場面・状況	(B)
言語活動の内容	(C)

(☆☆☆☆○○○○)

解答・解説

【中高共通】

【1】Part 1　C　　　Part 2　No.1　C　　　No.2　D　　　Part 3　1　C
　　2　A

〈解説〉スクリプトは非公開である。　Part 1　放送前に，グラフの要点を素早く読み取っておきたい。まず縦軸は月平均の残業時間，横軸は年度，2018年や2019年は他年度に比べて残業時間が多い，2020年は2011年以来の低水準となったことなどを把握する。また，凡例から30人以上の従業員がいる企業を対象にしたグラフであることも見て取れる。　Part 2　質問と選択肢の両方が読み上げられる四択問題と思われる。文字情報がないので，聞き逃さないように集中して臨みたい。Part 3　1　モノローグの案内やアナウンス，またダイアログがどこで行われているか，その場所を問われることは多いので，場所に特有のキーワードをもとにイメージするとよい。　2　本文で読み上げられた複数の英文を，端的に短く言い換えて選択肢にすることは多い。また，本文で使われている単語は誤答の選択肢に使われることが多い。

【中学校】

【1】(1)　（ウ）　　　(2)　学校運営協議会(制度)(コミュニティ・スクール)
　　(3)　（オ）　　　(4)　①　配慮　　　②　態度　　　(5)　①　(h)　　　②　(a)

　　③　(i)　　④　(f)

〈解説〉(1)　教育の機会均等を定めた教育基本法第4条からの出題。教育基本法は教育を受ける権利を国民に保障した日本国憲法に基づき，日本の公教育の在り方を全般的に規定する法律で昭和22(1947)年に制定され，制定後60年間の教育環境の変化を鑑みて平成18(2006)年に改正されている。教育基本法制定の由来と目的を明らかにし，法の基調をなしている主義と理想とを宣言する前文と18の条文から構成されている。　　(2)　学校運営協議会とは，保護者や地域住民などから構成されるものであり，学校運営の基本方針を承認したり，教育活動などについて意見を述べたりする取組を行う。学校運営協議会を設置している学校をコミュニティ・スクールと呼び，その根拠法が地方教育行政の組織及び運営に関する法律(地教行法)第47条の5である。　　(3)　中央教育審議会「『令和の日本型学校教育』の構築を目指して～全ての子供たちの可能性を引き出す，個別最適な学びと，協働的な学びの実現～(答申)」(令和3年1月26日)は，「各学校においては，教科等の特質に応じ，地域・学校や児童生徒の実情を踏まえながら，授業の中で『個別最適な学び』の成果を『協働的な学び』に生かし，更にその成果を『個別最適な学び』に還元するなど，『個別最適な学び』と『協働的な学び』を一体的に充実し，『主体的・対話的で深い学び』の実現に向けた授業改善につなげていくことが必要である」としている。その中にあるように，現在文部科学省は学校におけるICTの活用を推進しており，ICTを基盤とした先端技術や学習履歴などの教育ビッグデータの効果的な活用により，「誰一人取り残すことのない，公正に個別最適化された学び」の実現を目指している。なおSociety 5.0とは，サイバー空間(仮想空間)とフィジカル空間(現実空間)を高度に融合させたシステムにより，経済発展と社会的課題の解決を両立する，人間中心の社会(Society)のことで，平成28(2016)年1月閣議決定された「第5期科学技術基本計画」において日本が目指すべき未来社会の姿として初めて提唱された概念である。　　(4)　中学校学習指導要領(平成29年3月告示)は，同解説外国語編(平成29年7月)を参照しながら精読されたい。問題

文にある「聞き手，読み手，話し手，書き手に配慮しながら」とは，例えば「話すこと」や「聞くこと」の活動であれば，相手の理解を確かめながら話したり，相手が言ったことを共感的に受け止める言葉を返しながら聞いたりすることなどを指す。「主体的に外国語を用いてコミュニケーションを図ろうとする態度」とは，単に授業等においてだけでなく，学校教育外においても，生涯にわたり継続して外国語習得に取り組もうとする態度を指している。 (5) 出題の項では，設定された「具体的な課題等」の解決に向け，実際に英語を用いた言語活動の中で思考・判断・表現することを繰り返すことを通じて知識及び技能が習得され，学習内容の理解が深まり，学習に対する意欲が高まるなど，3つの資質・能力が相互に関係し合いながら育成される必要があることを述べている。 ア 英語で聞いたり読んだりした際にその内容を的確に理解できる，受容面での能力の育成について述べたもの。 イ アで身につけた受容面での能力を発信面での活動へ結びつけ，5つの領域が結びついた英語使用能力の育成が必要であることを述べたもの。 ウ イのように自分の持つ情報や考えを一方的に相手に伝えるのではなく，相手の情報や考えにも注意を払いながらやり取りすることで，互いの理解を深めることが重要であることを述べたもの。

【2】(1)（ア）　(2)（ウ）　(3)（イ）　(4)（ウ）　(5)（エ）
(6)（ウ）　(7)（ウ）　(8)（ア）　(9)（イ）　(10)（ウ）
〈解説〉(1)「ジェイソンは有名大学に合格したという知らせを受けたとき，喜びで(　　　)」とあるので，(ア)「いっぱいになった」だと考える。 (2)「牧師は，コミュニケーションは結婚の大事な(　　　)だと言った。それはすべての人間関係の基本部分だと言った」とあるので，(ウ)「要素」だと考える。 (3)「先週の冬まつりは大成功だった。1,500人(　　　)が来場した」とあるので，(イ)「〜(1,500人)もの」と考える。 (4)「メラニーは彼女の息子に科学のテストで85点(　　　)点数を取ってもらいたいと思った」とあるので，(ウ)「〜(85点)もの」

と考える。　(5)「マキコの両親は，ウルグアイは決して行くことの
ない(　　　)国だといつも思っていた。しかし，マキコがそこに引っ
越した時，彼女をたずねることに決めた」とあるので(エ)「遠い」だ
と考える。　(6)「アランダ学校の運動会は大雨のため(　　　)。学校
はその代わりに来週開催する予定である」とあるので，(ウ)「延期さ
れた」と考える。　(7)「その夫婦はその家がとても気に入ったが，
値段が(　　　)と判断した。代わりにもっと安い物を探した」とある
ので，beyond one's reach「手が届かない」という意味になる(ウ)だと考
える。　(8)「私たちは2つの地域の紛争はできるだけ早く平和的に解
決することを望んでいる。いかなる暴力的手段も(　　　)しない」と
あるので，(ア)「擁護する」だと考える。　(9)「私は，あなたが近く
の高校に行くかどうか決める前に(　　　)を調べるように提案します」
とあるので，(イ)「代替案，選択肢」だと考える。　(10)「スチュア
ートのそばを通りかかった歩行者は，彼を(　　　)まなざしで見た。
彼は喫煙しながら混雑した通りを歩いていた」とあるので，(ウ)「軽
蔑した」だと考える。

【3】(1)　①　イ　　②　ア　　(2)　①　カ　　②　ア　　(3)　①　オ
②　ア　　(4)　①　エ　　②　ウ　　(5)　①　エ　　②　ア
(6)　①　ウ　　②　イ　　(7)　①　ア　　②　ウ　　(8)　①　ウ
②　ア　　(9)　①　エ　　②　オ　　(10)　①　カ　　②　オ

〈解説〉(1)　(You had) better not stay up late (every night.)という文を作る。
〈had better not＋原形〉は「～しないほうがいい」，stay up lateで「遅く
まで起きている」という意味。　(2)　(The man has a wide range of
interests and) is never at a loss for (topics of conversation.)という文を作る。
be at a loss for…は「…に困る」という意味。　(3)　(No one) can blame
her for losing (the game last week.)という文を作る。blame人for…は「…
を～(人)のせいにする」という意味。　(4)　(Nancy) figured out a way
of accomplishing (the task in a better way.)という文を作る。figure out…は
「…を考え出す」，a way of…は「…のやり方」という意味。

(5) (Paul found) it very difficult to get (a job.)という文を作る。find it…to do〜「〜することは…だとわかる」という意味。itは形式目的語でto get a jobを指す。 (6) (If you had phoned me at home yesterday, my wife) could have picked you up (.)「もしあなたが昨日私に電話してくれていたら, 私の妻があなたを車で迎えに行けたのに」という仮定法過去完了の文を作る。〈If S＋had＋過去分詞〜, S＋助動詞過去＋have＋過去分詞〜〉にする。 (7) (In my country, many people) spend at least an hour driving to (and from work.)という文を作る。spend…doing〜は「〜するのに…を費やす」, at leastは「少なくとも」, to and from…は「…の行き帰り」という意味。 (8) (You) should have come to the party (, but you didn't.)という文を作る。〈should＋have＋過去分詞〉は「〜すべきだったのに」という意味。 (9) (The police estimated) the speed at which the truck (was traveling.)という文を作る。The police estimated the speedとthe truck was traveling at the speedの2つの文から成っている。 (10) (John) has spent a great deal of (money on the car.)という文を作る。a great deal of…は「多額の…, 大量の…」という意味。

【4】(1) 私たちが今日ここにいるのは, 勇気ある人たちが立ち上がり, そして危険を冒しながら自由は全ての人に与えられた権利であり, 壁のどちら側に住んでいるかや外見がどうであるかは関係ない, と主張したおかげである。 (2) some who will question whether we can act on such (3) 国家や国民が, 相違点によって規定されるのをよしとしていたら, 相互の隔たりは広がるのである。 (4) ④ ア ⑥ ウ (5) 暴力と不正に立ち向かうにあたって, 私たちは, ばらばらになるのではなく, 自由な国家, 自由な国民として一致団結しなければならない。 (6) (ア) progress (イ) destiny

〈解説〉(1) We're here today…for all peopleと, no matter what side of a wall …look likeの2つに分けて考える。前半のthoseは「人々」という意味で, who stood up and took risks to say that…for all peopleが後ろから修飾して, 「立ち上がり, 危険を冒して〜という人々」となる。人々が言っ

た内容はsayに続くthat以下に「自由は全ての人に与えられた権利である」と述べられている。後半のno matter what～は「たとえどんな～であろうと」という意味。「たとえ壁のどちら側に住んでいようと」と「たとえどんなふうに見えようとも」の2つから成っている。

(2)　(Now, I know that there are) some who will question whether we can act on such (a broad agenda.)「さて，このような広範な課題に基づいて私たちが行動できるのか，疑問に思う人もいるでしょう」という文になる。関係代名詞whoがあるので，someを先行詞にし「何人かの人」と考える。questionを動詞として捉え，question whether S＋V…「…かどうか疑問に思う」にする。act on…で「…に基づいて(に従って)行動する」，〈such a 形容詞＋名詞〉で「このような…」とする。　(3)　allow＋O＋to doは「Oが…するのを許す」，defineは「規定する」，gulfは「隔たり」という意味。　(4)　④　choose…over～は「～より…の方を選ぶ」という意味。　⑥　空所を含む文は「私たちの分断を埋め，希望を築き，私たちの責任を受け入れて，この世界を私たちが見つけたときよりも( )で平和なものにしようではありませんか」という意味。アは「破滅的な」，イは「伝染性の」，ウは「繁栄した」，エは「間違った」という意味。　(5)　下線部⑤の直前の文に「私たちの世界には，立ち向かわなければならない暴力と不正があります」とあり，itはそのviolence and injustice「暴力と不正」を指す。not by～but by…は「～によってではなく，…によって」という意味。split awayは「分裂する」，as…は「…として」という意味の前置詞。　(6)　(ア)　英文の意味は「何かの改善や発展，または何かの達成や完成に近づく過程」。これに相当するのはprogress「進歩」が適切。　(イ)　英文の意味は「ある人に起こること，または将来起こるであろうこと，特に，その人が変えたり避けたりすることができないこと」。これに相当するのはdestiny「運命」が適切。

【5】(1)　(イ)　(2)　A　(ア)　B　(エ)　(3)　現在進行形について教えるという決定をくだした場合，時としてドリルばかりの授業に陥

ってしまい，このような授業は多様性を欠き，本来目指しているものを達成するための最良の方法とはならないであろうということ。

(4) (エ)，(オ)

〈解説〉(1) ① 第2段落目の2文目に「授業のある時点，あるいはある日のあるグループの生徒にとって，どのようなアクティビティが最適なのかをまず考える」とある。 ② 第1段落の1文目に「生徒にどの言語スキルを身につけさせたいかを決定する必要がある」とある。 ③ 第1段落目の1文目に「どのような言語を導入し，生徒に学習，練習，研究，使用させるかを決定する必要がある」とある。 ④ 第1段落の1文目に「授業設計者は，興味と関心を喚起する可能性の高い内容を選択しなければならない」とある。 (2) A a variety of…で「様々な…」という意味。 B 空所Bの直前に「しかし，どんなに面白い内容でも，それに付随するアクティビティやタスクが想像力を欠いたものであれば，味気ないものになってしまう」とある。Bの直後には「特に魅力的でないテーマであっても，非常にうまく使うことができる」とある。ともに，使い方次第でよくも悪くもなることを述べているので，空所の前と後をつなぐのは，Similarly「同様に」が適切。 (3) 下線部は「プランニングの危険性の一つは，言語が主な焦点となる場合，それが教師が行うプランニングの最初にして唯一の決定であることだ」という意味。具体的な場面は下線部以降に，現在進行形を教えるのに，多様性を欠いたドリル主体の授業に陥る危険性が述べられている。 (4) (エ) ④の第2段落目の1文目「教科や内容の選択が教科書にある程度依存している場合でも，教科書のトピックをいつ使うか，あるいは他のトピックに置き換えるか，判断することができる」と一致する。 (オ) 最後の段落の「上に述べた要素について考えるとき，私たちは生徒に関する知識だけでなく，多様性と一貫性の適切なバランスを作り出す必要性についての信念も携えている」と一致する。

【6】(1) ① Could you tell me how to get to Iroha Airport? ② Which line should I take? ③ It takes about thirty minutes. (2) ① Every year, we have a school festival in November. Many people come and enjoy our festival. ② Our soccer team practices five days a week. We have been the champions in the local tournament several times. ③ If you are interested in our brass band, come to the music room on the third floor. (3) My favorite memory of junior high school was our school trip to Hiroshima. The three days I spent there were meaningful because I learned a lot. Especially, at the Hiroshima Peace Memorial Park, I learned about the importance of world peace. (41語)

〈解説〉(1) ① 生徒が道順を答えていることから判断する。観光客は道順を尋ねるので，Could you～?などの依頼表現を使うとよい。② どの線の電車に乗るか答えていることから判断する。③ 空港までの所要時間を尋ねているので，それに応答する文にする。

(2) ① 文化祭はschool festivalという。② 「数回優勝している」は，「数回優勝した経験がある」と考え，経験を表す現在完了を用いる。③ 「～階に」を表す前置詞はonを用いる。(3) ほかに部活動や生徒会活動，ボランティア活動などの話題も考えられる。最初に関係代名詞を使った文を考え，それを活かすようにスピーチを組み立てるとよい。関係代名詞は名詞の説明の仕方なので，「私たちの使うテニスコート(The tennis court we use)は近くの公園にある」，「私たちの催す文化祭(The school festival we hold)は地元の人に人気がある」，「私にはアメリカの音楽に興味のある友だち(a friend who is interested in American music)がいる」など，様々なものが考えられる。構成としては，まず，中学校の思い出が何なのかを述べ，次に思い出の内容を具体的に書き，最後にその思い出から学んだことなどを書くとよい。

【高等学校】

【1】(1) (ウ)　(2) 学校運営協議会(制度)(コミュニティ・スクール)
(3) (オ)　(4) (あ) 1 ⑥　2 ⑤　3 ①　4 ②

(い)　X　やり取り(やりとり)　　Y　発表

〈解説〉(1)　教育の機会均等を定めた教育基本法第4条からの出題。教育
基本法は教育を受ける権利を国民に保障した日本国憲法に基づき，日
本の公教育の在り方を全般的に規定する法律で昭和22(1947)年に制定
され，制定後60年間の教育環境の変化を鑑みて平成18(2006)年に改正
されている。教育基本法制定の由来と目的を明らかにし，法の基調を
なしている主義と理想とを宣言する前文と18の条文から構成されてい
る。　　(2)　学校運営協議会とは，保護者や地域住民などから構成され
るものであり，学校運営の基本方針を承認したり，教育活動などにつ
いて意見を述べたりする取組を行う。学校運営協議会を設置している
学校をコミュニティ・スクールと呼び，その根拠法が地方教育行政の
組織及び運営に関する法律(地教行法)第47条の5である。　　(3)　中央教
育審議会「『令和の日本型学校教育』の構築を目指して～全ての子供
たちの可能性を引き出す，個別最適な学びと，協働的な学びの実現～
(答申)」(令和3年1月26日)は，「各学校においては，教科等の特質に応
じ，地域・学校や児童生徒の実情を踏まえながら，授業の中で『個別
最適な学び』の成果を『協働的な学び』に生かし，更にその成果を
『個別最適な学び』に還元するなど，『個別最適な学び』と『協働的な
学び』を一体的に充実し，『主体的・対話的で深い学び』の実現に向
けた授業改善につなげていくことが必要である」としている。その中
にあるように，現在文部科学省は学校におけるICTの活用を推進して
おり，ICTを基盤とした先端技術や学習履歴などの教育ビッグデータ
の効果的な活用により，「誰一人取り残すことのない，公正に個別最
適化された学び」の実現を目指している。なおSociety 5.0とは，サイ
バー空間(仮想空間)とフィジカル空間(現実空間)を高度に融合させたシ
ステムにより，経済発展と社会的課題の解決を両立する，人間中心の
社会(Society)のことで，平成28(2016)年1月閣議決定された「第5期科学
技術基本計画」において日本が目指すべき未来社会の姿として初めて
提唱された概念である。　　(4)　高等学校学習指導要領(平成30年3月告
示)については，同解説外国語編・英語編(平成30年7月)を参照しなが

ら精読されたい。平成30年改訂の新学習指導要領より，外国語科の科目は「英語コミュニケーションⅠ，Ⅱ，Ⅲ」と，「論理・表現Ⅰ，Ⅱ，Ⅲ」に整理され，それぞれの具体的な活動内容や意義，配慮事項等が，一層明確に示されるようになった。出題以外の科目や段階ごとの目標も併せて理解しておきたい。また，従来一つの領域として扱われてきた「話すこと」が，改訂により「話すこと[やり取り]」と「話すこと[発表]」との二つの領域に分けられ，「聞くこと」，「読むこと」，「書くこと」と合わせて全五領域となった。領域ごとの目標も改訂されているので，確実に押さえておきたい。

【2】(1)　②　　(2)　④　　(3)　③　　(4)　②　　(5)　④　　(6)　④
〈解説〉(1) 「その地域は数多くの若い起業家を引き付けている」となる。
(2) expect…(人)to doで「…(人)が〜することを期待する」となる。
(3) 〈too＋形容詞＋a(an)＋名詞＋to do〉の語順にする。　(4) go and 動詞「〜しに行く」，apologize to…(人)「…(人)に謝る」。all concerned は「関係者全員」という意味。　(5) 「ジョセフは車に興味があり知識が豊富だったので，車が突然止まったとき，エンジンの知識を使って修理することができた」と考え，draw on「〜を利用する」を選ぶ。
(6) 「その薬はたった3分で頭痛を取り除くことができるとその広告は主張したが，エヴァンは(　　　　)。彼は鎮痛剤がそんなに早く効くと信じていなかった」とあることから，skeptical「疑わしい」と考える。

【3】(1)　opposed　　(2)　persuaded(talked)
〈解説〉(1)　ルーシーは，レストランで持ち帰りの料理を注文することは値段が高いし，脂肪や塩分が高いとして，ジェフの提案に反対していることがわかる。be opposed to doingで「〜することに反対する」という意味。toは前置詞。　(2)　マイクは，チームで全力を尽くす決意をし，どんなことがあっても決してあきらめないと言い，ロジャー氏の言葉に説得されたことがわかる。persuade[talk]人 into doingで「人を説得して…させる」という意味。

【4】(1) ① How about taking the train instead? ② We'd have to find someone to look after the dog, but it might be worth it. (2) The Japanese language is replete with English loan words. While many loan words retain their original English meaning and form, still more go through a variety of semantic and structural changes. For the latter, at least seven types of borrowing patterns are noticed. One of them is so-called "Japanese English."

〈解説〉(1) ① 「…していけば？」は提案と捉え，How about…?で表せる。 ②…を世話するは「look after…」，「…の価値がある」はbe worth …で表せる。 (2) 「…もあれば，(一方)～もある」は対照を表すwhile S +V…, S＋V.で表す。「後者のほうがずっと多く，それには少なくとも7種類のパターンが見られる」は，The latter is much more common, and there are at least seven different patterns to be found in it.とも表せる。

【5】(1) A ③ B ④ C ① D ③ (2) (あ) ④ (い) ③ (う) ①

〈解説〉(1) A 第2段落は救急対応装置の能力の話。空所を含む文は「遊泳者のピンチを発見したら，ドローンをリモコンで飛ばして，( )人のもとへ向かう」とあるので，in need「困っている」が入る。 B 空所の直前のWhen…reach the victim「溺れている人がいるとき，ドローンが離陸してわずか10秒で被害者に到達する」を先行詞として，「このことは，通常のライフガードの手順よりも速い」と続ける関係代名詞のwhichが入る。 C 空所を含む文は「この救助用ドローンは，ここドバイにある地域初の『スマートパーク』である『アル・マンザル・ビーチパーク』に( )数々のハイテク技術革新のひとつに過ぎない」という意味なので，救助用ドローンが公園に「設置された」と考える。 D 空所の直前の文で「政府は，スマートシティの実現に向け，さまざまな技術を導入することを検討している」と原因が述べられ，その結果として直後では「スマートパークの設置は，ドバイ市が目指している取り組みの一つである」と続く。接続詞

のsoは〈原因。So 結果〉という形で用いられる。　(2)　(あ)　第2段落の4文目の「音声通信システムが搭載されているので，被災者に話しかけ，ライフガードが到着するまでの行動を誘導することができる」が④と一致する。　(い)　第4段落の2文目の「ドバイ市によって開発されたこの公園(Al Mamzar Beach Park)は，より多くの訪問者を惹きつけるように設計されたスマートテクノロジーにあふれ，公共空間を近代化する新しい方法を提供するものである」と③が一致する。
(う)　第6段落の1文目の「灌漑システムは，スマートテクノロジーとセンサーを使って，草木が必要とする水の量を正確に検知する」と①が一致する。

【6】(1)　科学技術を持てば持つほど，我々はさらに進歩し，裕福になるということ。　(2)　(ウ)　(3)　書くことによって，知識や文学を時代や場所を越えて伝えることができるが，書物に依存することで，記憶力の低下を引き起こす。(59字)　(4)　(ウ)　(5)　Questioning (Question)

〈解説〉(1)　第1段落の3文目に「単純な方程式がある」とあり，それ以降にその方程式の内容があり，その内容を指して「この公理は～」と述べられている。　(2)　下線を含む文に「テクノロジーの良さを疑問視する人は，しばしばテクノロジー恐怖症やラッダイト(19世紀にテクノロジーの進歩に反対した労働者たち)と揶揄されることがある」とあり，(ウ)「テクノロジーの導入に反対する人たち」と一致する。

(3)　writing systemのプラスの影響が第3段落の4文目It has allowed both …で述べられ，マイナスの影響が6文目…the danger of writing is that…で述べられている。　(4)　第1段落では，テクノロジーはすべて善のものであり，人類の進歩の尺度だと信じ込まされていると述べられている。第2段落では，テクノロジーの恩恵を本当に受けているのは誰かという疑問が述べられている。第3段落では，文字システムのような無形のものもテクノロジーの一形態であり，プラス面とマイナス面があることが述べられている。第4段落ではテクノロジーの購入が誰

の恩恵になるのかと述べられている。筆者は全体を通してテクノロジーに懐疑的であり，使う側よりも作る側に恩恵があると思っていることから判断する。　(5)　(4)と同様に筆者が懐疑的であることと，最終文で「次にテクノロジーを買おうとするときは，『私の購入によって最も恩恵を受けるのは誰だろう？』と自問してみてほしい」と述べていることが，解答へのヒントである。

【7】(1)　教室内に現実的な雰囲気を作り出す助けになり，それによって生徒たちに英語という教科が，教室の外の生活と大きな関係があることを思い起こさせる。　(2)　映画のワンシーンを映し，生徒が学習した英語が使われていることに気付かせる。　(3)　・Word…restroom　Where seen…at school　・Word…priority seat　Where seen…on the train　(4)　生徒が自分はもうこれ以上は，上達しないのではないかと思い始める時期。　(5)　(A)　過去分詞の後置修飾　(B)　目的…「こどもの日」にちなんだ「わが家の料理」や「わが町(地域)」を共有する。　　場面…ALTとのT.Tにおける1分間スピーチ　状況…級友及びALTは上記教材を通して日本における「こどもの日」に関する基本情報を共有している。　(C)　"What is Children's Day in my Home / Town?" と題し，生徒は，(1)こどもの日にちなんで作られる料理，又は(2)こどもの日にちなんで行われる地域行事等について1分間スピーチをする。スピーチ後，同じ生徒がその内容について1つ質問し，級友やALTと即興的なやりとりを行う。

〈解説〉(1)　第2段落の最後に「観光地に住んでいるから，中等・高等教育で英語が重要な言語だから，海外のインターナショナルスクールに通っているからなど，特定の生徒にとって英語を学ぶことは非常に現実的な理由かもしれない」と述べられている。その後，下線部以降で，ポスターや壁に掲示された大きな図表がどういう影響を与えるか述べられている。　(2)　realiaは「実物教材」。解答のほかにも，駅にある英語表記の標識の写真や，有名な物語や童話のページから1パラグラフを提示したりすることなどが考えられる。　(3)　word…payment,

where seen…at the cash registerや，word…plant，where seen…in a garden
など，身の回りにある英単語とそれがある場所を書く。　(4)　下線部
④の直後のwhen以下に，plateauがどのような状態か述べられている。
(5)　(A)　受動態の文も多く含まれているので，英語表現として取り
上げてもよい。　(B)　言語活動の目的として，他のアジア諸国の「こ
どもの日」の行事などを共有するのもよい。　(C)　高等学校のコミュ
ニケーション科目における「話すこと[発表]」の言語活動には，発表
した内容について質疑応答をしたり，意見や感想を伝え合ったりする
活動が含まれることをおさえておこう。

2021年度　実施問題

【中高共通】

【1】放送される指示に従って答えなさい。

(Part 1)

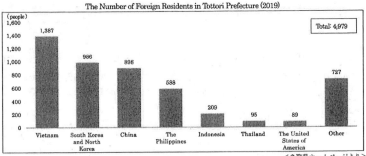

The Number of Foreign Residents in Tottori Prefecture (2019)

Total: 4,979

Vietnam 1,387
South Korea and North Korea 986
China 898
The Philippines 588
Indonesia 209
Thailand 95
The United States of America 89
Other 727

＜鳥取県ホームページより＞

(Part 2)

No. 1

　(1)

　(2)

No. 2

　(1)

　(2)

(Part 3)

　(A)　A lecture about contemporary art

　(B)　An art event at a prefectural office

　(C)　An art contest

　(D)　The opening of an art museum

(☆☆☆○○○○)

131

【中学校】

【１】次の各問いに答えなさい。

(1)　次の文は，教育公務員特例法に規定された条文である。条文中の空欄(①)・(②)にあてはまる最も適切な語句の組み合わせをア〜カから一つ選び，記号で答えなさい。

> 第21条　教育公務員は，その職責を遂行するために，絶えず (①)と(②)に努めなければならない。

	①	②
ア	研修	修養
イ	研修	実践
ウ	研究	研鑽
エ	研究	修養
オ	教育	実践
カ	教育	研鑽

(2)　次の①〜③の法令に規定されている条文を，ア〜カからそれぞれ一つずつ選び，記号で答えなさい。

①　教育基本法　　②　学校教育法　　③　地方公務員法

ア　第30条　すべて職員は，全体の奉仕者として公共の利益のために勤務し，且つ，職務の遂行に当つては，全力を挙げてこれに専念しなければならない。

イ　第7条　文部科学大臣は，教育職員の健康及び福祉の確保を図ることにより学校教育の水準の維持向上に資するため，教育職員が正規の勤務時間及びそれ以外の時間において行う業務の量の適切な管理その他教育職員の服務を監督する教育委員会が教育職員の健康及び福祉の確保を図るために講ずべき措置に関する指針(次項において単に「指針」という。)を定めるものとする。

ウ　第1条　教育は，人格の完成を目指し，平和で民主的な国家

及び社会の形成者として必要な資質を備えた心身ともに健康な
国民の育成を期して行われなければならない。

エ　第23条　公立の小学校等の教諭等の任命権者は，当該教諭等
(臨時的に任用された者その他の政令で定める者を除く。)に対
して，その採用(現に教諭等の職以外の職に任命されている者
を教諭等の職に任命する場合を含む。附則第5条第1項において
同じ。)の日から一年間の教諭又は保育教諭の職務の遂行に必要
な事項に関する実践的な研修(以下「初任者研修」という。)を
実施しなければならない。

オ　第66条　小学校は，当該小学校の教育活動その他の学校運営
の状況について，自ら評価を行い，その結果を公表するものと
する。

※第79条，第79条の8，第104条，第135条において，それぞれ
中学校，義務教育学校，高等学校，特別支援学校に準用。

カ　第34条　小学校においては，文部科学大臣の検定を経た教科
用図書又は文部科学省が著作の名義を有する教科用図書を使用
しなければならない。

※第49条，第49条の8，第62条，第28条において，それぞれ中
学校，義務教育学校，高等学校，特別支援学校に準用。

(3)　次のA及びBの各問いに答えなさい。

A　「中学校学習指導要領(平成29年3月告示)」第2章　第9節　外国
語　第1　目標(1)について，(①)〜(③)に入る最も適切な
語句を書きなさい。

　外国語の音声や語彙，表現，文法，言語の(①)などを理解
するとともに，これらの(②)を，聞くこと，読むこと，話す
こと，書くことによる実際のコミュニケーションにおいて活用で
きる(③)を身に付けるようにする。

B　「中学校学習指導要領(平成29年3月告示)」第2章　第9節　外国
語　第2　各言語の目標及び内容等　3　指導計画の作成と内容の
取扱い(1)について，(①)〜(⑨)に入る最も適切な語句を

a～rからそれぞれ一つずつ選び，記号で答えなさい。

ア　単元など内容や時間のまとまりを見通して，その中で育む
（　①　）の育成に向けて，生徒の（　②　）で深い学びの実現を
図るようにすること。その際，具体的な課題等を設定し，生徒
が外国語によるコミュニケーションにおける（　③　）を働かせ
ながら，コミュニケーションの（　④　），状況などを意識して
活動を行い，（　⑤　）の音声や語彙，表現，文法の知識を五つ
の（　⑥　）における実際のコミュニケーションにおいて活用す
る学習の充実を図ること。

イ　(省略)

ウ　実際に（　⑤　）を使用して互いの考えや気持ちを伝え合うな
どの（　⑦　）を行う際は，2の(1)に示す言語材料について理解
したり練習したりするための指導を必要に応じて行うこと。ま
た，小学校第3学年から第6学年までに扱った簡単な（　⑧　）や
基本的な表現などの学習内容を繰り返し指導し（　⑨　）を図る
こと。

エ　生徒が（　⑤　）に触れる機会を充実するとともに，授業を実
際のコミュニケーションの場面とするため，授業は（　⑤　）で
行うことを基本とする。その際，生徒の理解の程度に応じた
（　⑤　）を用いるようにすること。

(以下省略)

a　相手　　　　　　b　見方・考え方　　c　配慮
d　言語活動　　　　e　目的や場面　　　f　資質・能力
g　観点　　　　　　h　英語　　　　　　i　やり取り
j　意欲的・活動的　k　領域　　　　　　l　語句
m　主体的・対話的　n　興味・関心　　　o　定着
p　文法　　　　　　q　関連付け　　　　r　思考・判断

(☆☆☆◎◎◎)

【2】 次の(1)〜(15)の英文の( )に入る最も適切な単語または語句を
ア〜エからそれぞれ一つずつ選び，記号で答えなさい。

(1) After watching the marathon, Mark was (   ) to start jogging. He now
runs 8 kilometers a day.

ア created   イ astonished   ウ inspired   エ disturbed

(2) While Sara was on vacation, she became sick (   ) eating too much
food. After resting for a few hours, however, she felt better.

ア from   イ on   ウ at   エ to

(3) The photograph of the crowd was (   ), so it was hard to see their
faces clearly.

ア to the point   イ out of focus   ウ at its best

エ in the moment

(4) Last week, Monica's mother turned 80 years old. She planned a big
(   ) for her and about 50 guests attended.

ア reflection   イ prediction   ウ foundation

エ celebration

(5) When the old man was asked (   ) he became rich, he answered that it
was through hard work and nothing else.

ア what   イ who   ウ how   エ when

(6) Michael, who is a famous professional basketball player, said he had
been thinking about retirement for more than a year. He had (   ) his
basketball life to the Jets for eighteen years.

ア abandoned   イ alleviated   ウ donated   エ dedicated

(7) Dogs are known to have an (   ) sense of smell. It is at least a
thousand times as sharp as that of humans.

ア acute   イ obtuse   ウ indispensable   エ absolute

(8) Megan tried to (   ) her lost time with her son when she met him again
after a six-year separation.

ア catch up with   イ make up for   ウ keep up with

エ come down with

(9)　I wouldn't be in this position without you. Please accept this gift certificate as a (　　) of my appreciation for your help.

　　ア　compliment　　イ　deficit　　ウ　significance　　エ　token

(10)　After several stormy days that caused severe damage to the town, the sky was finally starting to (　　).

　　ア　put down　　イ　die down　　ウ　clear up　　エ　add up

(11)　The director was just making his introductory (　　) when his speech was suddenly interrupted by urgent business.

　　ア　remarked　　イ　remarks　　ウ　remarkable　　エ　remarkably

(12)　Mr. Magrheb was relieved to find that (　　) of the research had already been done by his colleagues.

　　ア　whole　　イ　another　　ウ　much　　エ　many

(13)　The fact that the metal deposits were located deep underground (　　) it more difficult for the company to extract them.

　　ア　made　　イ　got　　ウ　caused　　エ　allowed

(14)　The unique mechanisms inside the electric cleaner set it apart as the (　　) design currently on the United States market.

　　ア　innovatively　　イ　innovator　　ウ　more innovation

　　エ　most innovative

(15)　Perry Steel Company became one of the world's largest steel companies (　　) its commitment to quality control at all levels.

　　ア　because　　イ　owing to　　ウ　up　　エ　due

　　　　　　　　　　　　　　　　　　　　　　　(☆☆☆○○○○○)

【３】次の(1)～(10)の〔　　〕内の単語または語句を並べ替えてそれぞれ正しい英文を作るとき，(　①　)と(　②　)に入る単語または語句をそれぞれ一つずつ選び，記号で答えなさい。ただし，英文のはじめにくる単語または語句の頭文字も小文字にしてある。

(1)　〔ア　no　　イ　is　　ウ　she　　エ　succeeded　　オ　wonder
　　カ　in〕

It ( )(①)( )(②)( )( ) passing the exam.

(2) 〔ア decide イ made ウ to エ major オ you カ in〕

What ( )(①)( )(②)( )( ) education in college?

(3) 〔ア too イ cannot ウ careful エ be オ when〕

We ( )(①)( )(②)( ) we spend our money.

(4) 〔ア harder イ studied ウ wish エ had オ I〕

I ( )(①)( )(②)( ) when I was a student.

(5) 〔ア to イ find ウ awoke エ my sister オ me カ staring at〕

I ( )( )(①)( )(②)( ).

(6) 〔ア cannot イ up ウ breaking エ put オ him カ with キ promises〕

I ( )(①)( )(②)( )( )( ) so many times.

(7) 〔ア no イ wants ウ there エ war オ be カ to〕

Everyone ( )( )(①)( )(②)( ) in the world.

(8) 〔ア full イ speak ウ with エ mouth オ your〕

You mustn't ( )(①)( )(②)( ).

(9) 〔ア was イ understand ウ trying エ to オ what カ he〕

I didn't ( )(①)( )(②)( )( ) say.

(10) 〔ア the イ his ウ better エ for オ all〕

I like him ( )(①)( )(②)( ) stubbornness.

(☆☆☆○○○○○)

【4】次の英文は，1990年2月11日に，南アフリカ共和国元大統領のネルソン・マンデラ氏が釈放後に初めて行った演説の一部である。

　この英文を読み，(1)～(5)の各問いに答えなさい。

(前略)

①<u>It is our belief that the future of our country can only be determined by a body which is democratically elected on a nonracial basis.</u> Negotiations on the dismantling of apartheid will have to address the overwhelming demand of our people for a democratic, nonracial and unitary South Africa. There must be an end to white monopoly (n political power and a fundamental restructuring of our political and economic systems to ensure that the inequalities of apartheid are addressed and our society thoroughly democratized.

(中略)

②<u>Our struggle has reached a decisive moment. We call on our people to seize this moment so that the process towards democracy is rapid and uninterrupted.</u> We have waited too long for our freedom. We can no longer wait. Now is the time to intensify the struggle on all fronts. To relax our efforts now would be a (　③　) which generations to come will not be able to forgive. The sight of freedom looming on the horizon should encourage us to redouble our efforts.

It is only through disciplined mass action that our victory can be assured. We call on our while compatriots to join us in the shaping of a new South Africa. The freedom movement is a political home for ④<u>you</u> too. We call on the international community to continue the campaign to isolate the apartheid regime. To lift sanctions now would be to run the risk of aborting the process towards the complete eradication of apartheid.

Our march to freedom is irreversible. We must not allow fear to stand in our (　⑤　). Universal suffrage on a common voters' role in a united democratic and nonracial South Africa is the only way to peace and racial harmony.

In conclusion I wish to quote my own words during my trial in 1964. They are true today as they were then. I quote:

"I have fought against white domination, and I have fought against black domination. ₍₆₎I have cherished the ideal of a democratic and free society in which all persons live together in harmony and with equal opportunities. It is an ideal which I hope to live for and to achieve. But if needs be, it is an ideal for which I am prepared to die."

(英語で聴く　世界を変えた感動の名スピーチ　改訂第2版 より抜粋)

(1)　下線部①の英文を日本語にしなさい。

(2)　下線部②の英文を日本語にしなさい。

(3)　本文の内容を踏まえて, (　③　), (　⑤　)に入る最も適切な語をア～エから一つ選び, 記号で答えなさい。

   ③　ア　victory　　イ　mistake　　ウ　success　　エ　right

   ⑤　ア　past　　　イ　segregation　ウ　failure　　エ　way

(4)　下線部④が表すものを同じ段落の英文中から探し, 3語で書きなさい。

(5)　下線部⑥の英文を日本語にしなさい。

(☆☆☆◎◎◎◎)

【5】次の英文を読み, (1)～(6)の各問いに答えなさい。

≪　①　≫

Language ability has traditionally been considered, by language teachers and language testers alike, to consist of four skills: listening, reading, speaking and writing. Indeed, a model of language proficiency that has been very influential in language testing during the second half of this century describes language ability in terms of the four skills and several components (for example, grammar, vocabulary, and pronunciation). These four skills have traditionally been distinguished in terms of channel (audio, visual) and mode (productive, receptive). Thus listening and speaking involve the (　②　) channel, and receptive and productive modes, respectively, while reading and writing are in the (　③　) channel, and receptive and productive modes, respectively. (　ア　) However, is it adequate to distinguish the four skills simply in terms of channel and mode? If it is, then all language use that involves the audio channel and the productive mode could be considered speaking, while any language use in the visual channel and receptive mode would be (　④　). (　イ　)

We believe that it takes very little reflection to discover the (　⑤　) of this approach. First, it would classify widely divergent language use tasks or activities together under a single 'skill'. Consider, for example, how different are activities such as participating in a face-to-face conversation and listening to a radio newscast, even though both involve listening. Similarly, engaging in an electronic mail discussion probably has more in common with an oral conversation than with reading a newspaper, even though both the e-mail discussion and reading a newspaper involve the visual channel. Second, this approach fails to take into consideration the fact that language use is not simply a general phenomenon that takes place in a vacuum. We do not just 'read'; we read about something specific, for some particular purpose, in ⑥<u>a particular setting</u>. (　ウ　)

It is this conception of language use as the performance of specific situated language use tasks that provides, we believe, a much more useful means for characterizing what have traditionally been called language skills. We would thus not consider language skills to be part of language ability at all, but to be the contextualized realization of the ability to use language in the performance of specific language use tasks.

　　　　　　(Language Testing in Practice / Lyle F. Bachman, Adrian S. Palmer より抜粋)

(1)　≪　①　≫には，この英文全体のタイトルが入る。最も適切なものをア〜エから一つ選び，記号で答えなさい。

　　ア　Listening 'proficiency'

　　イ　Active Learning

　　ウ　Language 'skills'

　　エ　Audio Lingual Method

(2) (②)(③)(④)に入る最も適切な語を本文中から探し，それぞれ1語で書きなさい。

(3) 次の一文が入るのに最も適する部分を本文中の(ア)～(ウ)から一つ選び，記号で答えなさい。

That is, language use takes place, or is realized, in the performance of specific situated language use tasks.

(4) 本文の内容を踏まえて，(⑤)に入る最も適切な語をア～エから一つ選び，記号で答えなさい。

ア logic イ inadequacies ウ confirmation エ adequacy

(5) 筆者が，下線部⑥について対義語的に使っている語句を本文中から探し，2語で書きなさい。

(6) 本文の内容に合っているものをア～エから一つ選び，記号で答えなさい。

ア 言語能力は，4つの技能と，3つの要素のみからなると考えられてきた。

イ 言語技能をチャネルとモードという観点で区別することにより，適切に評価することができる。

ウ 口頭での会話に参加することは，電子メールによる議論に参加することよりも，新聞を読むことに近い。

エ 言語は，ある特定の状況の中で，何らかの目的を達成するために使用されるものである。

(☆☆☆☆○○○○)

【6】次の(1)～(4)の各問いに答えなさい。

(1) 次の①～⑤の用語の意味をア～オからそれぞれ選び，記号で答えなさい。

① CEFR ② SLA ③ CLIL ④ the Course of Study
⑤ BICS

ア 基本的対人伝達能力 イ 第二言語習得
ウ ヨーロッパ共通参照枠 エ 学習指導要領

オ　内容言語統合型学習

(2)　中学校の英語の授業で，買い物の場面における店員と客のやり取りを指導する。次の(条件)を踏まえて，(　①　)〜(　③　)に適する英文を一つずつ書き，モデルとして生徒に示す対話文を完成させなさい。

(条件)

　　・客は，青いセーターを探している。

　　・客は，自分にあったサイズのものを買いたい。

店員	客
May I help you?	(　①　)
OK. How about this one?	
	It looks nice. But it looks a little small for me. (　②　)
I'm sorry. We don't have bigger sizes in this color at the moment. But we have some other colors.	
	OK. Do you have any in dark colors?
Sure. How about this purple one? It is a really popular color.	
	It is beautiful. (　③　)
Sure. The fitting room is over there.	

(3)　中学3年生の英語の授業において，次の内容を生徒に英語で伝える時，それぞれどのように伝えるか，英語で書きなさい。

　　(語数及び文の数は問わない。)

　①　鳥取は住みやすい場所だと思うかどうか，を尋ねる時

　②　今日は将来住みたい場所について話してみよう，と提案する時

　③　なぜそう思うのか，を生徒に直接尋ねる時

(4)　中学3年生の英語の授業において，日本の伝統行事や有名な祭りを紹介するスピーチをさせる。その際，その中で分詞の後置修飾を用いた文を使わせたい。モデルとして提示するスピーチ原稿を40語程度で書きなさい。(文の数は問わない。)

(☆☆☆☆◎◎◎)

【高等学校】

【1】次の各問いに答えなさい。

(1) 次の文は，教育公務員特例法に規定された条文である。条文中の空欄(①)・(②)にあてはまる最も適切な語句の組み合わせをア〜カから一つ選び，記号で答えなさい。

> 第21条　教育公務員は，その職責を遂行するために，絶えず(①)と(②)に努めなければならない。

	①	②
ア	研修	修養
イ	研修	実践
ウ	研究	研鑽
エ	研究	修養
オ	教育	実践
カ	教育	研鑽

(2) 次の①〜③の法令に規定されている条文を，ア〜カからそれぞれ一つずつ選び，記号で答えなさい。

①　教育基本法　　②　学校教育法　　③　地方公務員法

ア　第30条　すべて職員は，全体の奉仕者として公共の利益のために勤務し，且つ，職務の遂行に当つては，全力を挙げてこれに専念しなければならない。

イ　第7条　文部科学大臣は，教育職員の健康及び棉祉の確保を図ることにより学校教育の水準の維持向上に資するため，教育職員が正規の勤務時間及びそれ以外の時間において行う業務の量の適切な管理その他教育職員の服務を監督する教育委員会が教育職員の健康及び福祉の確保を図るために講ずべき措置に関する指針(次項において単に「指針」という。)を定めるものとする。

　　ウ　第1条　教育は，人格の完成を目指し，平和で民主的な国家及び社会の形成者として必要な資質を備えた心身ともに健康な国民の育成を期して行われなければならない。

　　エ　第23条　公立の小学校等の教諭等の任命権者は，当該教諭等(臨時的に任用された者その他の政令で定める者を除く。)に対して，その採用(現に教諭等の職以外の職に任命されている者を教諭等の職に任命する場合を含む。附則第5条第1項において同じ。)の日から一年間の教諭又は保育教諭の職務の遂行に必要な事項に関する実践的な研修(以下「初任者研修」という。)を実施しなければならない。

　　オ　第66条　小学校は，当該小学校の教育活動その他の学校運営の状況について，自ら評価を行い，その結果を公表するものとする。
　　　※第79条，第79条の8，第104条，第135条において，それぞれ中学校，義務教育学校，高等学校，特別支援学校に準用。

　　カ　第34条　小学校においては，文部科学大臣の検定を経た教科用図書又は文部科学省が著作の名義を有する教科用図書を使用しなければならない。
　　　※第49条，第49条の8，第62条，第82条において，それぞれ中学校，義務教育学校，高等学校，特別支援学校に準用。

(3)　次の英文(高等学校の外国語教育における学習指導要領(平成22年5月文部科学省初等中等教育局)より抜粋)を読み，各問いに答えなさい。

＜English Communication Ⅰ＞

1. Objective

　To develop students' basic abilities such as accurately understanding and appropriately conveying information, ideas, etc., while fostering a positive (　X　) toward communication through the English language.

---

2. Contents

(1)　The following language activities, designed for specific language-use situations in order to encourage students to apply their abilities to understand and convey information, ideas, etc., should be conducted in English.

A. Understanding information, ideas, etc., and (　①　) the outline and the main points by listening to introductions to specified topics, dialogues, etc.

B. Understanding information, ideas, etc., and (　①　) the outline and the main points by reading explanations, stories, etc. Reading passages aloud so that the meaning of the content is expressed.

C. Discussing and exchanging opinions on information, ideas, etc., based on what one has heard, read, learned and experienced.

D. Writing brief passages on information, ideas, etc., based on what one has heard, read, learned and experienced.

(2)　To effectively conduct the language activities stated in (1), consideration should be given to the following instructional points.

A. Listening and speaking with due attention to the characteristics of English sounds, such as rhythm and intonation, speed, volume, etc.

B. Reading and writing with due attention to phrases and sentences indicating the main points, (　②　) phrases, etc.

C. Understanding and conveying matters, (　③　) facts, opinions, etc.

3. Treatment of the Contents

(1)　Based on general instruction to develop basic communication abilities given in lower secondary schools, the four areas of

145

language activities should be interlinked for (④) learning, while incorporating appropriate language activities involving speaking and writing about content heard or read.

(2)　Consideration should be given so that students master the items introduced in lower secondary schools and upper secondary schools through repeated instruction in accordance with students' circumstances, while experiencing various (⑤) language activities.

(あ)　本文中の(X)に入る最も適切な語を英語一語で答えなさい。

(い)　本文中の(①)～(③)に入る最も適切な語を，ア～オからそれぞれ一つずつ選び，(④)，(⑤)に入る最も適切な語を，カ～ケからそれぞれ一つずつ選び，記号で答えなさい。

①～③　[　ア　distinguishing　　イ　grasping

ウ　integrating　　エ　utilizing

オ　connecting　]

④，⑤　[　カ　abstract　　キ　situational

ク　comprehensive　　ケ　excessive　]

(☆☆☆◎◎◎)

【2】次の(1)～(6)の英文の( )に入る最も適切な語又は語句を，①～④の中からそれぞれ一つずつ選び，番号で答えなさい。

(1)　Although I woke up late yesterday morning, I ( ) be on time.

①　missed　　②　succeeded　　③　managed to　　④　could

(2)　Robert was afraid of her ( ) able to catch the last bus.

①　being not　　②　not being　　③　not be　　④　not to be

(3)　The newly built stadium will ( ) as many as 70,000 people.

①　fill　　②　seat　　③　give　　④　place

(4)　Twenty years ago, there were ( ) houses in this town.

①　good deal of　　②　good many　　③　so much a

④　a good many

(5)　Mary is not very (　　) with Chinese history.

①　famous　　②　familiar　　③　well-known　　④　well-learned

(6)　Hardly (　　) of the new compact cars have enough legroom for a tall

man like Paul.

①　neither　　②　one　　③　any　　④　many

(☆☆☆○○○○○)

【3】【例】にならって，次の(1)，(2)における会話体の英文(a)を英文(b)のように説明する時，それぞれの(　　)にあてはまる最も適切な語を英語一語で答えなさい。

【例】　(a)　"Go straight for three blocks," Susan said, "Turn left, and go past the bank and turn right. The train station is just around the corner. You can't miss it."

(b)　Susan (explained) the way to the train station.

(1)　(a)　"I have nothing to do with the case," David said, angrily. "I was nowhere near that convenience store when it was robbed."

(b)　David (　　) that he had robbed the convenience store.

(2)　(a)　"It's no use pretending to be innocent, Roger. I know you were at the place where Bill was killed last night." Edward said.

(b)　Edward (　　) Roger of killing Bill the previous night

(☆☆☆○○○)

【４】次の各問いに答えなさい。

(1) 次の会話の下線部①を英語にしなさい。

Cheryl：トム！本当に久しぶりね。	Cheryl：Tom！I haven't seen you in ages.
Tom　：シェリルかい？君だってわからなかったよ。だいぶやせたね。10歳は若く見えるよ。	Tom　：Cheryl? I barely recognized you！You're so much slimmer. You look 10 years younger.
Cheryl：それはどうかわからないけど。お褒めの言葉としていただいておくわ。	Cheryl：I'm not sure about that. But I'll take the compliment.
Tom　：それはそうと，秘けつは一体何なんだい？	Tom　：So what's your secret?
Cheryl：友人が素晴らしい個人トレーナーを勧めてくれたの。<u>①規則正しく運動をしたり，食事に関して気を使ったりするように，私のやる気を起こしてくれているのよ。</u>	Cheryl：My friend recommended a great personal trainer. ＿＿＿＿＿＿＿＿ ＿＿＿＿①＿＿＿＿．
Tom　：そうなんだ。明らかに効果があるみたいだね。	Tom　：Well, it's obviously working.

(旺文社　*2013年度版英検準1級過去6回全問題集*より抜粋)

(2) 次の文は，2010年に日本で女性初の民間旅客機機長となった藤明里さんのインタビューでの発言の抜粋です。下線部②を英語にしなさい。

> 多くの男性に言われました，日本でパイロットになるのは無理だ，特に民間旅客機のパイロットは，と。理由は聞きませんでしたが，彼らが「無理だ」と言うのは，当時，(民間旅客機の女性パイロットが)誰もいなかったからでしょう～中略～訓練前には毎回，鏡に向かい「私は機長だ」と言ったものです。弱さを外にさらしてはいけないと思いました。<u>②失敗して一番聞きたくないのは，現場はまだ女性には難しすぎる，という言葉でした。</u>

(朝日出版社　*CNN English Express 2019年10月号*より抜粋)

(3) 次の英文は，2017年2月14日付朝日新聞「天声人語」の英訳版です。この英文の見出しを10語程度の英語1文で答えなさい。

Teenagers who have just been accepted into university are now full of happy anticipation for their new lives starting this spring.

But The Asahi Shimbun's "Koe" (letters to the editor) section recently ran a letter from an Osaka high school student who was offered admission by recommendation to the university of her choice, but had to cancel her enrollment because she couldn't afford the tuition.

"If I become a parent in the future, I would never want my child to go through the same experience," she wrote.

This broke my heart.

There must be other young people in a similar predicament. It has been known for some years that Japan is stingy in supplying aid to financially strapped university students.

The nation is finally establishing a student grant that doesn't have to be repaid, but the amount of money earmarked and the number of eligible recipients is nowhere near adequate.

"More people today have come to accept the thinking that society at large has to support the welfare system," noted Junko Hamanaka, an educational sociologist. "But where education is concerned, this is still seen as the responsibility of each family."

A few years ago, a survey asked respondents to pick priority areas where taxpayers' money should be spent. Health care/ elderly care topped the list, followed by pension payments. Education was No.3 on the list.

The survey also found that only 20 percent to 30 percent of the respondents didn't mind spending more tax money to allow needy young people to receive a university education.

Without the backing of public opinion, government initiatives are not implemented.

"I fear an even wider gap will come to separate people who can lavish money on their children's education and the rest of society who can't," warned Hamanaka.

In most cases, what the Japanese refer to as "shogakukin" (scholarships) are more accurately "student loans" with interest.

With even national universities now charging steep tuition fees, many students are spending a great deal of their time working part-time jobs to eke out enough cash to pay for their basic living expenses and tutelage payments.

All Japanese universities can become tuition-free if the nation allocates just 1 percent of its consumption tax revenue to university education, according to one estimate.

Investing more in the future of our society is a matter that must not be put off any longer.

(原書房　天声人語　春　2017より抜粋)

(☆☆☆☆☆○○○○)

【5】次の英文を読み，各問いに答えなさい。

The American economy is on solid footing. Now in its 120th month of expansion, it shows few signs of bubbles about to burst. ⟨ X ⟩, ⟨ Y ⟩, and ⟨ Z ⟩. And perhaps most significantly, productivity is up. There is no denying that economic indicators are firmly positive.

These good numbers, however, are unlikely to change another set of numbers, regarding the geography of growth. Mark Muro of the Brookings Institution has calculated that over the last decade, the 53 largest American metro areas have (①) for 71 percent of America's total population growth, two-thirds of all of its employment growth, and a staggering three-quarters of all of its economic growth. In fact, half of all job growth in the United States took place in just 20 cities. (②), small towns in rural America have lost residents and barely contributed anything to economic growth.

This two-track economy has produced a two-track culture, with urbanites and rural Americans increasingly living in their own distinct worlds of news, entertainment and consumer goods. They live different lives and disagree deeply about politics —— a trend that is reflected in Washington.

Why is this happening? The economic trends can be explained by the digital revolution and globalization, in which brain work is more valuable, brawn work less so. The cultural forces are related to the recent rise of identity politics and backlash against immigration and multiculturalism. We see the forces that are pulling America apart. The question we should be focused on is, what can we do to bring the country (③)? Surely this has become the question of our times.

One answer that I have been increasingly drawn to is national service. There are many ways to design a national-service program, and a voluntary system will probably work better if it has strong (④), like loan forgiveness and tuition support, at its core. A 2013 study argued that current programs could feasibly be scaled up to 1 million volunteers without taking jobs from existing workers and would yield societal benefits worth more than four times the cost of the programs. And the programs that are already in operation, such as AmeriCorps, do good work and have stunningly high approval ratings from their alumni. Ninety-four percent say they gained a better (⑤) of differing communities, and 80 percent say the program helped their careers.

As Mickey Kaus noted in a prescient 1992 book, John F. Kennedy, the wealthy graduate of Choate and Harvard, famously served in World War II on a PT boat* alongside men who held jobs like mechanic, factory worker, truck driver and fisherman. Imagine if in today's America, the sons and daughters of hedge-fund managers, tech millionaires and bankers spent a year with the children of coal miners and farmers, working in public schools or national parks or the armed forces.

National service will not solve all of America's problems, but it might just help unite us as a nation, and that is the crucial first step forward.

(朝日出版社　*CNN English Express 2019年12月号*より抜粋)

注)　PT boat　哨戒用魚雷艇

(1)　次の(あ)〜(え)の問いの答えとして最も適切なものを，(A)〜(D)からそれぞれ一つずつ選び，記号で答えなさい。

(あ)　What is the main problem in America?

(A)　The economy has been expanding too rapidly.

(B)　Life in rural areas has been deteriorating.

(C)　America has become deeply divided.

(D)　Different people enjoy different national services.

(い)　What is the cause of the problem?

(A)　Population decline in the countryside

(B)　Cultural differences immigrants have caused

(C)　The government which encourages only economic development

(D)　Regional disparity in economic growth

(う)　What can help solve the problem?

(A)　Internship programs

(B)　Volunteer programs

(C)　Military service

(D)　Job hunting

(え)　Why is John. F. Kennedy mentioned in the passage?

(A)　Because Kennedy published a book about national service.

(B)　Because Kennedy was a famous graduate who worked as a mechanic.

(C)　To illustrate the importance of having people from different backgrounds work together.

(D)　To persuade readers to serve in the army.

(2)　本文中の　X ， Y ， Z にあてはめるのに適切でないものを，(A)〜(D)の中から一つ選び，記号で答えなさい。なお，文頭に来るべき語句も小文字で表記されている。

152

(A) unemployment is way down

(B) inflation is contained

(C) wages are moving up

(D) prices are decreasing

(3) 本文中の(①)～(⑤)に入る最も適切な語を，(A)～(D)から
それぞれ一つずつ選び，記号で答えなさい。

① (A) accounted   (B) spread   (C) looked

(D) reached

② (A) Moreover   (B) Likewise   (C) Meanwhile

(D) Namely

③ (A) alive   (B) forward   (C) back

(D) together

④ (A) presence   (B) measures   (C) initiative

(D) incentives

⑤ (A) popularity   (B) reward   (C) understanding

(D) reputation

(☆☆☆○○○○)

【6】次の英文を読み，各問いに答えなさい。

　　In the years since my coworkers and I succeeded in cloning a cow, I have
been asked a lot whether I would ever consider making a clone of myself.
There is, after all, a long and honorable history of medical scientists who have
tested their ideas on the most curious of experimental subjects — themselves.
Since the earliest days of medicine, researchers have swallowed bacteria,
injected vaccines, and even performed surgery on themselves. Usually,
①researchers double as subjects to make their experiments practical as well as
ethical. But not in the case of cloning. Whenever I have been asked whether I
would experiment on myself, I have had to explain how, even if the many
technical obstacles could be overcome, and a mini-me could be born without
risk, the answer would be the same. No. I have no intention of cloning myself.

One me is quite enough.

②If my clone were produced, living in my shadow would be very hard for him to bear. Imagine, when he would be a teenager, what he would make of being told that he is a genetic copy of a parent. Imagine what it would be like to know that you are the product of a scientific experiment. But more than this, imagine living under the burden of feeling that, both medically and psychologically, the future would no longer be open, that his life would follow the same path as his father's. My little identical twin would be an individual, a person in his own right, but he would have to handle the heavy burden of growing up to feel like my copy. He would watch each serious illness that struck me with fear, wondering whether it was his destiny to suffer in the same way.

The psychological and social impacts of cloning have been explored by Stephen Levick, a psychiatrist. Cloned children would have confusing and unusual relationships to their relatives. The clone would be the identical twin of the donor, who could also be his parent. Levick says that any parent motivated to clone himself or herself is bound to feel let down by the results. The narcissist is always (③) in his or her children and their failure to live up to perfection. They would surely feel entitled to expect a clone to be just like them, or their ideal image. Many people have already had to struggle under the burden of unrealistic parental expectations. For a cloned child the pressure could be extreme, even though parents know from their own experience that ④nurture is just as important as nature.

(旺文社　*2008　全国大学入試問題正解　英語(国公立大編)* より抜粋　一部改編)

(1)　下線部①の意味として最も適切なものを，(ア)～(エ)の中から一つ選び，記号で答えなさい。

(ア)　Researchers examine the result twice.

(イ)　Researchers carry out two experiments.

(ウ)　Researchers serve as an examinee as well.

(エ) Researchers have two different topics.

(2) 下線部②の理由を3つ，本文に即して日本語で答えなさい。

(3) 本文中の(③)に入る最も適切な語を，(ア)～(エ)の中から一つ選び，記号で答えなさい。

(ア) embarrassed (イ) bored (ウ) frustrated

(エ) disappointed

(4) 筆者が下線部④で述べているのはどのようなことか，本文の内容に即して分かりやすく日本語で説明しなさい。

(5) 本文で述べられている内容に合うものを，(ア)～(エ)の中から一つ選び，記号で答えなさい。

(ア) The author gave up conducting an experiment on himself.

(イ) We will be able to make a cloned child safely in the future.

(ウ) A cloned child couldn't be independent as a person.

(エ) A cloned child would feel more parental pressure than other children.

(☆☆☆◎◎◎◎)

【7】言語テストについて書かれた次の英文を読み，各問いに答えなさい。

Testing the language skills

Four major skills in communicating through language are often broadly defined as listening, listening and speaking, reading and writing. In many situations where English is taught for general purposes, these skills should be carefully integrated and used to perform as many genuinely communicative tasks as possible. Where ①this is the case, it is important for the test writer to concentrate on those types of test items which appear directly relevant to the ability to use language for real-life communication, especially in oral interaction. Thus, questions which test the ability to understand and respond appropriately to polite requests, advice, instructions, etc. would be preferred to tests of reading aloud or telling stories. In the written section of a test, questions requiring students to write letters, memos, reports and messages would be used in place of many of the more traditional compositions used in the past. In listening and reading tests, questions in which students show their ability to extract specific information of a practical nature would be preferred to questions testing the comprehension of unimportant and irrelevant details. Above all, there would be no rigid distinction drawn between the four different skills as in most traditional tests in the past, a test of reading now being used to provide the basis for a related test of writing or speaking.

Success in traditional tests all too often simply demonstrates that the student has been able to perform well in the test he or she has taken - and very little else. ②For example, the traditional reading comprehension test (often involving the comprehension of meaningless and irrelevant bits of information) measures a skill which is more closely associated with examinations and answering techniques than with the ability to read or scan in order to extract specific information for a particular purpose. In this sense, the traditional test may tell us relatively little about the student's general fluency and ability to handle the target language, although it may give some indication of the student's scholastic ability in some of the skills he or she needs as a student.

〜中略〜

Conversational exchanges

These drills are especially suitable for the language laboratory and can serve to focus attention on certain aspects of the spoken language, especially in those countries where English is taught as a foreign language and the emphasis is primarily on the reading skills. However, ③several of the test items themselves are far from in communicative in any sense at all and do not allow for authentic interaction of any kind. The essential element of constructive interplay with unpredictable stimuli and responses is absent from all these items as a result of the attempt to control the interaction taking place.

The item types range from items presenting the testees with situations in which they initiate conversations to incomplete conversations with the part of one speaker omitted (i.e.a one-sided dialogue). Tests containing such item types are on the whole reliable, but they cannot be described as being valid tests of speaking. If an opportunity is provided in other parts of the test for real oral interaction (i.e. genuine conversation and discussion), however, these controlled test items can be of some use in directing the attention of the students to specific language areas and skills.

Type 1   The testees are given a series of situations and are required to construct sentences on the lines of a certain pattern or group of patterns. Again, it is essential that two or three models be given to the testees so that they know exactly what is required. (The testees read or hear the situation and then make the appropriate responses, shown in the brackets.)

Examples:

Mrs Green lives in a flat. She doesn't like living in a flat and would like to live in a small house with a garden. (S*he wishes she lived in a small house with a garden.*)

It's raining heavily. Tom and Anna are waiting impatiently at home to set off on their picnic. (*They wish it would stop raining.*)

1.   Mr Black has a small car but his neighbours all have large cars. He would like a large car, too.
2.   Anna hasn't learnt how to swim yet but most of her friends can swim.
3.   Tom is waiting for Bill outside the cinema. The show is just about to start but Bill has not arrived yet.
4.   Mrs Robinson doesn't like living in towns; she wants to live in the country.

(etc.)

Type 2　This type of test item is similar to the previous type but not as strictly controlled. [　④　]

A friend of yours has forgotten where he has put his glasses. He cannot see too well without them. What will you say to him? (*Let me help you to look for them, etc.*)

You are on your way to school when it starts to rain heavily. Unfortunately, you and your friend have no raincoats. There is nowhere to shelter but your school is only a hundred yards away. What do you say to your friend? (*Shall we make a dash for it ? /Let's run the rest of the way.*)

1.　You are trying to get to the public library but you are lost. Ask a police officer the way.
2.　Your friend has just returned from a holiday abroad. What do you say to him?
3.　A waitress has just brought you the bill but has totalled it up incorrectly. What do you say to her?
4.　A friend of yours wants to see a film about a murder. You have already arranged to see it another evening, but you know she would be hurt if she knew. Make up an excuse.

Type 3　The students hear a stimulus to which they must respond in any appropriate way. (This test often relies on conventional greetings, apologies, acceptable ways of expressing polite disagreement, etc.)

Do you mind if I use your pencil for a moment?
(*Not at all/Certainly/Please do/Go ahead, etc.*)

What about a game of tennis?

(Yes, I'd love a game/All right. I don't mind/Don't you think it's a bit too hot?, etc.)

1. Please don't go to a lot of trouble on my behalf.
2. Oh dear, it's raining again. I hope it stops soon.
3. We shan't be late, shall we?
4. Karen asked me to say she's sorry she can't come tonight

Type 4   This is similar to the previous type of item, but the stimuli and responses form part of a longer dialogue and the situation is thus developed. Because of its total predictability, however, this type of item is sometimes referred to as a dialogue of the deaf！ The man in the dialogue below continues regardless of what the testee says.

You are on your way to the supermarket. A man comes up and speaks to you.

MAN : Excuse me. I wonder if you can help me at all. I'm looking for a chemist's.

PAUSE FOR TESTEE'S REPLY

MAN : Thank you. Do you know what time it opens?

PAUSE FOR TESTEE'S REPLY

MAN : Thanks a lot. Oh, er, by the way, is there a phone box near here?

PAUSE FOR TESTEE'S REPLY

MAN : Oh dear. I'll need some coins. Do you have any change for a 5 £ note?

PAUSE FOR TESTEE'S REPLY

MAN : Well, thanks a lot. You've been most helpful.

This dialogue clearly becomes absurd if, when asked where there is a chemist's, the testee replies, 'I'm sorry, I don't know,' and the man promptly thanks him and asks what time it opens. Nevertheless, the use of pre-recorded material of this kind makes it possible to use the language laboratory to test large numbers of students in a very short time.

Type 5　This item takes the form of an incomplete dialogue with prompts (shown in brackets in the following example) whispered in the student's ear.

> You are at the reception desk of a large hotel. The receptionist turns to address you.
> RECEPTIONIST : Can I help you?
> 　　(You want to know if there is a single room available.)
> 　　YOU : _____
> RECEPTIONIST : Yes, we have a single room with an attached bathroom.
> 　　(Ask the price.)
> 　　YOU : _____
> RECEPTIONIST : Thirty-four pounds fifty a night.
> 　　(You want to know if this includes breakfast.)
> 　　YOU : _____
> RECEPTIONIST : Yes, that's with continental breakfast
> 　　(You have no idea what 'continental breakfast' is.)
> 　　YOU : _____
> RECEPTIONIST : It's fruit juice, coffee, or tea and bread rolls.
> 　　(The receptionist is speaking too quickly. What do you say?)
> 　　YOU : _____
> RECEPTIONIST : Fruit juice, coffee, or tea and bread rolls.
> 　　(Book the room for two nights.)
> 　　YOU : _____
> RECEPTIONIST : Certainly. Room 216. The porter will take your bag

and show you where it is.

(Thank the receptionist.)

YOU : _____

(J. B. HEATON, *Writing English Language Tests*より抜粋)

(1) 下線部①のthisの内容を，本文の内容に即して日本語で答えなさい。

(2) 下線部②に即して，次の＜素材＞を読解の題材とし，高校2年生を対象に行う読解テストとして適切な問いを一つ，英語で具体的に示しなさい。

＜素材＞

Sudan is a large country in northeast Africa. It is a country with great promise. But it also has great problems.

In 1993 the people of Sudan suffered from war and hunger. Few people knew about this. Kevin Carter went there to work as a photographer. He wanted the world to see the problems of Sudan.

One day Carter saw a child. She was lying on the ground. He knew why the child was there. She was so hungry that she could not move. Suddenly a vulture appeared. He took this photo.

The photo appeared in newspapers all over the world. It made him famous. He won a Pulitzer Prize for it.

(平成18(2006)年度版*NEW CROWN English Series 3*
Lessson 7 "A Vulture and a Child" より抜粋)

---

(3) 下線部③の理由を，本文の内容に即して日本語で答えなさい。

(4) 本文の内容を踏まえて，[④] に入る文として最も適切なものを，(ア)〜(エ)の中から一つ選び，記号で答えなさい。

(ア) Some model responses are given by the examiner and the students can choose them or the patterns they wish.

(イ) Some model responses are given by the examiner and the students can't use the patterns they wish.

(ウ)　No model responses are given by the examiner and the students are free to use whatever patterns they wish.

(エ)　No model responses are given by the examiner and the students are free to change the situation.

(5)　Type 4での説明内容を次のような表にまとめた。本文の内容に即して，(A)，(B)に入れるべき説明を日本語で答えなさい。

タ イ プ 4	テストの特徴	・タイプ3と比較すると，対話が長く，場面設定がより発展的なものになる。 ・言うべき内容は簡単に予想がつく。
	テストとしての利点	(A)
	テストとして成立しなくなる状況	(B)

(6)　次に示すような場面・状況及び対話展開を設定して，あなたが Type 5で説明されているようなテストを生徒にする時，場面や状況に応じた生徒のそれぞれの発話をどのように促すか。(A)〜(D)に補うあなたの指示を，それぞれ英語で書きなさい。なお，英文の数は問わないこととする。

You are at a clothing store. The shop assistant turns to address you.

Shop assistant : Can I help you?

You　　　　　　　：＿＿＿＿＿＿(A)＿＿＿＿＿＿．

Shop assistant : The brand new coats just arrived yesterday.

You　　　　　　　：＿＿＿＿＿＿(B)＿＿＿＿＿＿．

Shop assistant : We have five colors.

You　　　　　　　：＿＿＿＿＿＿(C)＿＿＿＿＿＿．

Shop assistant : Yes, this is a large one.

You　　　　　　　：＿＿＿＿＿＿(D)＿＿＿＿＿＿．

Shop assistant : Yes, the fitting room is over there.

(☆☆☆◎◎◎◎)

解答・解説

【中高共通】

【1】Part 1　B　　Part 2　No. 1　(1)　C　　(2)　B　　No. 2　(1)　D
(2)　C　　Part 3　D

〈解説〉スクリプトは公表されていない。Part 1は，グラフの内容について正しく説明しているものを選択する問題と思われる。鳥取県在住の外国人の出身国に関するグラフである。グラフから読み取れる情報と，聞き取った情報とをうまく統合して答えられるかどうかが，解答のカギになるだろう。Part 2は，本文，質問文，選択肢とも問題用紙には印刷されておらず，音声のみで解答しなければならない。Part 3は選択肢のみ問題用紙に印刷されているので，事前に目を通し聴き取りのポイントをしぼっておきたい。選択肢から推測すると，何が開催されるのか(あるいは，何の催しに参加するのか)を聴き取る問題と思われる。

【中学校】

【1】(1)　エ　　(2)　①　ウ　　②　カ　　③　ア　　(3)　A　①　働き　　②　知識　　③　技能　　B　①　f　　②　m　　③　b
④　e　　⑤　h　　⑥　k　　⑦　d　　⑧　l　　⑨　o

〈解説〉(1)　教育公務員特例法第21条は，「研修」についての規定である。(2)　①　教育基本法第1条は「教育の目的」についての規定である。②　学校教育法第34条第1項は，小学校における「教科用図書その他の教材の使用」についての規定である。③　地方公務員法第30条は，「服務の根本基準」についての規定である。(3)　A　新学習指導要領における「知識・技能」に関する目標から出題されていることに着目したい。本目標での「外国語の音声や語彙，表現，文法，言語の働きなどを理解する」とは，基礎的・基本的な知識を確実に習得しながら，既存の知識と関連付けたり組み合わせたりしていくことにより，学習内容の深い理解と，個別の知識の定着を図るとともに，社会における様々な場面で活用できる概念としていくことである。また，「聞くこ

と，読むこと，話すこと，書くことによる実際のコミュニケーションにおいて活用できる技能を身に付ける」とは，一定の手順や段階を追って身に付く個別の技能のみならず，獲得した個別の技能が自分の経験やほかの技能と関連付けられ，変化する状況や課題に応じて主体的に活用できる技能として習熟・熟達していくということである。

Ｂ　出題箇所は，指導計画の作成に当たり，小・中・高等学校を通じた領域別の目標の設定という観点を踏まえ，小学校や高等学校における指導との接続に留意した上で，配慮すべき事項を示した項である。本項を熟読し用語等を正確に記憶しておくことが望ましいが，もし記憶していないとしても，学習指導要領に基づいた単元計画や指導案の作成をイメージしながら解答すれば，難解な問題ではないと思われる。例えば，ウで解答が求められている「互いの気持ちを伝えあうなどの言語活動」と「言語材料について理解したり練習したりするための指導」の区別は重要であり，新学習指導要領においては言語活動を核とした授業が求められている。同様に，アで解答が求められている「目的や場面，状況」については，言語活動に不可欠な要素である。

【２】(1)　ウ　　(2)　ア　　(3)　イ　　(4)　エ　　(5)　ウ　　(6)　エ
(7)　ア　　(8)　イ　　(9)　エ　　(10)　ウ　　(11)　イ　　(12)　ウ
(13)　ア　　(14)　エ　　(15)　イ
〈解説〉(1)　英文は「マークはマラソンを見た後に，ジョギングを始める気になった」の意味であり，be inspired to doは「～する気になる」の意味である。　(2)　英文は「サラは休暇中に大量に食べ過ぎて気分が悪くなった」の意味であり，became sick from Aは「Aが原因で体調が悪くなった」の意味である。　(3)　英文は「その群衆の写真はピントがずれているので，顔をはっきり見ることが難しかった」の意味であり，out of focusは「ピントがずれている」の意味である。　(4)　英文は「モニカは母に盛大な祝賀会を開くことを計画し，約50人の客が出席した」の意味であり，big celebrationは「盛大な祝賀会」の意味である。　(5)　英文は「その年配の男性がどのようにして裕福になった

かを尋ねられた時，彼は，とにかく一生懸命働いたと答えた」の意味である。　(6)　英文は「マイケルは18年間のバスケットボールの生活をJetsに捧げてきた」の意味であり，dedicatedは「捧げた」の意味である。　(7)　英文は「犬は鋭い嗅覚を持っていることで知られる」の意味であり，acuteは「鋭い」の意味である。　(8)　英文は「メーガンは6年間離れて暮らした息子に合った時，失った時間を取り戻そうとした」の意味であり，make up forは「～を取り戻す(返す)」の意味である。　(9)　英文は「あなたが助けてくれたことへのお礼の印として，この商品券を受け取ってください」の意味であり，as token of my appreciationは「私のお礼の印として」の意味である。　(10)　英文は「その町に甚大な被害をもたらした嵐の日々の後，ようやく空が晴れてきた」の意味であり，clear upは「晴れ上がる」の意味である。

(11)　英文は「その取締役の話が急に中断された時，彼は話の序言を言い出したところだった」の意味であり，introductory remarksは「序言」の意味である。　(12)　英文は「マグレブさんは調査のほとんどが既に同僚によって完了していることを知って安心した」の意味である。researchは一般的に不可算名詞であることに着目するとよい。

(13)　英文は「金属の鉱床が地中深くにあるという事実は，会社がそれらを採掘することをより困難にした」の意味であり，make O Cは「OをCにする」の意味である。　(14)　英文は「その電気掃除機は，独自の内部メカニズムによって，現在のアメリカ市場で最も革新的なものとして際立っている」の意味である。空欄の前がthe，後ろがdesignであるから，名詞を修飾する形容詞が入るとわかる。　(15)　英文は「ペリー製鉄会社はすべての段階における品質管理への取り組みのおかげで，世界で最も大きな製鉄会社の1つになった」の意味であり，owing toは「～のおかげで」の意味である。

【3】(1)　①　ア　　②　ウ　　(2)　①　オ　　②　ウ　　(3)　①　エ　②　ウ　　(4)　①　オ　　②　イ　　(5)　①　イ　　②　カ　(6)　①　エ　　②　カ　　(7)　①　カ　　②　ア　　(8)　①　ウ

②　エ　　(9)　①　オ　　②　ア　　(10)　①　ア　　②　エ
〈解説〉(1)　完成した英文はIt is no wonder she succeeded in passing the exam.であり，「彼女がその試験に合格したのは少しも不思議ではない」の意味である。　(2)　完成した英文はWhat made you decide to major in education in college.であり，「この大学で教育を専攻しようと決めたのはなぜですか」の意味である。　(3)　完成した英文はWe cannot be too careful when we spend our money.であり，「私たちはお金を使う時に，どんなに注意してもし過ぎることはない」の意味である。　(4)　完成した英文はI wish I had studied harder when I was a student.であり，「私は学生時代にもっと勉強しておけばよかったと思う」の意味である。
(5)　完成した英文はI awoke to find my sister staring at me.であり，「私が目を覚ますと姉が私を見つめていた」の意味である。　(6)　完成した英文はI cannot put up with him breaking promises so many times.であり，「私は彼が幾度となく約束を破ってきたことに我慢できない」の意味である。　(7)　完成した英文はEveryone wants there to be no war in the world.であり，「誰もが世界から戦争がなくなってほしいと思っている」の意味である。　(8)　完成した英文はYou mustn't speak with your mouth full.であり，「口をいっぱいにして話をしてはいけない」の意味である。　(9)　完成した英文はI didn't understand what he was trying to say.であり，「私は，彼が何を言おうとしていたか理解できなかった」の意味である。　(10)　完成した英文はI like him all the better for his stubbornness.であり，「彼の頑固さゆえに，よりいっそう私は彼が好きだ」の意味である。

【4】(1)　私たちの信念は，国の将来を決定できるのは，人種差別のない形で民主主義的に選出された組織しかないというものです。
(2)　私たちの闘争は，決定的な瞬間に達しています。私たちは国民に求めます，この機会を捉えて，民主主義に向かう過程を迅速で不断のものにしていくことを。　(3)　③　イ　　⑤　エ　　(4)　our white compatriots　(5)　私が大切にしてきたのは，すべての人が協調し，

平等の機会を持つ，民主的で自由な社会という理念です。

〈解説〉(1)　この文がいわゆる形式主語構文であることに着目すればよい。that節以下については，受動態の形になっていることは明らかであるので，基本に忠実に和訳していけばよいだろう。　(2)　1文目は短い文で構造も明快であるが，2文目はso thatの前後の節をうまくつなげて書けるかどうかがカギである。また，2文目の前半にあるcall on A to doは「Aに～するよう訴える(求める)」の意味である。　(3)　③を含んだ文は「現在の努力を緩めることは，後世の世代が許すことができない過ちであろう」の意味である。また，⑤を含んだ文は「私たちは恐怖が邪魔するのを許してはいけません」の意味である。　(4)　下線部④は「解放運動はあなたがたにとっても政治的な故郷になる」の意味であり，今まで南アフリカ共和国に住んでいた黒人だけでなく，新しい南アフリカ共和国を支持する白人を指す内容を探せばよい。(5)　a democratic and free societyとそれを修飾しているin whichの関係代名詞節を注意して和訳することができれば，文構造などは難しくない。

【5】(1)　ウ　　(2)　②　audio　　③　visual　　④　reading
　　　(3)　ウ　　(4)　イ　(5)　a vacuum　　(6)　エ
〈解説〉(1)　第1パラグラフをはじめとして，言語技能についての論が展開されていることに留意したい。また，いわゆる4技能のうち1つの技能に焦点を当てられていないことがわかれば，適切な選択肢は1つに定まるだろう。　(2)　②と③については，第1パラグラフ3文目に着目するとよい。リスニングとスピーキングは音声であり，リーディングとライティングは文字である。また，④については，空欄部を含んだ文の前半に，聴覚情報を処理する産出技能がスピーキングであると述べていることに着目すれば，視覚情報を処理する受容技能はリーディングであると推測できる。　(3)　補充する英文がThat isで始まっていることから，補充する英文が言い換えになっている箇所を探せばよい。specific situated language use tasksがキーフレーズであり，空欄前後に類似した表現が用いられている。　(4)　空欄部を含む英文は「このアプ

ローチの(　　　)を発見するには，ほとんど熟考しなくてよいと考えている」の意味である。これ以降の英文で，その理由が2つ述べられており，2つ目の理由についてthis approach fails to take into consideration という表現が用いられていることから，inadequacies「不完全性，不適切さ」が適切。　(5)　下線部を含んだ文では，リーディングは特定の状況において，特定の目的の下，そして何か特定の情報を読むことで行われると述べられている。よって，言語使用が実際の言語使用場面などから切り離されていることを意味する表現を探せばよい。vacuum は「孤立，真空」。　(6)　第3パラグラフの2文目に着目すればよい。

【6】(1)　①　ウ　　②　イ　　③　オ　　④　エ　　⑤　ア
(2)　①　I'm looking for a blue sweater.　　②　Do you have a bigger one?
③　Can I try it on?　　(3)　①　Do you think Tottori is a good place to live in?　　②　Where would you like to live in the future ? We'll talk about it today.　　③　Why do you think so?　　(4)　When we can see the full moon in September, we hold a traditional event called "Jugo-ya". We make dango from rice. It looks like the full moon. By making dango, we celebrate the harvest of the year and the beautiful moon. (40 words)

〈解説〉(1)　①　Common European Framework of Reference for Languages の略語である。もともとヨーロッパの言語習得状況に関するガイドラインであったが，この中で提唱されている「CAN-DOリスト」作成の取組みが日本でも普及しつつあり，日本の英語教育にも多大な影響を与えている。　②　Second Language Acquisitionの略語である。
③　Content and Language Integrated Learningの略語であり，言語によるコミュニケーションを通して，教科などの内容学習と言語学習を同時に達成しようとする指導方法のことである。日本の英語教育においても注目を集めている考え方である。　④　略語ではなく，基本的な用語なので確実に覚えておきたい。関連して，学習指導要領を告示している文部科学省の英名は，Ministry of Education, Culture, Sports, Science and Technology(MEXT)である。　⑤　Basic Interpersonal Communication

Skillsの略であり，日常生活など基本的なコミュニケーションで用いられる言語能力のことである。それに対して，学術的文脈など抽象的な思考が必要とされるコミュニケーションで用いられる言語能力を，Cognitive Academic Language Proficiency(CALP)という。併せて覚えておきたい。　(2)　買い物の場面におけるやり取りであることを考慮すれば，前後の文脈を踏まえて空欄に入る内容は容易に想像できるだろう。具体的に言えば，①は直後にHow about this one?とあることから，「青いセーターを探している」という内容を書けばよい。また，②は直後のWe don't have bigger sizes，③はThe fitting room is over there.のそれぞれに着目して，「大きいサイズはありますか」，「試着してもよいですか」と書けばよい。　(3)　いわゆるクラスルームイングリッシュが問われている。語数及び文の数に制限がないことから，あまり直訳的に考えないで，授業場面をイメージして生徒に対してどのように発話するかを考えればよい。解答例でも2文に分けているように，②は無理に1文で書こうとしない方がよいだろう。　(4)　日本の伝統行事や有名な祭りを紹介するという内容で，さらに分詞の後置修飾が自然に用いられているスピーチを書くことが求められている。文の数は制限がないものの，語数は40語程度に制限されていることから，分詞の後置修飾を無理にたくさん使用しようとして，不自然なスピーチにならないように注意したい。分詞の後置修飾としては現在分詞よりも過去分詞の方が書きやすいと考えられ，解答例にあるようなcalledの他にも，known asやmade byといった表現を使用することができるだろう。

【高等学校】

【1】(1)　エ　　(2)　①　ウ　　②　カ　　③　ア

(3)　(あ)　attitude　　(い)　①　イ　　②　オ　　③　ア　　④　ク　　⑤　キ

〈解説〉(1)　教育公務員特例法第21条は，「研修」についての規定である。

(2)　①　教育基本法第1条は「教育の目的」についての規定である。

②　学校教育法第34条第1項は，小学校における「教科用図書その他

の教材の使用」についての規定である。　③　地方公務員法第30条は，「服務の根本基準」についての規定である。　(3)　現行の学習指導要領(平成21年3月告示)の英訳版から，「コミュニケーション英語Ⅰ」に関する出題である。令和4年度施行予定の新学習指導要領(平成31年3月告示)ではないことに留意したい。　(あ)　外国語科の目標に関する記述である。日本語では「英語を通じて，積極的にコミュニケーションを図ろうとする態度を育成するとともに，情報や考えなどを的確に理解したり適切に伝えたりする基礎的な能力を養う」と書かれている。(い)　①　空欄後のthe outline and the main pointsに着目したい。日本語では「概要や要点をとらえる」と書かれている。　②　空欄前のphrases and sentences indicating the main pointsに着目したい。日本語では「内容の要点を示す語句や文，つながりを示す語句」と書かれている。　③　空欄後のfacts, opinionsに着目したい。日本語では「事実と意見などを区別して」と書かれている。　④　空欄前のthe four areas of language activities should be interlinked forに着目したい。日本語では「四つの領域の言語活動を有機的に関連付けつつ総合的に指導するもの」と書かれている。　⑤　空欄後のlanguage activitiesに着目したい。日本語では「多様な場面における言語活動を経験させ」と書かれている。

【２】(1)　③　　(2)　②　　(3)　②　　(4)　④　　(5)　②　　(6)　③
〈解説〉(1)　英文は「昨日の朝，私は寝坊したが，なんとか時間に間に合った」の意であり，manage toは「なんとか～する」の意味である。(2)　英文は「ロバートは彼女が最終バスに乗れないことを心配していた」の意であり，空欄前にあるherに着目すると，空欄には動名詞の否定形の形が入ることがわかる。　(3)　英文は「新しく建設されたスタジアムは70,000人を収容できるだろう」の意であり，seatは動詞で「収容する」の意味がある。　(4)　英文は「20年前にこの町には相当な数の住宅があった」の意であり，a good manyは「相当な数の」の意味である。　(5)　英文は「メアリーは中国史に詳しくはない」の意であり，

be familiar withは「～に詳しい(精通している)」の意味である。

(6) 英文は「新しいコンパクトカーには，ポールのような身長の高い人にとって十分な足元の広さがあるものはほとんどない」の意であり，hardly anyは「ほとんどない」の意味である。

【3】(1) denied　(2) accused

〈解説〉(1) (a) の英文は「『私はその事件とは全く関係がない。強盗事件が起こった時にそのコンビニの近くにはいなかった』とデイビッドは怒りながら言った」の意であり，デイビッドはコンビニ強盗をしたことを否定している。　(2) (a) の英文は「『ロジャー，無実を装っても無駄だよ。昨夜ビルが殺されたところに君がいたことは知っているよ』とエドワードが言った」の意であり，エドワードはロジャーのビル殺害を非難している。

【4】(1) He has motivated me to exercise regularly and be more careful about my diet.　(2) The last thing I wanted to hear from people if I failed was that it was still too hard out there for women.　(3) Japan still shows little desire to help needy students pay university fees. (12 words)

〈解説〉(1) いわゆる和文英訳の問題である。「規則正しく運動をする」と「食事に関して気を使ったりする」を並列に書くことができれば，文構造を複雑にしないで書くことができるだろう。　(2) この問題もいわゆる和文英訳の問題である。日本語をそのまま直訳すると難しいので，英訳しやすい日本語に置き換えるとよいだろう。例えば，「失敗した時に一番聞きたくない言葉は，現場はまだ女性には厳しすぎるということだ」のような形にすると，英語にした時の主部と述部の関係がわかりやすいだろう。　(3) 英文のタイトルを10語程度の1文の英語で書くことが求められており，難しい。まずは要約問題と同じように，英文の重要な部分を特定する必要がある。大阪の高校生が書いた投書の具体的な内容や，教育社会学者が話した内容などを統合すると，「日本では大学進学に必要な経済的サポートが行われていない」

という内容が共通しており，これを英語で表現すればよいだろう。

【5】(1) (あ) (C)　(い) (D)　(う) (B)　(え) (C)　(2) (D)
(3) ① (A)　② (C)　③ (D)　④ D　⑤ C

〈解説〉(1) (あ)　第2パラグラフ以降において，アメリカには格差による分断があることが述べられている。　(い)　主に第2パラグラフや第3パラグラフで述べられているように，アメリカの経済発展の裏には大きな地域格差がある。　(う)　問題の解決策は主に第5パラグラフで述べられている。　(え)　第6パラグラフの1文目の後半に，ジョン・F・ケネディは大統領になる前，第2次世界大戦中に整備員や工場労働者たちと同じ魚雷艇で仕事したとある。そして，同パラグラフの2文目では，仮定法を用いて，いわゆる富裕層の子息が，炭鉱夫や農夫などの子息と，公立学校や軍隊などで協働することを想像するように読者に求めている。このことから，いわゆる富裕層であっても富裕層だけと協働するのではなく，様々な人と協働することの必要性が説かれている。　(2)　空欄の前にはアメリカの経済が堅調であることが述べられていることから，経済にとってネガティブな指標を示す語句は不適切だといえる。　(3)　①　空欄を含む節は「アメリカにおける53番目までの大都市がアメリカの人口増加の71%を占めている」の意である。アメリカの経済発展は大都市の発展に起因しているのである。　②　①の解説とも関連するが，空欄前はアメリカの経済発展が大都市の発展に起因していることを述べている一方で，空欄後は地方の小さな町が経済発展には寄与していないことを述べている。よって，空欄前後で反対のことを述べるための接続詞が適切。　③　空欄を含む文の前に，アメリカが分断されているという問題が述べられている。よって，「団結させるにはどうしたらいいか」とするのが適切。

④　空欄を含む節は「もし，債権の免除や学費支援といった強力なインセンティブがその中核にあれば，自発的なシステムはほぼ間違いなく機能するだろう」の意である。　⑤　空欄を含む節は「94パーセントの人が，ほかのコミュニティをより理解できるようになったと言っ

ている」の意である。この前の文にあるAmeriCorpsは公共サービスに関わるボランティアの例であり，これらの活動がアメリカの分断への対策として機能することに着目する。

【6】(1) （ウ）　(2)　ティーンエイジャーになった時に親の遺伝子の複製だと言われ，自分が科学的実験の産物だと知り，医学的にも心理学的にも未来が開かれておらず，自分の父親と同じ道を歩むことになるのだと感じながら生きていくことになるから。　　(3)　（エ）

(4)　生まれつきに備わっているものと同じくらいどのように育つかも重要であるということ。　　(5)　（エ）

〈解説〉(1)　下線部の前の文を見ると，研究者自身が細菌を飲み込んだことや，ワクチンを自身に接種したことが書かれており，研究者が被験者を兼ねていることがわかる。　(2)　下線部は「もし私のクローンが作られたら，私の影で生きるのは非常に耐えがたいだろう」の意である。あとはこの文に続く3文がそれぞれ理由を示しているため，ほぼそのまま和訳をすればよい。　(3)　空欄を含む文は「ナルシストは，自身の子どもやその子どもたちが完璧ではないことに，いつも失望している」の意である。この文の前にあるis bound to feel let down by the resultsに着目するとよい。　(4)　下線部を含む文の2つ前の文に，クローンの親はクローンの子どもに自身の理想や自身と同じようになることを期待してよいと思うという記述がある。しかし，クローンだからといって，必ずしもその親と同じようになるとは限らず，教育などの環境要因も同様に重要であるということを書けばよい。　(5)　第3パラグラフの最後から2文目と最後の文に着目すると，クローンではない人も非現実な親からの期待という重荷にもがいているが，クローンの親はそのことを経験しているにも関わらず，クローンに対する期待が非常に大きいことが述べられている。

【7】(1)　言語によるコミュニケーションの主要技能である，聴く，聴き話す，読む，書くの4つの技能が注意深く統合され，それらを使っ

て純粋にコミュニカティブな課題が行われている場合。　　(2)　What made Carter famous?　　(3)　やり取りをコントロールしようとする結果，あらかじめ予測できない刺激・反応によって相互にやり取りするというこの活動の本質的な要素が脱落してしまうから。

(4)　(ツ)　　(5)　(A)　あらかじめ録音しておき，LL教室を利用して大勢の生徒を短時間で試験することができる。　　(B)　最初の質問に対して，「知らないですね。すみません。」と答え，次の質問がつながらなくなってしまう場合。　　(6)　(A)　You want to buy a coat.
(B)　Ask how many colors they have.　　(C)　Ask if there is a large one.
(D)　You want to try it on.

〈解説〉(1)　下線部を含む文の前の文の内容を書けばよい。代名詞が指す内容を答える問題では，基本的には代名詞の前または直後に着目するのがよい。　　(2)　下線部は「例えば，伝統的な読解テスト(たびたび，無意味で無関係な情報の断片の理解を含んでいる)は，特定の目的で特定の情報を取り出すために読む能力というよりは，試験や解答技術とより密接に関連した能力を測定している」の意である。したがって，英文の局所的な内容を問うような問題ではなく，英文の大局的な理解を問うような問題や，英文に明示的には書かれていないものの，十分推測可能な内容を問うような問題を書けばよいだろう。　　(3)　下線部を含む文の次の文に理由が説明されているので，この文の内容をまとめればよい。　　(4)　空欄のあるType 2は，Type 1ほど統制されていないもののType 1と類似しているとあるため，Type 1とType 2の違いに着目する。Type 1は決まった言語形式の文を作ることが求められており，受験者には問題の手順がわかるように2〜3の例を示す必要があることが述べられている。それに対して，Type 2の問題例を見ると，解答例の言語形式は完全に限定されているわけではない。また，問題文の中に受験者への質問文も含まれているため，受験者にとっては手順がわかりやすい形式になっている。したがって，「例を示す必要がなく，受験者が用いる言語形式を選ぶことができる」という選択肢が適切。　　(5)　Type 4のテストの利点(A)は，テストの下のパラグラフの

2文目に述べられており，テストとして成立しなくなる状況(B)は，同1文目に述べられている。Type 4のテストは，一連のやり取りにおける相手の発話のみを用意しておき，それぞれの発話の後に受験者に応答させるという形式である。そのため，相手の発話を録音しておけば，一度に多数の受験者にテストを実施することができる。一方で，最初の質問で「すみません。わかりません」と答えられてしまうと，それ以降の発話が続くことが不自然になってしまう。　(6)　Type 5のテストは，一連のやり取りにおける個々の発話について，テスト実施者が受験者に発話させたい内容の指示を与える形式になっている。したがって，解答する際には前後にある相手の発話を参考にしながら考える必要がある。まず，AはCan I help you?に対する応答であり，次の発話にあるcoatに着目する。次に，Bは次の発話にあるfive colorsに着目する。さらに，Cは次の文にあるthis is a large oneに着目する。最後に，Dは次の文にあるthe fitting room is over thereに着目する。解答する際に英文の数に制限はないが，生徒に発話させたい内容から逆算して，できるだけ1文で簡潔な指示を書きたい。

2020年度　実施問題

【中高共通】

【１】放送される指示に従い，答えなさい。

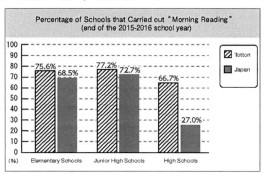

(Part 1)

(Part 2)
　No.1
　　(1)
　　(2)
　No.2
　　(1)
　　(2)
(Part 3)
　No.1
　No.2

(☆☆☆○○○○○)

【中学校】

【1】 次の(1)～(4)の各問いに答えなさい。

(1) 次の文は，教育に関する法令に記載された条文の一部である。下の問いに答えなさい。

> 第6条 法律に定める学校は，(   )を有するものであって，国，地方公共団体及び法律に定める法人のみが，これを設置することができる。

① (   )にあてはまる最も適切な語句を答えなさい。

② この文が記載された法令として最も適切なものを，次のア～オから1つ選び，記号で答えなさい。

ア 日本国憲法　　イ 教育基本法

ウ 学校教育法　　エ 地方教育行政の組織及び運営に関する法律

オ 教育公務員特例法

(2) 次の①，②の文は，文部科学省国立教育政策研究所が平成30年3月に発行したキャリア教育リーフレット「生徒が直面する将来のリスクに対して学校にできることって何だろう？」において，進路に関する主な相談機関について説明したものである。①，②の相談機関として最も適切なものを，ア～オからそれぞれ1つずつ選び，記号で答えなさい。

① 若者一人一人の状況に応じて，専門的な相談に乗ったり，各地域にある若者支援機関を紹介したりする施設。

② 労働者の最低限の労働条件を定めた労働基準法や，労働者の安全を守るための基準を定めた労働安全衛生法などに基づいて，労働者を保護するための仕事を行う機関。

ア 総合労働相談コーナー(都道府県労働局総務部)

イ 公共職業安定所

ウ 労働基準監督署

エ 職業能力開発促進センター

オ 地域若者サポートステーション

(3)　中学校学習指導要領(平成29年3月告示)「第2章　第9節　外国語　第1　目標」について，(　①　)～(　⑤　)に入る最も適切な語句を答えなさい。

---

(1)　(省略)

(2)　コミュニケーションを行う(　①　)や(　②　)，(　③　)などに応じて，日常的な話題や社会的な話題について，外国語で簡単な情報や考えなどを理解したり，これらを活用して表現したり伝え合ったりすることができる力を養う。

(3)　外国語の背景にある文化に対する理解を深め，聞き手，読み手，話し手，書き手に配慮しながら，(　④　)に外国語を用いてコミュニケーションを図ろうとする(　⑤　)を養う。

---

(4)　中学校学習指導要領(平成29年3月告示)「第2章　第9節　外国語　第2　各言語の目標及び内容等　英語　1　目標　(3)　話すこと[やり取り]」について，(　①　)～(　⑤　)に入る最も適切な語句を(a)～(j)からそれぞれ1つずつ選び，記号で答えなさい。

ア　(　①　)のある事柄について，簡単な語句や文を用いて(　②　)で伝え合うことができるようにする。

イ　日常的な話題について，(　③　)や自分の考え，気持ちなどを(　④　)し，簡単な語句や文を用いて伝えたり，相手からの質問に答えたりすることができるようにする。

ウ　社会的な話題に関して聞いたり読んだりしたことについて，考えたことや感じたこと，その(　⑤　)などを，簡単な語句や文を用いて述べ合うことができるようにする。

(a)　興味　　(b)　関心　　(c)　簡単な表現　　(d)　理由

(e)　整理　　(f)　即興　　(g)　事実　　　　　(h)　価値

(i)　構築　　(j)　根拠

(☆☆☆○○○○○)

178

【2】次の(1)～(20)の英文の(　　)に入る最も適切な単語または語句をそれぞれ1つずつ選び，記号で答えなさい。

(1)　Event planners noted that attendance at last night's awards ceremony was very (　　).

　　ア　empty　　イ　low　　ウ　lesser　　エ　few

(2)　IGY Corporation released a (　　) confirming its plans for expansion in Canada.

　　ア　state　　イ　stating　　ウ　statement　　エ　stated

(3)　The board of directors at Neumann Computing (　　) meets once a month.

　　ア　general　　イ　generalize　　ウ　generally　　エ　generalized

(4)　The construction on Highway 24 is expected to continue (　　) next year.

　　ア　until　　イ　across　　ウ　down　　エ　onto

(5)　Guests are required to pay their phone charges when they (　　) at the hotel reception desk.

　　ア　bring　　イ　check out　　ウ　remove　　エ　drop off

(6)　The mayor of Redbury has not (　　) reviewed the proposal to expand Grey Park.

　　ア　yet　　イ　soon　　ウ　very　　エ　after

(7)　Comments or suggestions concerning our room service (　　) welcome.

　　ア　is　　イ　are　　ウ　to be　　エ　being

(8)　Caritas Theater's advertising strategy has been to rely (　　) on digital media.

　　ア　increase　　イ　increases　　ウ　increasing　　エ　increasingly

(9)　Bedford Town Library has received nearly €5,000 in contributions (　　) the last 12 months.

　　ア　above　　イ　behind　　ウ　over　　エ　along

(10)　Dr. Woo is considered to be one of today's most influential economic policy analysts by (　　) in the field.

ア　other　　イ　others　　ウ　itself　　エ　themselves

(11)　When Dr. Patel's flight was canceled, she had to catch a train in order to arrive (　　) for the appointment.

ア　more punctual　　イ　punctuality　　ウ　punctual

エ　punctually

(12)　Belvin Movie Theaters will (　　) allow customers to purchase tickets on its Web site.

ア　yet　　イ　since　　ウ　ever　　エ　soon

(13)　There is a coffee machine (　　) located on the third floor of the Tabor Building.

ア　conveniently　　イ　slightly　　ウ　considerably

エ　eventually

(14)　Rather than wearing business attire on Tuesdays, staff may choose to wear casual clothing (　　).

ア　enough　　イ　despite　　ウ　instead　　エ　in case

(15)　Please read the following guidelines for (　　) books to the Hartleton Library.

ア　donate　　イ　donates　　ウ　to donate　　エ　donating

(16)　Ms. Choi is scheduled (　　) from her vacation next week.

ア　returning　　イ　returns　　ウ　returned　　エ　to return

(17)　The Kelvin Corporation is one of the largest (　　) of electronic supplies in the region.

ア　provide　　イ　providing　　ウ　providers　　エ　provided

(18)　The Gregory Conference Center is neither convenient to access to the city center (　　) is it near any train stations.

ア　and　　イ　but　　ウ　yet　　エ　nor

(19)　Researchers are required to update their (　　) contact information by Tuesday this week.

ア　person　　イ　personal　　ウ　personally　　エ　personalize

(20)　Department heads have submitted a list of subjects (　　) at the next conference.

ア to be raised イ are raised ウ were raised

エ are raising

【3】次の(1)～(10)の〔 〕内の単語または語句を並べ替えてそれぞれ
正しい英文を作るとき，(ア)と(イ)に入る単語または語句をそ
れぞれ1つずつ選び，番号で答えなさい。ただし，英文のはじめにく
る単語または語句の頭文字も小文字にしてある。

(1) 〔① will ② become ③ arrogant ④ less ⑤ you
⑥ the〕

The more knowledge you have, ( )(ア)( )(イ)( )
( ).

(2) 〔① no ② the issue ③ point ④ discussing
⑤ in ⑥ is〕

There ( )(ア)( )(イ)( )( ).

(3) 〔① as ② many ③ has ④ books ⑤ twice〕

He( )(ア)( )(イ)( ) as she has.

(4) 〔① ill ② person ③ speak ④ be ⑤ to
⑥ the last〕

He would ( )( )(ア)( )(イ)( ) of others.

(5) 〔① help ② laughing ③ couldn't ④ at ⑤ silly
⑥ his〕

I ( )( )(ア)( )(イ)( ) joke.

(6) 〔① in ② meeting ③ to ④ held ⑤ is
⑥ be〕

The ( )(ア)( )(イ)( )( ) Tottori.

(7) 〔① have ② want ③ magazine ④ whatever
⑤ you ⑥ may ⑦ to〕

You ( )( )(ア)( )(イ)( )( ) read.

181

(8) 〔① your　② Hong Kong　③ like　④ what

⑤ was　⑥ to　⑦ trip〕

Tell me (　)(　)(ア)(　)(イ)(　)(　).

(9) 〔① snow　② going　③ prevented　④ heavy

⑤ me　⑥ from〕

The (　)(　)(ア)(　)(イ)(　)home.

(10) 〔① a jacket　② gets　③ case　④ in

⑤ with you　⑥ it〕

Take (　)(　)(ア)(　)(イ)(　) cold.

(☆☆○○○○○)

【4】次の英文は，2016年5月27日に，アメリカ合衆国前大統領のバラク・オバマ氏が広島平和記念公園で行なった演説の一部である。この英文を読み，(1)〜(4)の各問いに答えなさい。

(前略)

That is (　①　) we come to Hiroshima, so that we might think of people we love, the first smile from our children in the morning, the gentle touch from a spouse over the kitchen table, the comforting embrace of a parent. We can think of ㋐those things and know that those same precious (　②　) took place here 71 years ago. Those who died — they are like us. Ordinary people understand this, I think. They do not want more war. ㋑They would rather that the wonders of science be focused on improving life and not eliminating it. When the choices made by nations — when the choices made by leaders — reflect this simple wisdom, then the (　③　) of Hiroshima is done.

The world was forever changed here, but today, ㋒(city / the / of / this / go/ their / day / children / through / will / in / peace). What a precious thing that is. It is (　④　) protecting and then extending to every child. That is a future we can choose, a future in which Hiroshima and Nagasaki are known not as the (　⑤　) of atomic warfare but as the start of our own moral awakening.

(オバマ広島演説Obama's Hiroshima Speech　朝日出版社)

182

(1)　本文中の(　①　)〜(　⑤　)に入る最も適切な単語をア〜エから
それぞれ1つずつ選び，記号で答えなさい。

　①　ア　how　　　　イ　it　　　　　　ウ　why
　　　エ　right
　②　ア　tragedies　イ　moments　　ウ　happenings
　　　エ　morning
　③　ア　pain　　　　イ　instruction　ウ　sorrow
　　　エ　lesson
　④　ア　worth　　　イ　worse　　　ウ　worst
　　　エ　worthless
　⑤　ア　fall　　　　イ　dawn　　　ウ　explosion
　　　エ　end

(2)　下線部㋐の内容を日本語で簡潔に3つ答えなさい。

(3)　下線部㋑の英文を日本語にしなさい。

(4)　下線部㋒の(　　)内の単語を正しく並べ替えて書きなさい。

(☆☆☆○○○○)

【5】次の英文を読み，(1)〜(4)の各問いに答えなさい。(問題作成の都合
上，一部省略してある。)

Fragmentation was very much a characteristic of the Industrial Age. Power
blocks such as countries, societies and even educational systems (　①　)
according to territory, borders and boundaries. 　ア　 The Industrial Age
was marked by strategies of position and physically based resources.
　イ　 This has resulted in sweeping changes in how societies, and the
educational systems that serve them, operate. In the Knowledge Age, the two
main strategies are of movement and unlimited resources, (　②　) the
significance of ideas, creativity and intelligence. 　ウ　 It is (　③　)
surprising that such a seismic change in global culture pressurizes change
within educational systems. Integration, convergence and participative
learning are three key characteristics of Knowledge Age organizations which

183

are influencing decisions on what, and how, we teach young people.

The key performance drivers of the Knowledge Age society are commonly (④) as the "Knowledge Triangle." This triangle integrates education, research and innovation, which are the core features for managing successful change and adaptation. These are also core issues influencing how we can reshape the ways in which we teach languages. (中略) Much CLIL classroom practice involves the learners being active participants in ⑤developing their potential for acquiring knowledge and skills through ⑥a process of inquiry and by ⑦using complex cognitive processes and means for problem solving. When the teacher pulls back from being the donor of knowledge and becomes the facilitator, as is often found in CLIL practice, forces are unleashed which empower learners to acquire knowledge whilst actively engaging their own and peer-group powers of perception, communication and reasoning.

(Content and Language Integrated Learning / Do Coyle, Philip Hood, David Marsh)

(1) 本文中の(①)～(④)に入る最も適切な単語または語句をア～エからそれぞれ1つずつ選び，記号で答えなさい。

① ア operator　　イ operatic　　ウ operated
　 エ operates

② ア despite　　イ since　　ウ although
　 エ because of

③ ア hardly　　イ hardy　　ウ hard
　 エ hardship

④ ア mesmerized　　イ accustomed　　ウ measured
　 エ cited

(2) 次の一文が入るのに最も適する部分を，本文中の　ア　～　ウ　から1つ選び，記号で答えなさい。

　　But globalization and the emergence of the new technologies have moved us into a new era, the Knowledge Age.

(3) 下線部⑤～⑦について，それぞれの内容を一言で表している単語

を本文中から探し，英語で答えなさい。

(4) CLIL(Content and Language Integrated Learning)の教授法における，教師の担うべき役割を表す単語を本文中から探し，英語で答えなさい。

(☆☆☆○○○○)

【6】次の英文を読み，(1)～(6)の各問いに答えなさい。(問題作成の都合上，一部省略してある。)

I'm very optimistic about where the world will be 50 years from now. I hope I'm around to see it, but I think we can already see the shape of things in some ways.

| ア | A human population which was growing at a very rapid rate is now growing at a slower rate because, as we become successful, families have chosen to have less (①), and so we can see a peak population that makes it possible to think about living within the resource constraints that we have.

We can also see a (②) in violence. It's amazing now because we hear about all the violent things around the world, but every century the world has had a lot less war, a lot less violent deaths, and ③we've come to value the work that's been done in other countries, making great products and really think together about humanity's common future. | イ |

The pace of innovation will need to surprise us in some ways. What form this great energy source will be that will avoid us, destroying the (④), that's an invention that's very, very important. How much care will we give towards making sure ⑤(left, that, poorest, are, not, several billion, completely, the, out)? You know, there's been a little bit of progress there, but the inequity level still should concern us quite a bit.

| ウ | For example how important will robots be in 50 years? Maybe 20 years ago, people when they first heard about robots thought, "Wow, that's pretty scary. (⑥)" But then when it didn't really happen, they, you know, stopped thinking about it ― ⑦(almost, the, only, a, it's, like, in,

185

curiosity, movies) or toys, and yet clearly in the decades ahead, the cost, the capabilities will mimic what we've seen in science fiction, and so we'll have to see how we take advantage of that.

　　エ　You know, as we're living longer, how do we find fulfillment? What does a working career look like in terms of timing? The world will have aged, on average, and that brings with it very interesting (⑧).

It's not without challenges, but the path of extended lifespan, more science, more global understanding, sense of our common humanity, more education, more ability to watch a great course and not give up the curiosity that you're born with but try to think about the world and where it can go and how you can (⑨) to it — I think all of these things are taking more advantage of our innate capabilities, and will ⑩allow us to make 50 years from now a far better place than even what we have today.

　　(成功者10人の声で聞く！　改訂版　起業家の英語「ビル・ゲイツ」　コスモピア株式会社)

(1)　本文中の(②)(④)(⑧)(⑨)に入る最も適切な単語をア〜エからそれぞれ1つずつ選び，記号で答えなさい。

② 　ア　declaration　　イ　decline　　　ウ　increase
　　エ　fluctuation

④ 　ア　relevance　　　イ　evacuation　　ウ　environment
　　エ　development

⑧ 　ア　problems　　　イ　longevity　　ウ　developments
　　エ　values

⑨ 　ア　contribute　　イ　continue　　ウ　confirm
　　エ　confront

(2)　本文中の(①)に入る最も適切な単語を答えなさい。

(3)　下線部⑤と⑦の(　)内の単語を，それぞれ正しく並べ替えて書きなさい。

(4)　次の一文が入るのに最も適する部分を本文中の　ア　〜　エ　から1つ選び，記号で答えなさい。

186

And then there are things that are harder to predict.

(5) 下線部③と⑩の英文を日本語にしなさい。

(6) 本文中の(⑥)に入る最も適切な英文をア～エから1つ選び，記号で答えなさい。

ア　What did you say?　　イ　Where do you live?

ウ　What does it mean?　　エ　How have you been?

(☆☆☆☆◎◎◎◎◎)

【7】次の(1)～(4)の各問いに答えなさい。

(1) 次の①～⑥に示される文法事項を表す英語を，ア～カの中からそれぞれ1つずつ選び，記号で答えなさい。

① 形容詞　　② 助動詞　　③ 接続詞　　④ 不定詞

⑤ 受け身　　⑥ 関係代名詞

ア　adjective　　　　イ　infinitive　　　　ウ　relative pronoun

エ　passive voice　　オ　auxiliary verb　　カ　conjunction

(2) 中学1年生の英語の授業において，不定冠詞aとanの使い分けについて指導する際，aとanそれぞれに続く例として示す名詞を英語で5つずつ書きなさい。ただし，全ての語の最初の文字が異なること。

(3) 中学3年生の英語の授業において，携帯電話をテーマに議論させるために英語で指示を出したい。次の内容を生徒に英語で伝える時，それぞれどのように伝えるか，英語で書きなさい。

① 知っている言葉を使って，携帯電話を英語で説明してください。

② 質問があれば，遠慮なく聞いてください。

③ 中学生が携帯電話を持つことは，良いことだと思いますか？

(4) 中学2年生の英語の授業において，「今一番行ってみたい国」について英作文をさせたい。また，その中で不定詞の名詞的用法と，副詞的用法を使わせたい。モデルとして提示する英作文を50語程度で書きなさい。(文の数は問わない。)

(☆☆☆◎◎◎)

【高等学校】

【１】次の各問いに答えなさい。

(1)　次の文は，教育に関する法令に記載された条文の一部である。下の問いに答えなさい。

> 第6条　法律に定める学校は，(　　　)を有するものであって，国，地方公共団体及び法律に定める法人のみが，これを設置することができる。

①　(　　　)にあてはまる最も適切な語句を答えなさい。

②　この文が記載された法令として最も適切なものを，次のア～オから1つ選び，記号で答えなさい。

ア　日本国憲法　　イ　教育基本法
ウ　学校教育法　　エ　地方教育行政の組織及び運営に関する法律
オ　教育公務員特例法

(2)　次の①，②の文は，文部科学省国立教育政策研究所が平成30年3月に発行したキャリア教育リーフレット「生徒が直面する将来のリスクに対して学校にできることって何だろう？」において，進路に関する主な相談機関について説明したものである。①，②の相談機関として最も適切なものを，下のア～オからそれぞれ1つずつ選び，記号で答えなさい。

①　若者一人一人の状況に応じて，専門的な相談に乗ったり，各地域にある若者支援機関を紹介したりする施設。

②　労働者の最低限の労働条件を定めた労働基準法や，労働者の安全を守るための基準を定めた労働安全衛生法などに基づいて，労働者を保護するための仕事を行う機関。

ア　総合労働相談コーナー(都道府県労働局総務部)
イ　公共職業安定所
ウ　労働基準監督署
エ　職業能力開発促進センター
オ　地域若者サポートステーション

(☆☆☆◎◎◎)

【2】次の英文(高等学校の外国語教育における学習指導要領(平成22年5月文部科学省初等中等教育局)※抜粋)を読み，各問いに答えなさい。

＜Ⅴ. English Expression Ⅰ＞

1. Objective

　　To develop students' abilities to evaluate facts, opinions, etc. from multiple perspectives and communicate through reasoning and a range of expression, while fostering a 　X　 attitude toward communication through the English language.

2. Contents

　(1)　The following 　Y　, designed for specific language-use situations in order to encourage students to apply their abilities to understand and convey information, ideas, etc., should be conducted in English.

　　A. Impromptu speaking on a given topic. Speaking concisely in a style suitable for the audience and purpose.

　　B. Writing brief passages in a style suitable for the audience and purpose.

　　C. (①)information, ideas, etc., based on what one has heard, read, learned and experienced.

　(2)　To effectively conduct the 　Y　 stated in (1), consideration should be given to the following instructional points.

　　A. Speaking with due attention to the characteristics of English sounds such as rhythm and intonation, speed, volume, etc.

　　B. Writing with due attention to phrases and sentences indicating the main points, connecting phrases, etc. and reviewing one's own writing.

　　C. Learning presentation methods, expressions used in presentations, etc. and (②)them to real-life situations.

　　D. (③) one's own opinion by comparing what one has heard

189

or read with opinions from other sources, and identifying
similarities and differences.

3. Treatment of the Contents

(1) Based on general instruction to develop basic communication
abilities given in lower secondary schools, students should be
instructed so as to improve their abilities to convey information,
ideas, etc., while focusing on [Y] involving speaking and
writing.

(2) Instruction on speaking and writing should be conducted more
effectively through (④) with listening and reading activities.

(3) Consideration should be given so that students master the items
introduced in lower secondary schools and upper secondary schools
through repeated instruction in accordance with students'
circumstances, while experiencing various situational [Y].

(1) 本文中の[X]に入る最も適切な語を英語一語で答えなさい。

(2) 本文中の[Y]に入る最も適切な語句を英語二語で答えなさい。

(3) 本文中の(①)～(③)に入る最も適切な単語または語句を，
ア～オからそれぞれ1つずつ選び，(④)に入る最も適切な単語を，
カ～クから1つ選び，記号で答えなさい。なお，文頭に来るべき語
句も小文字で表記されている。

①～③　［ア　applying　　　　　　イ　listening
　　　　ウ　summarizing and presenting　エ　translating
　　　　オ　forming］

④　　　［カ　communication　　　　キ　integration
　　　　ク　interaction］

(☆☆○○○○○)

【3】次の(1)～(10)の英文の( )にあてはまる最も適切な単語または語
句を，①～④の中からそれぞれ1つずつ選び，番号で答えなさい。

(1) After the restaurant started to provide free Wi-Fi, the number of customers (　) about long wait times decreased sharply.

① complain　② complained　③ complaining
④ complains

(2) The manager did not give a precise explanation for the delay, but said the reason had (　) with problems in the company's distribution network.

① to do　② been doing　③ done　④ been done

(3) The results of the consumer survey are (　) in the next issue of Economy Insider Magazine.

① releasing　② to be released　③ releases　④ to release

(4) (　) so many people ill, the principal decided to close the school for two days.

① Regarding　② Reported　③ Since　④ With

(5) In his final speech the president paid (　) to all his employees, who had worked very hard for his company.

① attribute　② attention　③ tribute　④ contribution

(6) We often hear it (　) that Japanese are very punctual.

① says　② saying　③ said　④ to be said

(7) Cathy had cause for jealousy; but she was (　) a child to guess the cause at once.

① something of　② more of　③ too much of
④ very little of

(8) As the time is running (　), we kindly ask you to submit the application form as soon as possible.

① shortly　② shorted　③ short　④ shortage

(9) Medical science has made remarkable progress. (　), we still haven't found a fully effective treatment for cancer.

① Rather　② Nevertheless　③ Despite　④ Besides

(10) The admissions test is only three weeks away, so he is really going to have to double (　) on his studies.

　① down　② book　③ charge　④ deal

（☆☆○○○○○）

【4】次の(1)〜(4)の各問いに答えなさい。

(1)　次の会話の【状況】をふまえ，下線部①を英語にしなさい。

【状況】ある企業に勤める外国人の社員たちが，時間外労働を減らす方法について会話をしている。	
A：①時間外労働を減らすことは，コスト削減になると思う んだよね。 B：うん。それは明らかよ。でもどうやって。 C：1つには，年末の休暇中に，もっとたくさんの臨時職員 を雇うことだね。	A：　　　　　　①　　　　　　. B：Yes. That's clear. But how can we do that? C：One way to do it is to hire more temp staff during the 　year-end holidays.

(2)　次の文の下線部②を英語にしなさい。

　　現代の日本語には英語由来の単語がたくさん含まれている。それならば英語話者にとって日本語は易しくなるはずだが，実情は必ずしもそうではない。②英語の単語がその語と分からないほど短縮されたり，聞き慣れない発音に変わったりすることが少なくない。たとえば，「ロス」がロサンジェルスのことだと分かるアメリカ人は10万人に1人もいないだろうし，「ホーム」の語源がプラットフォームだと見抜くアメリカ人は100万人に1人もいないだろう。

（文英堂　*Unicorn English Communication 3*より抜粋）

(3)　次の英文の主旨を，5語〜10語の英語で答えなさい。

　　The early form of the necktie originated in the 17th century from Croatian soldiers hired to fight in France. The Croatian soldiers tied cloths around their necks to hold up their uniforms and as decoration. The king of France liked the style so much that he had his own guards wear the accessory and named the ties *cravat* from the French word for Croatian. To this day *cravat* is the French word for necktie. The tie as we know it today came in the 1920's when advances in materials and construction led to ties that returned to their original shape after being untied. This also allowed for a variety of ways for them to be tied such as the most common and simple four-in-hand knot or symmetrical and thick Windsor knot.

（旺文社　*TOEFL ITP*　テストリーディング問題攻略より抜粋）

(4) 次の英文は，CNNインターナショナルに所属するジャーナリストのKristie Lu Stoutへのインタビューの一部を抜粋したものである。文中の下線部に入る適切な英文を答えなさい。

Interviewer ： You studied Mandarin Chinese at university in Beijing.
_____?

Kristie Lu Stout ： For me, being bilingual helped open the door to a career in journalism. Being bilingual opened the door to new friendships, opened a door to a greater understanding of an entire different culture and people.

And one other thing that I do like (and this may sound strange) about my lifelong pursuit of learning Mandarin—because I still work with a Chinese tutor every week—it is a very humbling pursuit, right, because it's like the old saying by a Chinese philosopher: "The further one goes, the less one knows." The more you study a language, the more you realize you don't know about that.

(朝日出版社 *CNN English Express* 2019年5月号より抜粋)

(☆☆☆○○○○)

【5】 次の英文を読み，あとの(1)～(3)の各問いに答えなさい。

This month, on a trip to Tokyo, IMF chief Christine Lagarde had a message for Prime Minister Shinzo Abe of Japan: "Abenomics," his signature basket of economic policies aimed at ①boosting growth, desperately needs revamping. That's because the Japanese population is aging dramatically.

In September, Japan hit a new record: nearly 70,000 people over 100 years of age. It already had the most per capita in the world. And 27 percent of the population is 65 or older, compared to less than 9 percent globally.

All this has ②stunning implications for Japan's economy. In less than 50 years, the working population could shrink by nearly half. Already, firms complain of labor shortages, and the ratio of job openings to applicants has reached a 40-year high.

All this means that Japan could lose a percentage point of GDP growth over the next three decades, according to the IMF. Some proposed solutions include worker robots or a freer immigration system, but there's one ③woefully underused resource right at home: women.

Women in their prime have actually flooded the workforce in Japan in recent years. The female labor-force-participation rate has now surpassed that of the U.S. But as a recent Brookings report notes, almost 32 percent of prime-age female workers in Japan are part-time. Compare that to 18 percent of female workers in that same age group in the United States and less than 5 percent of Japanese men.

So why is this happening? Discrimination is undoubtedly part of it. Japanese women complain of being put on a "mommy" or noncareer track ─ X ─ a management track─by companies, which, of course, causes many to drop out.

But part of the problem is Japan's work culture, which is notoriously punishing and characterized by long hours. Many women who want to have children feel that they cannot participate in career-track work. And women seem to ④shoulder the burden of childcare. Look at the amount of time Japanese women spend in unpaid labor, close to four hours per day; and Japanese men, just 41 minutes, the lowest among all OECD countries.

If Japan were able to match Sweden's female-employment rates, it could add $579 billion to its GDP, according to Price-waterhouseCoopers. Abe knows this. In 2013, he pledged to enact policies meant to bring women equitably into the workforce, dubbed "womenomics." For a deeply conservative leader of a highly traditional country, he set an extraordinary goal: women in 30 percent of leadership positions by 2020.

The Abe government has passed important reforms, but Japan is nowhere close to reaching that goal. In fact, the government has since halved the target to just 15 percent, but women now hold just 4 percent of managerial positions, according to Bloomberg. That's because genuine gender ⑤<u>parity</u> would require real changes in the work culture in Japan, and the Abe administration hasn't fully attempted those.

The issue of bringing women more meaningfully into the workforce is often framed as something about virtue—it's important because it's the right thing to do. True, but virtue is not the main operating principle of business or government. What Japan makes clear is that women should also be equal at work because the economy will actually depend on it.

(朝日出版社 *CNN English Express* 2019年月1号より抜粋)

(1) 次の(あ)～(え)の問いの答えとして最も適切なものを，(A)～(D)からそれぞれ1つずつ選び，記号で答えなさい。

(あ) What percentage of the world population is 65 or older?

    (A) Less than 9 percent

    (B) Nearly 17 percent

    (C) Around 18 percent

    (D) More than 25 percent

(い) What important labor resource has Japan been underusing?

    (A) Women

    (B) Robots

    (C) Foreign workers

    (D) Retired workers

(う) How does employment of women in Japan compare with that in other countries?

    (A) The rate of employment of women is higher in the U.S. than in Japan.

    (B) Japan has now surpassed Sweden in female-employment rates.

    (C) The percentage of part-time female workers is higher in Japan than in the U.S.

    (D) All of the above

(え) What percentage of women are in leadership positions in Japan?

 (A) 4 percent (B) 15 percent (C) 30 percent

 (D) 32 percent

(2) 下線部①〜⑤と同じ意味の語句を，(A)〜(D)の中からそれぞれ1つずつ選び，記号で答えなさい。

 ① (A) experience (B) sustain (C) control

  (D) accelerate

 ② (A) other (B) surprising (C) normal

  (D) essential

 ③ (A) reportedly (B) relatively (C) terribly

  (D) definitely

 ④ (A) take on (B) take after (C) take against

  (D) take from

 ⑤ (A) equality (B) discrimination (C) role

  (D) issue

(3) 　X　内に入る最も適切な語句を，(A)〜(D)の中から選び，記号で答えなさい。

 (A) as opposed to (B) relevant to (C) equivalent to

 (D) related to

(☆☆○○○○○)

【6】次の英文を読み，あとの(1)〜(5)の各問いに答えなさい。

 In phone gaming, the market is dominated by free-to-play games, games which cost nothing to download but provide opportunities for players to spend money to ①enhance their experience. Money can be spent on in-game items that speed up play or provide bonuses. In some multiplayer games, these items can be bequeathed to other teammates, thereby helping their chances against opponents. In theory, the free-to-play model lets players try out a game before spending any money, allowing them to decide if they like it before paying.

 In practice, many players end up not paying at all. Either they trudge through the game's obstacles without the benefits paid items would afford them, or they simply abandon the game in favor of another free game. Most of those who do pay only spend a small amount, about on par with a game that asks you to pay up front. Yet ②these free-to-play games top the top-grossing charts. Where does all the money come from?

These games primarily make their money from "whales": players who spend much more money than the average player. To be on the threshold for being a whale, one should spend over a hundred dollars a month on a game, though some spend thousands a month. Even though these players make up a miniscule amount of a game's player base—often less than one percent—they account for more than half of a game's revenue.

Whales are a profitable resource for game makers, but a tenuous one. One reason whales spend is the effect they can have on other players. They can both dominate opponents in combat and provide massive amounts of aid to teammates. In some sense, other players are "content" for the whales. Whales enjoy ③occupying this place of power over other players. However, since whales are so much more powerful, regular players can become disenfranchised. Who wants to play if you're just going to be beaten by whales who have paid their way to success? If non-paying players abandon the game, then the whales won't have anyone to show off against. This causes the whales to abandon the game and the whole enterprise collapses.

(旺文社　*TOEFL ITP* テストリーディング問題攻略より抜粋)

(1)　次の日本文は，この英文における第一段落の目的を表したものである。(　)を補うのに最も適切な言葉を答えなさい。

　「無料ゲームの(　)を提示すること。」

(2)　下線部①の語に最も近い意味を表す語を選び，記号で答えなさい。

　(ア)　trivialize　　(イ)　attach　　(ウ)　lengthen　　(エ)　improve

(3)　下線部②の理由を，60字以内の日本語で答えなさい。

(4)　下線部③の語に最も近い意味を表す語を選び，記号で答えなさい。

　(ア)　betraying　　(イ)　inhabiting　　(ウ)　discovering

197

(エ)　shortening

(5)　お金を払わないプレーヤーが "whales" にとって重要である理由を，20字以内の日本語で答えなさい。

(☆☆☆○○○○○)

【7】次の英文を読み，あとの(1)～(6)の各問いに答えなさい。

　　The aims of a language teaching course are very often defined with reference to the four 'language skills': understanding speech, speaking, reading and writing. These aims, therefore, relate to the kind of activity which the learners are to perform. But how can we characterize this activity? What is it that learners are expected to understand, speak, read and write? The obvious answer is: the language they are learning. But what exactly do we mean by ①this? We might mean a selection of lexical items recorded in a dictionary combined with syntactic structures recorded in a grammar. In this view, the teaching of a language involves developing the ability to produce correct sentences. Many teachers would subscribe to ②this view and it has been productive of a good deal of impressive language teaching material. ③In some respects, however, it is unsatisfactory. We may readily acknowledge that the ability to produce sentences is a crucial one in the learning of a language. It is important to recognize, however, that it is not the only ability that learners need to acquire. Someone knowing a language knows more than how to understand, speak, read and write sentences. He also knows how sentences are used to communicative effect.

～中略～

　　The learning of a language, then, involves acquiring the ability to compose correct sentences. That is one aspect of the matter. But it also involves acquiring an understanding of which sentences, or parts of sentences are appropriate in a particular context. The first kind of ability depends upon a knowledge of the grammatical rules of the language being learned. We can demonstrate this knowledge by producing strings of sentences without regard to context:

> The rain destroyed the crops.
> The cat sat on the mat.
> The unicorn is a mythical beast.
> Poor John ran away.
> The farmer killed the duckling.
> John loves Mary.
> My tailor is rich.

To produce sentences like this is to manifest our knowledge of the language system of English. We will say that they are instances of correct English ④*usage*. But of course we are not commonly called upon simply to manifest our knowledge in this way in the normal circumstances of daily life. We are generally required to use our knowledge of the language system in order to achieve some kind of communicative purpose. That is to say, we are generally called upon to produce instances of language ⑤*use*: we do not simply manifest the abstract system of the language, we at the same time realize it as meaningful communicative behaviour.

～中略～

I want now to consider some examples of how language is presented in the classroom and how this presentation, in concentrating on usage, may sometimes involve an inappropriate use of language. The following is an example of a familiar oral drill in which the learner is required to repeat a sentence pattern by using different 'call-words'

Teacher : Book.

Pupils 　 : There is a book on the table.

Teacher : Bag.

Pupils 　 : There is a bag on the table.

Teacher : Pen.

Pupils 　 : There is a pen on the table.

Teacher : Under the table.

Pupils 　 : There is a pen under the table.

Teacher : On the floor.

Pupils 　 : There is a pen on the floor.

What is going on here? We have a series of responses to a verbal cue but these responses are not replies in any normal sense. The pupils are demonstrating their knowledge of usage by manipulating the sentence pattern but they are not doing so for any other purpose.

Let us now adjust the drill so that we get what appears to be a more normal question and answer sequence:

Teacher : What is on the table?

Pupils 　 : There is a book on the table.

Teacher : What is on the floor?

Pupils 　 : There is a bag on the floor.

Teacher : Where is the bag?

Pupils 　 : The bag is on the floor.

Teacher : Where is the book?

Pupils 　 : The book is on the table.

Here we can recognize that some account is taken of use. To begin with, for the pupils to give an answer there must be a book on the table and a bag on the floor: there must be some simple situation to refer to. The pupils are not simply spinning sentences out without any reference to what the words mean, as they are in the first drill. But although there is some concern for use in this respect, it is still usage which has the dominant emphasis. Although the pupils' response is a reply to a question and not just a reaction to a prompt, the *form* of the reply is inappropriate. We can compare the drill with the following exchanges where the replies take on a more normal appearance:

A : What is on the table?

B : A book.

A : Where is the bag?

B : On the floor.

Even in this form, however, ⑥the language cannot necessarily be regarded as demonstrating appropriate use. To see why this is so, we have to ask ourselves: 'Why does A ask this question?' If a book is seen to be on the table, and a bag seen to be on the floor, and if everybody is aware of the location of these objects, then why does A need to ask where they are? If there is a book on the table in front of the whole class, then, as has been pointed out, the question is contextualised to the extent that it refers to something outside language and is not just a manipulation of the language itself. But by the same token, the fact that there *is* a book on the table, visible to everybody, makes it extremely unnatural to ask if it is there. Thus the provision of a situation may lead away from usage in one respect but lead back to usage in another. Only if the pupils know that the teacher cannot see the bag and is genuinely looking for it does his question as to its whereabouts take on the character of natural use. The following classroom exchange, for example, would commonly take on this genuine quality of real communication:

Teacher : Where's the duster?

Pupils　 : Under your chair.

　　(H. G. Widdowson, *Teaching Language as Communication* より抜粋,

201

一部改編)

(1)　下線部①のthisの内容を，本文の内容に即して日本語で答えなさい。

(2)　下線部②のthis viewの内容を，本文の内容に即して具体的に日本語で説明しなさい。

(3)　下線部③の理由を，本文の内容に即して日本語で答えなさい。

(4)　下線部④，⑤について，*usage*と*use*はそれぞれどのようなものであるか，本文の内容に即して日本語で説明しなさい。

(5)　下線部⑥の理由を，本文の内容に即して日本語で答えなさい。

(6)　本文の内容に即して，具体的な言語材料と設定する状況や場面を日本語で記述し，想定される教師と生徒，あるいは生徒同士のやり取りを英語で書きなさい。

(☆☆☆◎◎◎◎)

解答・解説

【中高共通】

【1】Part 1　B　　　Part 2　No.1　(1)　D　　　(2)　B　　　No.2　(1)　A
(2)　A　　　Part 3　No.1　C　　　No.2　B

〈解説〉Part 1は，グラフの内容について適切な説明文を選択する問題と思われる。朝の読書を実施している小中高校の割合を，日本全体と鳥取県とで比較したグラフである。数値の正確な聞き取りができるか，「〜倍」「〜より多い／少ない」などの比較の表現が身についているかが解答のカギとなるだろう。Part 2とPart 3は，本文，質問文，選択肢ともすべて音声のみで解答しなければならず，高い集中力が必要である。放送が2度ある場合は，1度目で概要をつかみ，2度目で細部まで聞き取る方法が有効であるが，放送が1度しかない場合は，聞き取れない箇所があっても気にせずに大意を把握することに集中しよう。細

部にこだわって，その後に流れる英文を聞き逃してしまわないように注意したい。落ち着いて試験に臨めるよう市販のリスニング教材等を活用して，音声のみの問題に慣れておくことが必要である。

【中学校】

【1】(1) ① 公の性質　② イ　(2) ① オ　② ウ

(3) ① 目的　② 場面　③ 状況　④ 主体的　⑤ 態度

(4) ① (b)　② (f)　③ (g)　④ (e)　⑤ (d)

〈解説〉(1)　教育基本法は，教育を受ける権利を国民に保障した日本国憲法に基づき，日本の公教育の在り方を全般的に規定する法律。法制定の由来と目的を明らかにし，法の基調をなしている主義と理想とを宣言する前文と18の条文から構成され，出題の第6条は学校教育について定めている。文部科学省は「公の性質を有する」の意味について，「広く解すれば，おおよそ学校の事業の性質が公のものであり，それが国家公共の福利のためにつくすことを目的とすべきものであって，私のために仕えてはならないという意味とする。狭く解すれば，法律に定める学校の事業の主体がもともと公のものであり，国家が学校教育の主体であるという意味とする。」としている。　(2)　キャリア教育リーフレットは文部科学省のシンクタンクである国立教育政策研究所がキャリア教育のさらなる充実に資するため，実践に役立つパンフレットを作成し，全国の学校や教育委員会等へ配布しているもの。アの総合労働相談コーナー(都道府県労働局総務部)は，勤めた会社で何か問題が起きたときに，専門の相談員がいろいろな相談に乗り，問題解決のための支援をする機関。イの公共職業安定所(ハローワーク)は，職業の紹介や失業したときの失業給付金の支給などを行うほか，公共職業訓練のあっせんや，会社を辞めたくなったようなときの相談にも応じる機関。エの職業能力開発促進センターは，求職者などに，就職に向けて必要な知識・技能を身につけるための職業訓練を実施する機関。　(3), (4)　中学校学習指導要領からの出題。中学校学習指導要領は平成29年3月に告示され，令和3年度から全面実施となる。平成29年

3月告示の学習指導要領や解説を精読するとともに，新旧対照表で平成20年3月告示の学習指導要領との違いを確認しておきたい。

【2】(1) イ　　(2) ウ　　(3) ウ　　(4) ア　　(5) イ　　(6) ア
(7) イ　　(8) エ　　(9) ウ　　(10) イ　　(11) エ　　(12) エ
(13) ア　　(14) ウ　　(15) エ　　(16) エ　　(17) ウ　　(18) エ
(19) イ　　(20) ア

〈解説〉(1) "was very (　　)"の主語はattendance「出席(者数)」なので，これに対応する形容詞としてはイlow「低い」が適切。アemptyは「空っぽの」，ウlesserは「より小さい，より少ない」，エfewは「ほとんどない」の意味。　　(2) "release a statement"で「声明を発表する」の意味となるのでウが適切。アstateには名詞の用法があるが，「状態」の意味なので文脈に合わず誤り。イとエは動詞state「〜を述べる」の現在分詞と過去分詞だが，直前に冠詞aがあり空欄には名詞が入るため誤り。　　(3) 空欄の文中の位置，そして空欄に入るのが1語であることから，空欄は動詞meetsを修飾する副詞だと考えられるためウgenerally「通常は」が適切。アgeneral「全般的な，一般の」は形容詞，イgeneralizeとエgeneralizedは「〜を一般化する」の意味を持つ動詞の活用形なので誤り。　　(4) 空欄にはアuntilを入れ，「24号線の工事は来年まで続くと予想される」とするのが適切。イacross「〜を横切って」，ウdown「〜を下って」，エonto「〜の上へ」は文脈に合わず誤り。　　(5) 空欄にはイcheck outを入れ，「客はホテルの受付デスクでチェックアウトするとき，電話代を支払うことが求められる」とするのが適切。アbring「〜を持っていく」，ウremove「〜を取り除く」，エdrop off「外れる，落ちる，減る」は文脈に合わず不適切。　　(6) yetは現在完了の否定文で「まだ」，疑問文で「もう」の意味で使われるためアyetが適切。イsoon「すぐに」，ウvery「とても」，エafter「〜の後で」は文脈に合わず誤り。　　(7) 文の主語"Comments or suggestions"が複数形なのでイareが適切。　　(8) 空欄は動詞relyを修飾する副詞なのでエincreasingly「ますます」が適切。他の選択肢は動詞increase「〜を増

やす」の活用形なので誤り。 (9) 前置詞overには期間を表す用法があるためウが適切。ア above「～の上に」，イ behind「～の後ろに」，エ along「～に沿って」は文脈に合わず誤り。 (10) 問題文は受け身文であり，空欄には Dr.Woo を今日最も影響力のある経済政策分析家の1人だと考えている動詞 consider の動作主が入るため，イ others「他の人々」が適切。他の選択肢は consider の動作主にはならないので誤り。(11) 空欄には自動詞 arrive を修飾する副詞が入るのでエ punctually「時間通りに」が適切。他の選択肢は副詞でないので誤り。 (12) 空欄にはエ soon を入れ，「Belvin Movie Theater は，すぐに客がウェブサイトでチケットを購入できるようにするだろう」とするのが適切。ア yet「まだ，もう」，イ since「～以来」，ウ ever「これまでに」は文脈に合わず誤り。 (13) 空欄にはア conveniently を入れ，「Tabor Building の3階には都合よくコーヒー自動販売機が置かれている」とするのが適切。イ slightly「わずかに」，ウ considerably「かなり」，エ eventually「最終的に」は文脈に合わず誤り。 (14) 空欄にはウ instead を入れ，「火曜日はビジネス向けの服装を身に着けるのではなく，その代わりにスタッフはカジュアルな服装を選んでもよい」とするのが適切。ア enough「十分に」，イ despite「～にもかかわらず」，エ in case「念のため」は文脈に合わず誤り。 (15) 空欄は前置詞 for の直後なので動名詞のエ donating「～を寄付すること」が適切。不定詞のウ to donate には名詞的用法があるが，前置詞の後に不定詞を入れることはできない。

(16) "be scheduled to do" で「～する予定になっている」の意味となるので，不定詞のエ to return が適切。 (17) "one of the＋最上級＋複数形の名詞" で「最も～な人・物の1つ」の意味となるので，ウ providers「供給者」が適切。他の選択肢は複数形の名詞ではないため誤り。 (18) 空欄にはエ nor「～もまた…ない」を入れ，「The Gregory Conference Center は市内にアクセスするのに便が良いわけではないし，駅に近いわけでもない」とするのが適切。nor は否定的な内容を重ねるときに使う接続詞で，よく neither とともに用いられる。(19) "their ( ) contact information" という空欄の位置から，ここに

は名詞contact information「連絡先情報」を修飾する形容詞が入るため，イpersonal「個人的な」が適切。　(20)　1つの節に活用する本動詞は“have submitted” の1つだけなので，イ～エは誤りでアto be raisedが適切。

【3】(1) ア ④　イ ⑤　(2) ア ①　イ ⑤　(3) ア ⑤イ ②　(4) ア ②　イ ③　(5) ア ②　イ ⑥(6) ア ⑤　イ ⑥　(7) ア ④　イ ⑤　(8) ア ⑦イ ②　(9) ア ③　イ ⑥　(10) ア ④　イ ⑥

〈解説〉(1) “the 比較級, the 比較級”「より～なほど，より…」の構文を使い，“The more knowledge you have, the less arrogant you will become.”「多くの知識を持つほど，傲慢でなくなるだろう」とする。

(2) “There is no point in -ing”「～しても無駄だ」の構文を使い，“There is no point in discussing the issue.”「その問題を議論しても無駄だ」とする。　(3)　倍数表現を“as 形容詞／副詞 as～”の直前に置くと，「～の○倍…である」の意味になる。本問では“He has twice as many books as she has.”「彼は彼女の2倍の本を持っている」とする。　(4) “the last person to do”「決して～しない人物」の構文を使い，“He would be the last person to speak ill of others.”「彼は決して他人の悪口を言わない」とする。“speak ill of～”で「～の悪口を言う」の意味。　(5) “cannot help -ing”「～せずにはいられない」の構文を使い，“I couldn't help laughing at his silly joke.”「彼のばかげた冗談に笑わずにはいられなかった」とする。“laugh at～”で「～を笑う」の意味。　(6)　be動詞＋不定詞の予定を表す用法を使い，“The meeting is to be held in Tottori.”「会議は鳥取で開催されることになっている」とする。　(7)　whatever＋名詞は関係詞whatを強調した形で，「どんな～でも」の意味。本問ではその構文を使い，“You may have whatever magazine you want to read.”「お読みになりたい雑誌をどれでもお取りください」とする。(8) “what～ like”「～はどのようなものか」の構文を使い，“Tell me what your trip to Hong Kong was like.”「あなたの香港への旅行はどのよ

うなものであったかを教えてください」とする。 (9) "〜prevent …
from -ing"「〜は…が—するのを妨げる」の語法を使い，"The heavy
snow prevented me from going home."「大雪により私は家に帰れなかっ
た」とする。 (10) "in case〜"「〜の場合に備えて」の構文を使い，
"Take a jacket with you in case it gets cold."「寒くなる場合に備えて上着
を持って行ってください」とする。

【4】(1) ① ウ ② イ ③ エ ④ ア ⑤ イ
(2) ・朝起きて，最初に見る子ども達の笑顔。 ・食卓越しに伴侶か
ら優しく触れられること。 ・親からの心安らぐ抱擁のこと。
(3) 彼らは科学の驚異を人々の生活を奪うためではなく，むしろ向上
させるためだけに使ってほしいと思っているのです。 (4) the children
of this city will go through their day in peace
〈解説〉(1) ① 空欄にはウを入れ，"That is why we come to Hiroshima"
「それが私たちが広島に来る理由だ」とするのが適切。アを入れると
"That is"の補語が"how we come to Hiroshima"「広島に来る方法」と
なり，文脈に合わないため誤り。また，空欄にイitとエrightを入れる
と"That is"の補語となる名詞節が形成されないので誤り。 ② 空
欄にはイを入れ，"those same precious moments took place"「同じ貴重な
瞬間が生じた」とするのが適切。他の選択肢は，空欄の内容が"the
first smile 〜 of a parent"を指すため，文脈に合わない。 ③ 空欄を
含む文の"this simple wisdom"は下線部イの内容を指すため，エを入
れて"the lesson of Hiroshima is done"「広島の教訓が成される」とする
のが適切。アpain「苦痛」，イinstruction「指示」，ウsorrow「悲しみ」
は"this simple wisdom"の内容と合わないため誤り。 ④ 空欄には
アを入れて"be worth −ing"「〜する価値がある」の語法とするのが適
切。 ⑤ "not 〜 but…"「〜ではなく…」の構文が使われているため，
"the (⑤) of atomic warfare"は"the start of our own moral awakening"
「私たち自身が持つモラルの目覚めの始まり」と反対の内容となると
考えられる。したがって，空欄にはイを入れ，"the dawn of atomic

warfare"「核戦争の幕開け」とするのが適切。　(2)　those thingsは，前文の第1パラグラフ1文目 "the first smile～ of a parent" の内容を指す。(3) "would rather (that) ～"「～してほしい」の構文と，"improving life" と "not eliminating it (= life)" の対比に注目する。　(4)　並べ替え問題では，一度に文全体を作ろうとせず，セットで使う語がないかを探し，それらを組み合わせて文を作るとよい。本問では "will go through"「～を経験するだろう」，"in peace"「平和に」がそうである。

【5】(1)　①　ウ　　②　エ　　③　ア　　④　エ　　(2)　イ
(3)　⑤　education　　⑥　research　　⑦　innovation
(4)　facilitator

〈解説〉(1)　①　第1パラグラフ2文目では，"such as countries, societies and even educational systems" が "Power blocks" を修飾して長い名詞句を形成し，文の主語として機能している。空欄はその直後にあるので動詞が入ると考えられるが，ここでは "the Industrial Age"「産業化時代」のことについて言及しているので，過去形のウoperated「機能した」が適切。アoperator「操作者」，イoperatic「オペラの」は動詞でないので誤り。エoperatesは動詞だが過去形でないので誤り。　②　空欄にはエbecause ofを入れ，前後を因果関係でつなげるのが適切。アdespite「～にもかかわらず」，イsince「～以来」は空欄前後の文脈に合わないので誤り。ウalthough「～だけれども」は接続詞だが，空欄の後に節が続いていないので誤り。　③　空欄には直後の形容詞surprisingを修飾する副詞が入るのでアhardly「ほとんど～ない」が適切。イhardy「我慢強い」，ウhard「難しい，熱心な」，エhardship「困難」はいずれも副詞ではないので誤り。　④　"cite～ as …"「～を…として挙げる」の受け身が使われているのでエが適切。アmesmerized「魅了された」，イaccustomed「慣れた」，ウmeasured「測った」は文脈に合わず誤り。　(2)　挿入文は新時代の "the Knowledge Age" を導入する文となっている。また，文頭にButがあることから，挿入文は反対の内容，つまり旧時代の "the Industrial Age" に関する内容の後に来る。

本文の第1パラグラフの1～3文目までは"the Industrial Age"について書かれているが，4文目に"This has resulted in sweeping changes"「このことが劇的な変化につながった」とあり，5文目で"the Knowledge Age"が初めて登場する。以上のことから，空欄イで話題が"the Industrial Age"から"the Knowledge Age"に変わったと考えられる。

(3) ⑤ 下線部は「知識や技能を獲得する潜在能力を発達させる」なのでeducationが適切。 ⑥ 下線部は「調査のプロセス」なのでresearchが適切。 ⑦ 下線部は「複雑な認知プロセスや問題解決の方法を用いること」なのでinnovationが適切。 (4) 第2パラグラフ5文目を見ると，CLILの実践では，教師が知識を与えるのではなくファシリテーターとなることが書かれている。

【6】(1) ② イ ④ ウ ⑧ ア ⑨ ア (2) ① children

(3) ⑤ that the poorest several billion are not completely left out

⑦ it's almost like only a curiosity in the movies (4) ウ

(5) ③ 私達は，他の国々の取り組みを尊敬し， ⑩ 今から50年後の世界を今よりずっと良いものにすることを可能にしてくれる(と思います)。 (6) ウ

〈解説〉(1) ② 第3パラグラフ2文目で，戦争や暴力による死が減少しているとあるため，イdecline「減少」が適切。アdeclaration「宣言」，ウincrease「増加」，エfluctuation「変動」は文脈に合わず誤り。

④ 第4パラグラフは，技術革新，エネルギー源などについて書かれている。この文脈に照らすと"destroying the (④)に入るのはウenvironmentが適切。アrelevance「関連性」，イevacuation「避難」，エdevelopment「発達，開発」は文脈に合わず誤り。 ⑧ "bring with it～"で「～をもたらす」の意味。この動詞句の主語thatは，世界が高齢化するという直前の内容を指すので，そのことがもたらすものとしてはアproblems「問題」が適切。イlongevity「長寿」，ウdevelopments「発達」，エvalues「価値観」は文脈に合わず誤り。 ⑨ "contribute to～"で「～に貢献する，～に寄与する」の意味。 (2) 第2パラグラフ1文

209

目前半を見ると，人口増加率が以前に比べて低くなっているとあるため，"families have chosen to have less (children)" とするのが適切。
(3)　⑤ "the poorest"，"left out"「除外される」のようにセットで使われる語句を見つけて組み合わせていくとよい。　⑦ "almost like"，"a curiosity"，"in the movies" がセットで使われるため，これらを他の語と組み合わせて文を作っていく。　(4)　挿入文の内容は「予測するのがより難しいものがある」の意味。There構文は新しいトピックを導入する機能を持ち，挿入文の後は予測困難なものについて書かれていると考えられるので，直後でロボットについて書かれている内容からウが適切だと考えられる。　(5)　③ "come to do" で「〜するようになる」の意味。valueは動詞で「〜を高く評価する，〜を尊重する」の意味を持つ。また，"that's (= that has) been done in other countries" がthe workを修飾することにも注意したい。　⑩ "allow〜 to do" で「〜が…するのを許す」の意味。また，"make〜 …"「〜を…にする」の第5文型が使われており，目的語が "50 years from now"，補語が "a far better place" となっている。ここでfarは比較級betterの強調で，比較対象はthan以降の部分。　(6)　空欄は，人々が20年前にロボットについて初めて聞いたときの発言なので，話の内容がわからずに聞き返しているウ「どういうことですか」が適切。

【7】(1)　①　ア　　②　オ　　③　カ　　④　イ　　⑤　エ　　⑥　ウ
(2)　aに続く例…①　cat　　②　desk　　③　fan　　④　girl
⑤　house　　anに続く例…①　apple　　②　egg　　③　umbrella
④　orange　　⑤　hour　　(3)　①　Describe a cellphone in English by using words you already know.　　②　Feel free to ask me if you have any questions.　　③　Do you think that using a cellphone is good for junior high school students?　　(4)　I love K-pop so much, so I want to visit Korea to see K-pop concerts. If I can meet real K-pop stars, I'll be very excited. I must study the Korean language to speak with them. Korea has good food, too. I want to try some spicy food when I am there. (52words)

〈解説〉(1)　基本的な文法用語を表す英語は確認しておくこと。

(2)　不定冠詞のanに続くのは最初の音が母音(日本語のアイウエオに相当する音)となる単語である。解答例のhourは綴りで見ると最初が子音(h)だが，発音で見ると最初の音は母音/áuər/なので不定冠詞のanを使う。一方，不定冠詞aに続くのは最初の音が子音(母音以外の音)となる単語である。　(3)　①　意味のまとまりに分けると「(あなたが)知っている言葉を使って」，「(あなたが)携帯電話を英語で説明してください」となる。前者は関係代名詞(解答例ではthatが省略されている)と「by -ing」の語法を用いて表す。後者は命令文を使って表現する。

②　意味のまとまりに分けると「(あなたが)質問を持っていれば」，「(あなたが)遠慮なく聞いてください」となる。「遠慮なく～してください」は，解答例以外に，"Please don't hesitate to do" としてもよい。

③　意味のまとまりに分けると「中学生が携帯電話を持つことは良いこと」，「(あなたは)～だと思いますか？」となる。前者は動名詞を使って表現できる。　(4)　内容の面に関して，その国に行きたい理由をいくつか具体的に述べるとよい。また，文法の面に関して，不定詞の名詞的用法と副詞的用法を使うことが求められていることから，「～すること」，「～するために」という表現を上記の理由の中に組み込みたい。

【高等学校】

【1】(1)　①　公の性質　　②　イ　　(2)　①　オ　　②　ウ

〈解説〉(1)　教育基本法は，教育を受ける権利を国民に保障した日本国憲法に基づき，日本の公教育の在り方を全般的に規定する法律。法制定の由来と目的を明らかにし，法の基調をなしている主義と理想とを宣言する前文と18の条文から構成され，出題の第6条は学校教育について定めている。文部科学省は「公の性質を有する」の意味について，「広く解すれば，おおよそ学校の事業の性質が公のものであり，それが国家公共の福利のためにつくすことを目的とすべきものであって，私のために仕えてはならないという意味とする。狭く解すれば，法律

に定める学校の事業の主体がもともと公のものであり，国家が学校教育の主体であるという意味とする。」としている。　(2)　キャリア教育リーフレットは文部科学省のシンクタンクである国立教育政策研究所がキャリア教育のさらなる充実に資するため，実践に役立つパンフレットを作成し，全国の学校や教育委員会等へ配布しているもの。アの総合労働相談コーナー(都道府県労働局総務部)は，勤めた会社で何か問題が起きたときに，専門の相談員がいろいろな相談に乗り，問題解決のための支援をする機関。イの公共職業安定所(ハローワーク)は，職業の紹介や失業したときの失業給付金の支給などを行うほか，公共職業訓練のあっせんや，会社を辞めたくなったようなときの相談にも応じる機関。エの職業能力開発促進センターは，求職者などに，就職に向けて必要な知識・技能を身につけるための職業訓練を実施する機関。

【２】(1)　positive　　(2)　language activities　　(3)　①　ウ　　②　ア
③　オ　　④　キ
〈解説〉(1)　高等学校学習指導要領(平成21年3月告示)における「第5　英語表現Ⅰ」の英訳から出題されている。「1　目的」の項の「英語を通じて，積極的にコミュニケーションを図ろうとする態度を育成するとともに」に該当する箇所なので，positiveが適切。　(2)「2　内容　(1)」の項の「次のような言語活動を英語で行う」に該当する箇所なので，language activitiesが適切。　(3)　①「2　内容　(1)　ウ」の項の「情報や考えなどをまとめ，発表する」に該当する箇所なので，ウsummarizing and presentingが適切。　②「2　内容　(2)　ウ」の「実際に活用する」に該当する箇所なので，アapplyingが適切。　③「2　内容　(2)　エ」の「自分の考えをまとめたりする」に該当する箇所なので，オformingが適切。　④「3　内容の取扱い　(2)」の項の「聞くこと及び読むこととも有機的に関連付けた活動を行うことにより」に該当する箇所なので，キintegrationが適切。

【3】(1) ③　(2) ①　(3) ②　(4) ④　(5) ③　(6) ③
(7) ③　(8) ③　(9) ②　(10) ①

〈解説〉(1) "(　) about long wait times" はcustomersを修飾して「長い待ち時間について不満を言っている客」の意味となるため，現在分詞の③complainingが適切。　(2) "have to do with 〜" は「〜と関係がある」の意味である。　(3) releaseは「〜を発表する」の意味で主語が"The results of the consumer survey" なので，受け身の②to be releasedが適切。be動詞＋to不定詞で予定を表す用法が使われている。他の選択肢は能動態なので誤り。　(4) 空欄には④を入れて"with＋目的語＋補語" の付帯状況「大勢が病気なので」とする。①前置詞Regarding「〜に関して」の後には名詞が入るが，その場合illが浮いてしまうので誤り。②過去分詞Reported「報告されて」が空欄に入る場合，受け身の分詞構文の可能性が考えられるが，その場合the principalがreportedの主語となり誤り。また，空欄の後は主語＋動詞の形ではないので，③接続詞Since「〜以来」，「〜なので」も誤り。　(5) "pay tribute to 〜"で「〜に賛辞を送る」の意味となる。①attribute「特性」，②attention「注意」，④contribution「貢献」は，社長が熱心に働いた社員に送るものという文脈に合わず誤り。　(6) hearは知覚動詞の1つ。知覚動詞＋目的語の後に入る動詞は，原形不定詞，現在分詞，過去分詞のいずれかである。また，hearの目的語itは後ろのthat節を指し，空欄に入る動詞の意味上の主語であるため，③saidが適切。①saysと④to be saidは原形不定詞，現在分詞，過去分詞ではないため誤り。②sayingを空欄に入れると，意味上の主語がit(＝that節)では意味が通らなくなるため誤り。　(7) 空欄には③too much of 〜「度を超した〜」を入れ，「Cathyはすぐにその(嫉妬の)理由を推測するにはあまりに子どもであった」とするのが適切。①something of 〜「ちょっとした〜」，②more of 〜「どちらかというと〜」，④very little of 〜「ほとんど〜ない」は文脈に合わないため誤り。　(8) "run short"で「不足する，なくなる」の意味である。　(9) 空欄は，1文目「医学は目覚ましく進歩した」と2文目「未だにガンに対する十分に効果的な治療法を見つけられないでい

る」をつなげる単語であるため，②Nevertheless「それにもかかわらず」
が適切。①Rather「それどころか」，④Besides「さらに」は文脈に合わ
ず誤り。③Despite ～「～にもかかわらず」は後ろに名詞を伴う前置詞
なので誤り。　(10)　"double down on ～"で「～を強化する」の意味
となる。"double-book"は「重複して予約を受ける」，"double-charge
～"は「～に二重請求を行う」，"double-deal"は「二重に取引をする」
の意味であるため，文脈に合わず誤り。

【４】(1)　I think that cutting down on overtime work will help us reduce costs.
(2)　English words are sometimes shortened in a manner that makes them
unrecognizable, or given strange pronunciations.　(3)　How ties
originated in France.　(4)　What would you say are the benefits of being
bilingual?

〈解説〉(1)　下線部①を意味のまとまりに分けると，「(Aが)～と思う」，
「時間外労働を減らすことはコスト削減になる」になり，前者は"I
think that ～"で表現できる。後者は「時間外労働を減らすことが，私
たちがコストを減らすのを助けてくれる」と捉え，使役動詞helpを使
って表現できる。　(2)　下線部②を意味のまとまりに分けると，1
「英語の単語が短縮されることが少なくない」，2「(英語の単語が)その
語と分からないほど」，3「(英語の単語が)聞きなれない発音に変わる
ことが少なくない」の3つになる。2のまとまりは1のまとまりを修飾
しており，"in a manner that ～"「～という方法で」を使って表現でき
る。　(3)　英文の趣旨はフランスでのネクタイの起源である。
(4)　インタビュアーの質問に対し，Kristie Lu Stoutは，バイリンガル
であることが，ジャーナリストとしてのキャリアや，新しい友人，異
なる文化や人々へのより深い理解につながったなどと答えている。し
たがって，下線部では，バイリンガルであることにどのようなメリッ
トがあるかを問うていると考えられる。

【5】(1) （あ）(A) （い）(A) （う）(C) （え）(A)
(2) ① (D) ② (B) ③ (C) ④ (A) ⑤ (A)
(3) (A)

〈解説〉(1) （あ） 第2パラグラフ3文目の "compared to less than 9 percent globally" から，世界の65歳以上人口は9％未満とわかる。 （い） 第4パラグラフ2文目 "there's one woefully underused resource right at home: woman" から，女性の労働力が活用されていないことがわかる。 （う） 第5パラグラフ3文目と4文目では，働き盛りの日本女性の32％がパートタイムであり，同年齢層の米国女性 (18％) に比べて高いと述べているので，(C)と一致する。(A)は，第5パラグラフ2文目と逆のことを述べているので誤り。第8パラグラフ1文目でスウェーデンについて触れているが，仮定法で書かれており現実の状況とは異なるため，(B) も誤り。選択肢(A), (B)が誤りであるため，(D)の「上記(の選択肢)はすべて正しい」も誤りとなる。 （え） 第9パラグラフ2文目に，「女性管理職はわずか4％しかいない」と述べられている。 (2) ① boostは「〜を促進する」なので，(D) accelerateが適切。(A) experienceは「〜を経験する」，(B) sustainは「〜を持続する」，(C) controlは「〜を制御する」。 ② stunning「驚くほど」なので，(B) surprisingが適切。
(A) other「他の」，(C) normal「普通の」，(D) essential「不可欠な」は誤り。 ③ woefullyは「ひどく」なので，(C) terriblyが適切。
(A) reportedlyは「伝えられるところによると」，(B) relativelyは「比較的」，(D) definitelyは「確かに」。 ④ shoulderは「〜を負う」なので，(A) take onが適切。(B) take after「〜に似ている」，(C) take against「〜に反感を持つ」，(D) take from「〜から取る，〜から引き継ぐ」は誤り。
⑤ parityは「同等であること」なので，(A) equalityが適切。
(B) discrimination「差別」，(C) role「役割」，(D) issue「問題」は誤り。
(3) 空欄Xの前後には反対の内容を表す語句があるため，(A) as opposed to「〜とは対照的に」が適切。(B) relevant toと(D) related to「〜に関連して」，(C) equivalent to「〜と同等で」は誤り。

【6】(1)　定義　　(2)　(エ)　　(3)　主にクジラと呼ばれる，平均的プレーヤーよりもはるかに多くのお金を費やすプレーヤーたちからお金を得ているから。(54字)　　(4)　(イ)　　(5)　自分の力を誇示する相手が必要だから。(18字)

〈解説〉(1)　第1パラグラフでは，無料ゲームがどのようなゲームかが説明されていることから「定義」が適切。　(2)　enhance「～を高める」に最も近い意味なのは (エ) improve。(ア) trivialize「～をつまらなくする」，(イ) attach「～をくっつける」，(ウ) lengthen「～を伸ばす」である。　(3)　下線部②に「無料ゲームが興行収益番付の最上位にある」とあり，直後の第2パラグラフ最終文に「その全てのお金はどこから来るのだろう」とある。したがって，下線部②の理由は第3パラグラフ1文目の内容をまとめたものとなる。　(4)　下線部③occupyingはoccupy「～に居住する」の動名詞で，最も近い意味なのは (イ) inhabiting。(ア) betraying「～を裏切ること」，(ウ) discovering「～を発見すること」，(エ) shortening「～を短縮すること」は誤り。　(5)　第4パラグラフではクジラと呼ばれるプレーヤーが多額のお金を費やす理由が書かれている。クジラと呼ばれるプレーヤーとお金を払わないプレーヤーとの関係は同パラグラフ8文目に具体的に書かれており，その内容をまとめる。

【7】(1)　学習者が学んでいる言語　　(2)　ある言語を教えるということは，正しい文を作り出す能力を伸長させることを伴うという考え方。(3)　1つの言語を身につけようとするとき，正しい文を作り出す能力が重要であることは誰もが認めるところであるが，コミュニケーションを行うためにそれらの文をどのように使うかについても知っている必要があるから。　　(4)　*usage*は英語の言語体系についての知識によって正しい文を作ることで，*use*はコミュニケーション上の目的を達するために，それらの知識を使用することである。　　(5)　Aさんにとって，本が机の上にあり，カバンが床の上にあることが明らかな状況の中で，Aさんがこのような質問を行うのは極めて不自然なことであ

り，*use*の域に達していないから。　(6)　言語材料…How do you feel? How about～？など相手の気持ちをたずねる表現　状況・場面設定…列車でのマナーをテーマにして，次のような表現を確認し，生徒同士で列車でのマナーについてお互いが感じていることを質問しあう。

・wear backpacks　　・speak loudly　　・eat food　　・sit in priority seats　　・listen to loud music　　・litter　　・talk on phones

やり取り…　Student A : How do you feel when people are listening to loud music on the train?

Student B : I hate it. How about you?

Student A : I don't like it either. How about eating food on the train?

Student B : It's OK. Actually, I do that myself.

〈解説〉(1)　下線部①は前文(第1パラグラフ5文目)の"the language they (= learners) are learning"を指す。　(2)　下線部②は前文(第1パラグラフ8文目"the teaching of a language involves developing the ability to produce correct sentences"を指す。　(3)　下線部③の理由は第1パラグラフ11～14文目に記述されており，それらの内容をまとめる。

(4)　第2パラグラフ1～3文目を見ると，言語学習には正しい文を作ることと，特定の文脈で適切な語句や文を理解することが関わっている。第3パラグラフ1, 2文目で，前者は英語の言語体系に関する知識によるもので，これが*usage*だとされている。一方，第3パラグラフ4, 5文目で後者は言語体系の知識をコミュニケーション上の目的を達成するために使うこととされ，これが*use*だとされている。　(5)　第8パラグラフ3文目から，もし誰もが机の上の本や床の上のカバンが見えていたら，AさんがBさんにそれらの位置をたずねる必然性はない。したがって，その場合はコミュニケーション上の目的(例．Aさんは本やカバンが見えず見つけたいと思っている)を達成するために言語体系の知識を使う*use*には至っていない。　(6)　本文の内容と照合すると，「言語材料」では指導の中でどの言語知識を扱うかを考える。「状況や場面」は，コミュニケーションを行う必然性が生じるように「設定」する。「や

り取り」では，以上の状況や場面でコミュニケーションを図る中で当
該の言語知識がどのように使われるのかを想定する。

2019年度　実施問題

【中学校】

【1】放送される指示に従い，答えなさい。

(Part 1)

(1)　　　　　　　(2)　　　　　　　　　　(3)

(Part 2)

(1)　　　　　　(2)　　　　　　(3)

(Part 3)

(1)　　　　　　(2)　　　　　　(3)

(Part 4)

(1)　　　　　　(2)　　　　　　(3)

(☆☆☆○○○○)

【2】次の各問いに答えなさい。

(1)　次の①～⑤の文章は，教育に関係する法令に記載された条文の一部である，①～⑤が記載された法令として最も適切なものを，下のア～コからそれぞれ1つずつ選び，記号で答えなさい。

①　第11条　校長及び教員は，教育上必要があると認めるときは，文部科学大臣の定めるところにより，児童，生徒及び学生に懲戒を加えることができる。ただし，体罰を加えることはできない。

②　第30条　地方公共団体は，法律で定めるところにより，学校，図書館，博物館，公民館その他の教育機関を設置するほか，条例

で，教育に関する専門的，技術的事項の研究又は教育関係職員の
研修，保健若しくは福利厚生に関する施設その他の必要な教育機
関を設置することができる。

③　第94条　地方公共団体は，その財産を管理し，事務を処理し，
及び行政を執行する権能を有し，法律の範囲内で条例を制定する
ことができる。

④　第4条　すべて国民は，ひとしく，その能力に応じた教育を受
ける機会を与えられなければならず，人種，信条，性別，社会的
身分，経済的地位又は門地によって，教育上差別されない。

⑤　第52条　小学校の教育課程については，この節に定めるものの
ほか，教育課程の基準として文部科学大臣が別に公示する小学校
学習指導要領によるものとする。

　　ア　日本国憲法　　　　　イ　教育基本法
　　ウ　学校教育法　　　　　エ　学校教育法施行令
　　オ　学校教育法施行規則　カ　学校図書館法
　　キ　地方教育行政の組織及び運営に関する法律
　　ク　社会教育法　　　　　ケ　地方公務員法
　　コ　教育公務員特例法

(2)　次の文章は，中学校学習指導要領(平成29年3月告示)第1章総則で
示された，各教科等の指導に当たり配慮する事項の一部である。
(　①　)～(　⑤　)にあてはまる最も適切な語句を答えなさい。

　　第1の3の(1)から(3)までに示すことが偏りなく実現されるよう，
単元や題材など内容や時間のまとまりを見通しながら，生徒の主体
的・(　①　)で深い学びの実現に向けた授業改善を行うこと。

　　特に，各教科等において身に付けた(　②　)及び技能を(　③　)し
たり，思考力，(　④　)，表現力等や学びに向かう力，人間性等を
発揮させたりして，学習の対象となる物事を捉え思考することによ
り，各教科等の特質に応じた物事を捉える視点や考え方(以下「見
方・考え方」という。)が鍛えられていくことに留意し，生徒が各教
科等の特質に応じた見方・考え方を働かせながら，(　②　)を相互

に関連付けてより深く理解したり，（　⑤　）を精査して考えを形成
したり，問題を見いだして解決策を考えたり，思いや考えを基に創
造したりすることに向かう過程を重視した学習の充実を図ること。

(3) 「中学校学習指導要領」(平成20年3月告示)第2章第9節外国語にお
ける，指導計画の作成上の配慮事項について，（　①　）〜（　⑤　）
に入る最も適切な語句を下の(a)〜(i)の中からそれぞれ1つずつ選び，
記号で答えなさい。

　　指導計画の作成に当たっては，次の事項に配慮するものとする。

　ア　各学校においては，生徒や地域の実態に応じて，学年ごとの
　　　目標を適切に定め，3学年間を通して英語の目標の実現を図る
　　　ようにすること。

　イ　2の(3)の言語材料については，学習段階に応じて平易なもの
　　　から難しいものへと段階的に指導すること。

　ウ　音声指導に当たっては，日本語との違いに留意しながら，
　　　（　①　）などを通して2の(3)のアに示された言語材料を継続し
　　　て指導すること。また，音声指導の補助として，必要に応じて
　　　発音表記を用いて指導することもできること。

　エ　（　②　）に当たっては，生徒の学習負担に配慮し筆記体を指
　　　導することもできること。

　オ　語，連語及び慣用表現については，運用度の高いものを用い，
　　　（　③　）することを通して定着を図るようにすること。

　カ　（　④　）の使い方に慣れ，（　③　）できるようにすること。

　キ　生徒の実態や教材の内容などに応じて，コンピュータや情報
　　　通信ネットワーク，教育機器などを有効活用したり，ネイティ
　　　ブ・スピーカーなどの協力を得たりなどすること。また，ペア
　　　ワーク，グループワークなどの(　⑤　)を適宜工夫すること。

(a)　活用　　　　(b)　言語活動　　(c)　思考

(d)　発音練習　　(e)　文字指導　　(f)　ICT

(g)　辞書　　　　(h)　学習形態　　(i)　学習環境

（☆☆☆◎◎◎）

【3】次の英文の(　　)に入る最も適切な単語又は語句をア～エからそれ
ぞれ1つずつ選び，記号で答えなさい。

(1)　The safety instructions describe important techniques for moving heavy
baggages without (　　) one's back.
　　ア　injuring　　　イ　to injure　　　ウ　injure　　　エ　injured

(2)　Visitors to the company must wear name tags at all times for the purpose
of (　　).
　　ア　identify　　　イ　identifying　　　ウ　identity　　　エ　identification

(3)　The microphone stopped working just as the emcee was (　　) the
winner.
　　ア　announce　　　イ　announcing　　　ウ　announcement
　　エ　announcer

(4)　Please ensure that everyone (　　) the departure time of the plane.
　　ア　knows　　　イ　know　　　ウ　have known　　　エ　is known

(5)　Richard Theater productions are funded mainly through private (　　).
　　ア　medications　　　イ　extractions　　　ウ　donations
　　エ　formations

(6)　Tom got the job, (　　) he was not the most experienced applicant.
　　ア　even though　　　イ　because　　　ウ　in spite of
　　エ　resulting in

(7)　Karen was praised by her boss (　　) her dedication and hard work.
　　ア　for　　　イ　as　　　ウ　since　　　エ　against

(8)　Please (　　) using cell phones during takeoff and landing.
　　ア　admit to　　　イ　reply to　　　ウ　care for　　　エ　refrain from

(9)　(　　)the ongoing bad weather, every outdoor event has been canceled.
　　ア　Thanks to　　　イ　Due to　　　ウ　In response　　　エ　Despite

(10)　Ken is a really (　　) person, so he cleans his room every day.
　　ア　nutritious　　　イ　vague　　　ウ　temporary　　　エ　neat

(11)　Mr. Deen was a really strict teacher. He did not (　　) students who
talk in his classroom.

ア   contrast   イ   delete   ウ   straighten   エ   tolerate

(12)   Mr. Grant was offered a nice promotion at his company's New York office, but he (   ) the job because he did not want to move to a big city.

ア   broke into   イ   broke up   ウ   brought back

エ   turned down

(13)   Most of the scientific community agrees that global warming is a dangerous (   ) that is a great threat to the health of the planet.

ア   admission   イ   misconception   ウ   intention

エ   phenomenon

(14)   The day before final exams started, no one (   ) walking around the campus. Every student was inside studying.

ア   seeing   イ   will see   ウ   was seeing   エ   was to be seen

(15)   Kate spent a long time searching for the shop. She (   ) found it after asking two different people for directions.

ア   cruelly   イ   eventually   ウ   unfortunately

エ   increasingly

(16)   In order to (   ) for a job as an assistant chef at the restaurant, Mike took a cooking course.

ア   protest   イ   qualify   ウ   betray   エ   illustrate

(17)   Mary kept talking about somebody in the room, but John was not sure who she was (   ) to.

ア   fading   イ   referring   ウ   maintaining   エ   supplying

(18)   The little boy asked his father not to (   ) him by kissing him in front of his friends.

ア   envy   イ   exaggerate   ウ   embarrass   エ   enlarge

(19)   A typhoon warning was (   ) along the coast all afternoon. People were asked to stay indoors.

ア   in fashion   イ   on demand   ウ   in effect   エ   on duty

(20)   When Judy gave her presentation, she spoke loudly (   ) of the people in the back of the room.

　　ア　for a change　　イ　for the benefit　　ウ　at the sight

　　エ　at the expense

(☆☆○○○○○)

【４】次の(1)～(10)の〔　　〕内の単語または語句を並べ替えてそれぞれ正しい英文を作るとき，（　ア　）と（　イ　）に入る単語または語句をそれぞれ1つずつ選び，番号で答えなさい。ただし，英文の初めにくる単語または語句の頭文字も小文字にしてある。

(1)　〔①　asked　　②　as　　③　your　　④　do　　⑤　superior　⑥　should〕

　　You (　　) (　　) (　ア　) (　　) (　イ　) (　　).

(2)　〔①　not　　②　the　　③　to　　④　money　　⑤　mention〕

　　She does not have the time, (　　) (　ア　) (　　) (　イ　) (　　), to go anywhere this month.

(3)　〔①　I'm　　②　goes　　③　used　　④　saying　　⑤　without　⑥　that〕

　　It (　　) (　　) (　ア　) (　　) (　イ　) (　　) to hot weather.

(4)　〔①　no　　②　learning　　③　less　　④　than　　⑤　is　⑥　important〕

　　Sleeping (　　) (　　) (　ア　) (　　) (　イ　) (　　).

(5)　〔①　happen　　②　what　　③　will　　④　do　　⑤　think　⑥　you〕

　　(　　) (　　) (　ア　) (　　) (　イ　) (　　) if it snows?

(6)　〔①　that　　②　takes　　③　we　　④　for　　⑤　granted　⑥　it　　⑦　will〕

　　She (　　) (　　) (　ア　) (　　) (　イ　) (　　) (　　) always be there to help her.

(7)　〔①　but　　②　galleries　　③　what　　④　was the　⑤　enjoyed most　　⑥　she〕

　　She thought that the restaurants and hotels were excellent, (　　) (　　)

224

(ア)( )(イ)( ).

(8) 〔① avoid ② slowly ③ to ④ as ⑤ having

⑥ so〕

Alice drove her car very ( ) ( ) (ア) ( ) (イ) ( )

an accident.

(9) 〔① travel ② to ③ decision ④ his

⑤ objected to ⑥ Kim's parents〕

( ) ( ) (ア) ( ) (イ) ( ) alone in Europe and

Asia.

(10) 〔① job ② more ③ the ④ called

⑤ experience ⑥ for〕

Our boss said that ( ) ( ) (ア) ( ) (イ) ( ) with

computers.

(☆☆○○○○○)

【5】次の英文を読み，後の(1)～(4)の各問いに答えなさい。

Physicists find themselves in a position not unlike that of Alfred Nobel himself. Alfred Nobel invented the most powerful explosive ever (①) up to his time — a means of destruction par excellence. In order to atone for this, in order to relieve his human conscience, he (②) his awards for the promotion of peace and for the achievement of peace.

Today, ⑦the physicists who participated in forging the most formidable and dangerous weapon of all time are harassed by an equal feeling of responsibility, not to say guilt. We cannot (③) warning and warning again. We cannot and should not slacken in our efforts to make the nations of the world — and especially their governments — (④) the unspeakable disaster they are certain to provoke unless they change their attitude toward each other and toward the task of shaping the future.

We helped in creating this new weapon ④(to / from / prevent / order / enemies / it / achieving / the / in / mankind / of) ahead of us — which, given

225

the mentality of the Nazis, would have meant inconceivable destruction and the enslavement of the rest of the world. We delivered this weapon into the hands of the Americans and the British people as (　⑤　) of the whole of mankind, as fighters for peace and liberty.

But so far we fail to see any guarantee of peace. We do not see any guarantee of the freedoms that were promised to the nations in the Atlantic Charter. ⑦The war is won, but the peace is not.

　　注　par excellence：一段と優れた　　forging：鍛造
　　　　provoke：引き起こす　　inconceivable：想像もつかない
　　　　(改訂版　英語で聴く　世界を変えた感動の名スピーチ／
　　　　株式会社KADOKAWA)

(1)　本文中の(　①　)～(　⑤　)に入る最も適切な単語または語句を
　　ア～エからそれぞれ1つずつ選び，記号で答えなさい。
　　①　ア　knew　　　　イ　known　　　　ウ　knows
　　　　エ　know
　　②　ア　encompassed　イ　condemned　　ウ　constructed
　　　　エ　instituted
　　③　ア　struggle with　イ　settle with　　ウ　desist from
　　　　エ　fall into
　　④　ア　aware of　　　イ　dishonest in　　ウ　cruel to
　　　　エ　remarkable for
　　⑤　ア　authors　　　イ　governors　　　ウ　trustees
　　　　エ　unfortunates
(2)　下線部⑦の英文を日本語にしなさい。
(3)　下線部④の(　　)内の単語を正しく並べ替えて書きなさい。
(4)　下線部⑦のように話者が考える理由は何ですか。日本語で説明し
　　なさい。

　　　　　　　　　　　　　　　　　　　　(☆☆○○○○○)

226

【6】次の英文を読み，後の(1)～(4)の各問いに答えなさい。(本文には出題の都合上，省略した箇所がある。)

A broader view of development

In order to enhance professional and personal (①), teachers sometimes need to step outside the world of the classroom where the concentration, all too frequently, is on knowledge and skill alone. There are other issues and (②) which can be of immense help in making their professional understanding more profound and their working reality more rewarding.

Learning by learning

Ⓐ(ourselves / one of / the / learners / ways of / our teaching practice / reflecting upon / is / become / to / best) so that our view of the learning-teaching process is not always influenced from one side of that relationship. By voluntarily submitting ourselves to a new learning experience especially (but not only) if this involves us in learning a new language, our view of our students' (③) can be changed. We might suddenly find out how frightening it is to speak in class; perhaps we will realize that many 'communicative' (④) are mundane, or realize how difficult it is to speak when we have nothing much to say; we might be surprised by how much we want to go through texts word for word. ⒷIt can be eye-opening to find out how important our teacher's approval is for us, how susceptible we are to teacher criticism, or to realize how important it is for the teacher to set us clear goals and guide us in other ways.

ⒸThose who teach a language which they themselves learned as a foreign or second language will have highly relevant memories of the experience. Teachers who teach their first language will not have the same history. However, in both cases, continuing as a learner will offer significant insights into the whole business in which we are engaged as (⑤).

(The Practice of English Language Teaching / Jeremy Harmer)

(1)　本文中の(　①　)〜(　⑤　)に入る最も適切な単語をア〜オから
それぞれ1つずつ選び, 記号で答えなさい。ただし, 1つの語は1度
しか使えないものとする。

ア　professionals　　イ　experience　　ウ　growth　　エ　practices
オ　activities

(2)　下線部Ⓐの(　　　)内の単語または語句を, 以下の日本語の内容に
合うように並べ替えて書きなさい。

『自らの教育実践を振り返る最良の方法は, 教師自身が学習者に
なることです。』

(3)　下線部Ⓑで, どんなことに気づくことが新鮮な驚きをもたらして
くれると言っているか。日本語で3つ答えなさい。

(4)　下線部Ⓒの英文を日本語にしなさい。

(☆☆☆○○○○)

【7】次の英文を読み, 後の(1)〜(7)の各問いに答えなさい。

　"Aren't you feeling lonely without me being near you?" a mother asked in a
letter to her 6-year-old daughter who died in the harrowing disaster that struck
Japan's northeastern Tohoku region in March 2011. "Are you playing happily
with your friends? Are you eating well?"

　"I want to see you again, even if it is in a (　①　)," the mother writes. "I
want to embrace you."

　Her letter to her deceased daughter is included in "Hiai" (sorrowful love),
②(letters / a / written / who / their / loved / of / ones / collection / by / the / in /
people / lost / disaster). The collection was compiled by Kiyoshi Kanebishi, a
professor at Tohoku Gakuin University, as a record of personal (　③　)
caused by the Great East Japan Earthquake.

　In another letter in the book, a widow writes about why she talks every day
to the family Buddhist altar dedicated to her (　④　) husband. Otherwise,
she writes, he is likely to say, "(　⑤　)" when she meets him again in the
future as an old woman with a wrinkled face.

"When we laugh here, you also laugh with us, don't you?"says one (⑥   ) in a letter written by a woman to her deceased younger sister.

| ア |

Six years since the crushing calamity, many of the people bereaved of their loved ones still continue struggling with a profound sense of loss and mourning.

Back then, the post-disaster reconstruction was (⑦   ) to Japan's postwar regeneration.

⑧Various ideas were proposed as to how a new future should be built for the nation through a process as dramatic as Japan's rise from the ashes after the end of World War Ⅱ.

| イ |

But the expectations for a new future appear to have been replaced by inertia.

⑨Evacuees from areas affected by the nuclear disaster are still suffering from verbal abuse and prejudice.

As the landscapes of devastated cities and towns change, the initial impact of the experience inevitably weakens over time. Memories of what happened on that day become increasingly hazy and eventually die out.

| ウ |

A huge banner was recently hung on the side of a building in Tokyo's Ginza district ⑩(when / show / was / high / to / the tsunami / of / the / hit / how / city / Ofunato / it), Iwate Prefecture, on that day.

As I looked up at the red line on the banner indicating the maximum height at which the tsunami was observed, roughly as high as a five-story building, I felt dizzy.

It was a balmy weekend day when Ginza was bustling with shoppers.

The chilling sign made me appreciate afresh our ordinary, uneventful daily lives and also aware of how easily they could be destroyed.

(原書房「天声人語2017春」より "To relive our 3/11 experiences

now and then is hard but necessary")

(1) 本文中の(①)に入る最も適切な単語を答えなさい。

(2) 下線部②と⑩の( )内の単語を，それぞれ正しく並べ替えて書きなさい。

(3) 本文中の(③)(④)(⑥)(⑦)に入る最も適切な単語をア～エからそれぞれ1つずつ選び，記号で答えなさい。

  ③　ア　probabilities　　イ　tragedies　　ウ　satisfactions

    エ　revelations

  ④　ア　last　　　　　　イ　own　　　　　ウ　forward

    エ　late

  ⑥　ア　girl　　　　　　イ　sentences　　ウ　passage

    エ　victim

  ⑦　ア　compared　　　イ　comparing　　ウ　combined

    エ　combining

(4) (⑤)に入る最も適切な英文をア～エから1つずつ選び，記号で答えなさい。

  ア　Why are you here?

  イ　Who are you?

  ウ　I've wanted to see you.

  エ　Nice to see you.

(5) 次の一文が入るのに最も適する部分を本中の　ア　～　ウ　から1つ選び，記号で答えなさい。

  That's why we need to make efforts to relive and revisit our experience of the disaster from time to time.

(6) 下線部⑧と⑨を日本語にしなさい。

(7) 銀座で幕を見た時，筆者がめまい以外に感じたことを日本語で答えなさい。

(☆☆☆☆○○○○)

【8】 次の各問いに答えなさい。

(1)　中学校1年生の授業において,「文字の読み方」には,文字の「名称の読み方」と「文字が持っている音」の両方があることを理解させ,練習させたい。次の①〜④の母音字の「名称の読み方」及び「文字が持っている音」を理解し,練習させるのに適する単語をそれぞれ答えなさい。ただし,例のように指定された母音字に下線を引くこと。

　　　例　a　　「名称の読み方」c<u>a</u>pe　　「文字が持っている音」<u>a</u>pple
　　　①　e　　「名称の読み方」　　　　　「文字が持っている音」
　　　②　i　　「名称の読み方」　　　　　「文字が持っている音」
　　　③　o　　「名称の読み方」　　　　　「文字が持っている音」
　　　④　u　　「名称の読み方」　　　　　「文字が持っている音」

(2)　中学校3年生の英語の授業において,英語で指示を出したい。次の内容を生徒に英語で伝えるとき,どのように伝えるか。3文の英語で書きなさい。

　　【内容】
　　　・今日は日本の学校とアメリカの学校がどのように違うかということについてスピーチを聞きます。
　　　・もうすでに発表の順番を決めてあります。
　　　・最初に,ひとみさんのスピーチを聞きましょう。

(3)　中学校3年生の英語の授業において,「中学校の思い出」というスピーチをさせたい。導入としてモデルを提示する際,どのようなモデルを提示するか。5文の英語で1つのモデルを書きなさい。(本文前後のあいさつ文は除く。語数は問わない。)

(4)　中学校3年生に5文型の違いについて説明したい。【第1文型】【第2文型】は下のような例文を提示した。【第3文型】【第4文型】【第5文型】はどのような例文を提示するか。それぞれ1文ずつ書きなさい。

　　【第1文型】　　Birds fly.　　【第2文型】　　I am a student.
　　【第3文型】
　　【第4文型】

231

【第5文型】

(☆☆☆◎◎◎)

【高等学校】

【1】放送される指示に従い，答えなさい。

(Part 1)

(1)

(2)

(Part 2)

(1)　　　　　　　　(2)　　　　　　　　(3)

(Part 3)

(☆☆☆◎◎◎◎◎)

【2】次の①〜⑤の文章は，教育に関係する法令に記載された条文の一部である。①〜⑤が記載された法令として最も適切なものを，後の(ア)〜(コ)からそれぞれ1つずつ選び，記号で答えなさい。

①　第11条　校長及び教員は，教育上必要があると認めるときは，文部科学大臣の定めるところにより，児童，生徒及び学生に懲戒を加えることができる。ただし，体罰を加えることはできない。

②　第30条　地方公共団体は，法律で定めるところにより，学校，図書館，博物館，公民館その他の教育機関を設置するほか，条例で，教育に関する専門的，技術的事項の研究又は教育関係職員の研修，保健若しくは福利厚生に関する施設その他の必要な教育機関を設置することができる。

③　第94条　地方公共団体は，その財産を管理し，事務を処理し，及び行政を執行する権能を有し，法律の範囲内で条例を制定することができる。

④　第4条　すべて国民は，ひとしく，その能力に応じた教育を受ける機会を与えられなければならず，人種，信条，性別，社会的身分，経済的地位又は門地によって，教育上差別されない。

⑤　第52条　小学校の教育課程については，この節に定めるもののほか，教育課程の基準として文部科学大臣が別に公示する小学校学習指導要領によるものとする。

(ア)　日本国憲法　　　　　(イ)　教育基本法
(ウ)　学校教育法　　　　　(エ)　学校教育法施行令
(オ)　学校教育法施行規則　(カ)　学校図書館法
(キ)　地方教育行政の組織及び運営に関する法律
(ク)　社会教育法　　　　　(ケ)　地方公務員法
(コ)　教育公務員特例法

(☆☆☆◎◎)

【3】次の英文(高等学校の外国語教育における学習指導要領(平成22年5月文部科学省初等中等教育局)　※抜粋)を読み，各問いに答えなさい。

<English Communication Ⅰ>
1. Objective
　To develop students' basic (　X　) such as accurately understanding and appropriately conveying information, ideas, etc., while fostering a positive attitude toward (　Y　) through the English language.
2. Contents
　(1)　The following language activities, designed for specific language-use situations in order to encourage students to apply

their abilities to understand and convey information, ideas, etc., should be conducted in English.

A. (　①　) information, ideas, etc., and grasping the outline and the main points by listening to introductions to specified topics, dialogues, etc.

B. (　①　) information. ideas, etc., and grasping the outline and the main points by reading explanations, stories, etc. Reading passages aloud so that the meaning of the content is expressed.

C. (　②　) opinions on information, ideas, etc., based on what one has heard, read, learned and experienced.

D. (　③　) brief passages on information, ideas. etc., based on what one has heard, read, learned and experienced.

(2) To effectively conduct the language activities stated in (1), consideration should be given to the following instructional points.

A. Listening and speaking with due attention to the characteristics of English sounds, such as rhythm and intonation, speed, volume, etc.

B. Reading and writing with due attention to phrases and sentences indicating the main points, connecting phrases, etc.

C. Understanding and conveying matters, distinguishing facts, opinions, etc.

3. Treatment of the Contents

(1) Based on general instruction to develop basic communication abilities given in lower secondary schools, the four areas of language activities should be interlinked for comprehensive learning, while incorporating appropriate language activities involving speaking and writing about content heard or (　④　).

> (2) Consideration should be given so that students master the items introduced in lower secondary schools and upper secondary schools through repeated instruction in accordance with students' circumstances, while (⑤) various situational language activities.

(1) 本文中の(X)，(Y)に入る英単語一語を，本文中から抜き出してそれぞれ答えなさい。

(2) 本文中の(①)～(③)に入る最も適切な単語又は語句を，ア～エから選び，(④)(⑤)に入る最も適切な単語を，カ～ケから選び，それぞれ記号で答えなさい。

①～③ [ア Understanding   イ Writing

ウ Discussing and exchanging   エ Translating]

④，⑤ [カ summarizing   キ experiencing

ク read   ケ mastered]

(☆☆◎◎◎◎◎)

【4】次の(1)～(7)の会話や英文の(   )にあてはまる最も適切な単語又は語句を，それぞれ①～④の中から1つずつ選び，番号で答えなさい。

(1) A: I feel like sleeping all day long today.

B: Not a chance. Time is precious. You have to make it (   )!

① count   ② punctual   ③ pass   ④ up

(2) A: I see you're working overtime again today.

B: I know. I (   ) there were more hours in the day.

A: Well, that's never going to happen, so maybe you'd be better off asking someone to help you with the project instead.

① want   ② hope   ③ expect   ④ wish

(3) A: You've just put the teapot in the fridge.

B: (   )! How silly of me!

① So have you   ② So I have   ③ That's it

235

④　There are you

(4)　He's very lucky in the sense (　　) he's got such kind parents.

①　that　　②　now that　　③　which　　④　while

(5)　"Welcome to Tottori Grand Hotel. We provide guests with (　　) they need as far as business conference services go."

①　somebody　　②　something　　③　anytime　　④　whatever

(6)　My father has never invested in real estate; (　　), he carefully watches property values.

①　similarly　　②　moreover　　③　nevertheless　　④　indeed

(7)　Given that the students' team was only put together last month, its performance has been (　　) so far.

①　excepting　　②　exception　　③　exceptional

④　exceptionally

(☆☆○○○○○)

【５】次の(1)～(4)各問いに答えなさい。

(1)　次の会話の【状況】をふまえ，下線部①を英語にしなさい。

> 【状況】ある企業に勤める20代の男性社員2人が，終業後に，更衣室で会話をしている。
>
> A:どうして泣いているんだい？
>
> A:Why are you crying?
>
> B:ジェーンが僕と結婚したくないって言ってるんだ。
>
> B:Jane says she doesn't want to marry me.
>
> A:まぁ，①世の中，そんなもんさ。
>
> A:Well ＿＿＿＿＿＿＿＿.

(David Thayne・鈴木衣子著「ニュアンスの違いがわかる英会話表現」より抜粋)

(2) 次の文の下線部②を英語にしなさい。

> そんなエジソンの最大の理解者が，母のナンシーでした。エジソンの好奇心や疑問を大切にし，自宅に実験室を構え，研究に打ち込むエジソンを支えます。
>
> 12歳のとき，エジソンは事故で耳がほとんど聞こえなくなりました。しかし，彼はこう考えます。「②これで雑音がなくなり，集中力が増すではないか」

（「ギフト〜E名言の世界〜2010年4月号」NHK出版より抜粋）

(3) 次の英文は，2009年9月8日，アメリカ合衆国前大統領のバラク・オバマ氏が，バージニア州アーリントンの高校を訪れ，集まった生徒及び中継を視聴する全米の児童・生徒に向けて，直接語りかけた教育演説からの抜粋である。この一節の主旨を端的に伝える小見出しを，英語一文で作成しなさい。

> I know that sometimes you get that sense from TV that you can be rich and successful without any hard work, that your ticket to success is through rapping or basketball or being a reality TV star. Chances are you're not going to be any of those things.
>
> The truth is, being successful is hard. You won't love every subject that you study. You won't click with every teacher that you have. Not every homework assignment will seem completely relevant to your life right at this minute. And you won't necessarily succeed at everything the first time you try.
>
> That's okay. Some of the most successful people in the world are the ones who've had the most failures. JK Rowling ⋯ who wrote *Harry Potter*, her first Harry Potter book was rejected 12 times before it was finally published. Michael Jordan was cut from his high school basketball team. He lost hundreds of games and missed thousands of shots during his career. But he once said,"I have failed over and over and over again in my life, and that's why I succeed."

(「[対訳]オバマから子どもたちへ Obama Speaks to America's Schoolchilrdren」朝日出版社より抜粋，一部改変)

(4)　次の指示に従って解答しなさい。

　　マーシャ・クラッカワー著「日本人の英語力」(小学館)で，英語では，ある程度まとまった文章は，次の文章の組み立て方に示すような構成にするという約束がある，と述べられている。このことに関し，筆者は「常に，まったくこのとおりでなければならないというわけではありませんが，大まかな線はこの流れに沿って行ったほうが，わかりやすいと思います。」と述べている。

　　この文章の組み立て方に従って，ある用件を伝えるための英語メール文を作成した。以下の【条件】をふまえ，英語メール文中の下線部を補うのにふさわしい英語を一文で答えなさい。

文章の組み立て方

1.　Introduction

　　a. Hook

　　b. General statement(s)

　　c. Thesis statement

2.　Body

　　a. Topic sentence

　　b. Support(s)

　　c. Concluding sentence

3.　Conclusion

　　a. Restatement

　　b. Advice / Warning / Something to think about

　　c. Summary

【条件】

・あなたは30代の社会人であり，このメール文の書き手である。
・メール文の送り先はあなたの友人であり，あなたとは別の職場に勤務する30代の英国人である。この英国人は，ミカ(Mika)と職場が同じであり，ミカとも顔見知りの間柄である。

英語メール文

Guess who I met at the party yesterday? A guy by the name of John Smith, who was a friend of Mika's while she was in the U.S. He has lost her email address but would like to see her. Is it possible for you to let Mika know that John is here in Tokyo? Mika might want to see him too. His phone number is 090-1234-5678. ＿＿＿＿＿＿＿＿＿＿＿＿＿? John would really appreciate it if he could see her, He leaves on Tuesday. I hope they can get in touch.

(マーシャ・クラッカワー著「日本人の英語力」より抜粋，一部改変)

(☆☆☆○○○)

【6】次の(1)〜(3)の英文は，ユネスコ協会が示す持続可能な開発目標(SDGs)のいずれかのgoalから一部のtargetを抜き出したものである。それぞれの英文が示すgoalがどれであるか，以下に示す1〜17のロゴの中から1つずつ選び，番号で答えなさい。

(1)

-By 2030, ensure access for all to adequate, safe and affordable housing and basic services and upgrade slums

-Strengthen efforts to protect and safeguard the world's cultural and natural heritage

-By 2030, significantly reduce the number of deaths and the number of people affected and substantially decrease the direct economic losses relative to global gross domestic product caused by disasters, including water-related disasters, with a focus on protecting the poor and people in vulnerable situations

(2)

-By 2025, prevent and significantly reduce marine pollution of all kinds, in particular from land-based activities, including marine debris and nutrient pollution

-By 2020, sustainably manage and protect marine and coastal ecosystems to avoid significant adverse impacts, including by strengthening their resilience, and take action for their restoration in order to achieve healthy and productive oceans

-Minimize and address the impacts of ocean acidification, including through enhanced scientific cooperation at all levels

(3)

-End all forms of discrimination against all women and girls everywhere

-Eliminate all forms of violence against all women and girls in the public and private spheres, including trafficking and sexual and other types of exploitation

-Eliminate all harmful practices, such as child, early and forced marriage and female genital mutilation

（国際連合広報センターホームページ 2030アジェンダより抜粋）

（☆☆◎◎◎）

【7】次の英文を読み，以下の(1)(2)の各問いに答えなさい。

＜Overview＞

Global vaccination coverage - the proportion of the world's children who receive recommended vaccines - has stalled over the past few years.

During 2016, about （　a　） % of infants worldwide (116.5 million infants) received 3 doses of diphtheria-tetanus-pertussis(DTP3) vaccine, protecting them against infectious diseases that can cause serious illness and disability or be fatal. By 2016, （　b　） countries had reached at least 90% coverage of DTP3 vaccine.

＜Global immunization coverage 2016＞

A summary of global vaccination coverage in 2016 follows.

Hepatitis B is a viral infection that attacks the liver. Hepatitis B vaccine for infants had been introduced nationwide in 186 countries by the end of 2016.

Global coverage with 3 doses of hepatitis B vaccine is estimated at 84％ and is as high as 92％ in the Western Pacific. In addition, 101 countries introduced one dose of hepatitis B vaccine to newborns within the first 24 hours of life, and the global coverage is 39％.

Pneumococcal diseases include pneumonia, meningitis and febrile bacteraemia, as well as otitis media, sinusitis and bronchitis. Pneumococcal vaccine had been introduced in 134 countries by the end of 2016, including three in some parts of the country, and global coverage was estimated at 42％.

Polio is a highly infectious viral disease that can cause irreversible paralysis. In 2016, 85％ of infants around the world received three doses of polio vaccine. Targeted for global eradication, polio has been stopped in all countries except for Afghanistan, Pakistan and Nigeria. Countries without polio have been infected by imported virus, and all countries - especially those experiencing conflict and instability - remain at risk until polio is fully eradicated.

Rubella is a viral disease which is usually mild in children, but infection during early pregnancy may cause fetal death or congenital rubella syndrome, which can lead to defects of the brain, heart, eyes, and ears. Rubella vaccine was introduced nationwide in 152 countries by the end of 2016, and global coverage was estimated at 47％.

Yellow fever is an acute viral haemorrhagic disease transmitted by infected mosquitoes. As of 2016, yellow fever vaccine had been introduced in routine infant immunization programmes in 35 of the 42 countries and territories at risk for yellow fever in Africa and the Americas. In these 42 countries and territories, coverage is estimated at 45％.

(世界保健機構(WHO)ホームページより抜粋，一部改変)

(1) 次のグラフを参考に，本文中の(a)(b)に入る数字を算用数字で答えなさい。

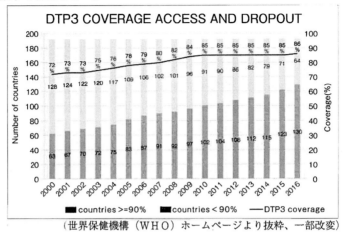

（世界保健機構（WHO）ホームページより抜粋、一部改変）

(2) 次の各図表中の X ， Y に入る最も適切な疾病の名称を，本文中から抜き出して答えなさい。

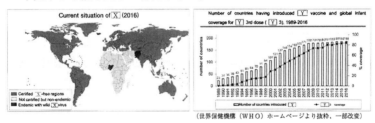

（世界保健機構（WHO）ホームページより抜粋、一部改変）

(☆☆◎◎◎◎)

【8】次の英文は，2001年7月に，英国科学振興協会から相談を受けた心理学者リチャード・ワイズマンが，インターネットを用いてLaughLabというサイトを立ち上げ，世界中の人々の協力を仰ぎながら，「世界一おかしなジョーク」探求を進めた実験プランについて述べたものである。この英文を読み，以下の(1)〜(5)の各問いに答えなさい。

Participants were asked to rate each joke on a five-point scale ranging from "not very funny" to "very funny". To simplify our analysis, we combined the "4" and "5" ratings to make a general "yes, that is quite a funny joke" category. We could then order the jokes on the basis of the percentage of responses that fell into this category. If the joke really wasn't very good, then it might have only 1 percent or 2 percent of people assigning it a "4" or "5" rating. In contrast, the real ribticklers would have a much higher percentage of top ratings. At the end of the first week, we reviewed some of the leading submissions. Most of the material was pretty poor, and so tended to obtain low percentages. Even the top jokes fell well short of the 50 percent mark. Around 25-35 percent of participants found the following jokes funny, and so they came towards the top of the list:

A teacher decided to take her bad mood out on her class of children and so said, "Can everyone who thinks they're stupid, stand up!" After a few seconds, just one child slowly stood up. The teacher turned to the child and said, "Do you think you're stupid?" "No…" replied the child, "…but I hate to see you standing there all by yourself." [1]

Did you hear about the man who was proud when he completed a jigsaw within thirty minutes, because it said "five to six years" on the box? [2]

The top jokes had one thing in common - they create a sense of (　①　) in the reader. The feeling arises because the person in the joke appears stupid (like [2]), or makes someone in a position of power look foolish (like [1]).

We were not the first to notice that people laugh when they feel superior to others. The theory dates back to around 400 BC, and was described by the Greek scholar Plato in his famous text *The Republic*. Proponents of this "superiority" theory believe that the origin of laughter lies in the baring of teeth akin to "the roar of triumph in an ancient jungle duel". Because of these animalistic and primitive associations, Plato was not a fan of laughter. He thought that it was wrong to laugh at the misfortune of others, and that hearty laughter involved a loss of control that resulted in people appearing to be (②) fully human. In fact, the father of modern-day philosophy was so concerned about the potential moral damage that could be caused by laughter that he advised citizens to limit their attendance at comedies, and never to appear in this lowest form of the dramatic arts.

(Richard Wiseman, Quirkology より抜粋)

(1) この文で紹介されているratingはどのように行われたのか，100字程度の日本語で述べなさい。

(2) ジョーク[2]について解説した次の英文において，(　)を補うのに最も適切な英単語一語を答えなさい。

The man in joke [2] mistakenly believes that it usually takes five to six years to complete the puzzle, and so he boasts that he is very capable of doing it in a much shorter time. But, in fact, the written message of "five to six years"means that the puzzle is designed for children whose (　) is five to six.

(3) 本文中の(①)を補うのに最も適切な英単語一語を，本文中から抜き出して答えなさい。

(4) 本文中の(②)を補うのに最も適切な語句を，ア～エから選び，記号で答えなさい。

　ア　nothing but　　イ　just like　　ウ　less than　　エ　close to

(5) プラトンのポリスの人々へのアドバイスを，プラトンが語っているかのように書き直した。この英文中の空欄(ア)(イ)を補うのに最も適切な英単語一語をそれぞれ答えなさい。

"Go and see comedies as (ア) as possible, and never (イ) in a comedy, since it is the lowest form of dramas."

(☆☆☆☆◎◎◎)

【9】次の英文を読み，以下の(1)〜(5)の各問いに答えなさい。

Questions in the classroom

Teachers' questioning behaviour has been the focus of a good deal of research in second language classrooms. Questions are fundamental in engaging students in interaction and in exploring how much they understand. Two types of questions that have been extensively examined are referred to as 'display' questions (to which the teacher already knows the answer) and 'genuine' or 'referential' questions (to which the teacher may not know the answer). The role they play in classroom interaction has been examined in a number of studies.

Study 6: Teachers' questions in ESL classrooms

①Michael Long and Charlene Sato(1983) examined the forms and functions of questions asked by teachers in ESL classrooms and compared them with questioning behaviours observed outside the classroom between native and non-native speakers.They were particularly interested in differences between the quantity of 'display' and 'information' ('genuine' or 'referential') questions. Audio recordings made of the interactions between teachers and students in six adult ESL classes revealed that teachers asked more display questions than information questions. In the native speaker/non-native speaker conversations outside the classroom, referential questions were more frequent than display questions. The researchers concluded that teacher-learner interaction is a 'greatly distorted version of its equivalent in the real world', and they argued that the interactional structure of classroom conversation should be changed.

Even though language teaching methods have changed since the Long and Sato study, other classroom studies on teachers' questioning behaviour have also reported disproportionately higher numbers of display questions. In the context of communicative language teaching, teachers have been urged to use fewer display questions because they are thought to lead to short simple responses that require little cognitive effort on the part of the learner. Instead, they have been encouraged to ask more referential (or genuine) questions since the latter are thought to require more cognitive processing and to generate more complex answers.

More recently, however. a re-evaluation of display questions has taken place. This is based on the observation that there are different ways in which display questions can be asked in classrooms. One is for the teacher to ask a series of questions in a drill-like format such as 'Do you have a brother?', 'Does he have a brother?', 'Do you have a sister?', 'Does she have a sister?' In this context, display questions do not have a meaningful or communicative purpose. In other contexts, however, display questions can serve important pedagogic and interaction functions. The study below describes teachers' use of display questions in a more positive light.

Study 7: Scaffolding and display and referential questions

In a case study of one teacher's adult ESL class, Dawn McCormick and Richard Donato (2000) explored how the teacher's questions were linked to her instructional goals. Working within sociocultural theory, the researchers chose ②the concept of scaffolding to investigate teacher questions as 'mediational tools within the dialogue between the teacher and students'. As we saw in the previous Chapters, scaffolding refers to a process in which, for example, a more knowledgeable (or expert) speaker helps a less knowledgeable (or novice) learner by providing an interactional framework that the learner can build on.

McCormick and Donato identified six functions of scaffolding (for example, drawing the novice's attention to the task, and simplifying or limiting the task demands). The researchers examined another function - the teacher's use of questions during the scaffolded interactions - and how it contributed to class participation and learner comprehension. ③In the example

247

below, they argue that the teacher's use of the display question 'Who usually lives in palaces?' serves an important pedagogic function because it draws the learners attention to the word 'palace' through the display question and facilitates the learners' comprehension of the world.

> Teacher　: Palace? (　ア　)
>
> Student 1 : Like castle?
>
> Student 2 : Special place, very good.
>
> Student 3 : Very nice.
>
> Teacher　: Castle, special place, very nice. (　イ　)
>
> Students　: Kings.
>
> Teacher　: Kings, and queens, princes, and princesses. (　ウ　)
>
> Students　: Yeah.
>
> Student 4 : Maybe beautiful house?
>
> Teacher　: Big beautiful house, yeah, really big. (　エ　)

McCormick and Donato suggest that questions should be examined within the framework of scaffolded interaction and with reference to the teacher's goals in a particular lesson or interaction.

Study 8: Open and closed questions

Another distinction similar to the one between display and genuine questions is that between ④open and closed questions. Closed questions typically have only one possible answer and they usually lead to simple one-word responses, making them quick and easy to respond to. Open questions have more than one possible answer and invite elaboration, typically leading to longer and more complex answers, including, for example, explanation and reasoning. In **content and languag-integrated learning** (CLIL) classes in Austria, Christiana Dalton-Puffer (2006) observed and audio recorded the types of questions asked by English teachers, as well as the responses students gave to them. Students produced a greater quantity and quality of output after open questions. In addition, open questions that asked learners not just for facts but also for reasons or explanations led to the most complex linguistic outcomes. Dalton-Puffer concluded that asking more complex open questions would benefit learners in these CLIL classrooms but that this level of question/response interaction requires a high level of competence in the foreign language on the part of the teacher.

(Patsy M. Lightbown / Nina Spada, *How Languages are Learned* より抜粋，一部改変)

(1) 下線部①にある1983年のLongとSatoによる研究の結果，2人の研究者はどのような結論を導いたのか，本文の内容に即して日本語で説明しなさい。

(2) 下線部②にあるscaffoldingとはどのようなものか，本文の内容に即して日本語で説明しなさい。

(3) 下線部③にある 'Who usually lives in palaces?' の一言は，本文中に示される教師と生徒達とのインタラクション例であればどこに来るか，最も適切な箇所を(ア)～(エ)から1つ選び，記号で答えなさい。

(4) 下線部④について，open questions と closed questions はそれぞれどのような質問であるか，本文の内容に即して日本語で説明しなさい。

(5) 以下の【状況】で□□に示す文章をコミュニケーション英語Ⅰの題材として指導するとき，あなたが指導者であればどのような open question と closed question を生徒に問うか。それぞれ1つずつ，英語で作成しなさい。なお，質問を構成する英文の数は問わないこととする。

【状況】

　対象　高校1年生

　人数　40名

　時期　1学期(7月中旬)

　科目　コミュニケーション英語Ⅰ

Never Give Up!

Last spring, Cathy started a part-time job at a French restaurant near her college. Cathy had never worked in a restaurant before, and the first week was very hard for her. The restaurant was busy, and Cathy worked until late most evenings. Sometimes, the chef got angry with her for doing things wrong. One evening, she broke some plates, and later she spilled water on a customer's clothes. After that, Cathy thought about quitting.

However, she decided to stay, and after a while, she began to enjoy the job. There was another student from Cathy's college working at the restaurant, and they became friends. Cathy started to get used to the work, and she made fewer mistakes. Recently, the chef has even taught her how to cook some French dishes. Cathy will make the dishes for her family during her next vacation from college.

(☆☆☆◎◎◎◎)

解答・解説

【中学校】

【 1 】Part 1　(1)　C　　(2)　C　　(3)　D　　Part 2　(1)　A　　(2)　A
(3)　C　　Part 3　(1)　B　　(2)　A　　(3)　C　　Part 4　(1)　C
(2)　A　　(3)　C

〈解説〉スクリプトは公表されていない。Part1 は提示されているイラストについて，適切な説明文を選択する問題と思われる。放送前にイラストをよく見て，「だれが」「何をしている」情景なのか正確に把握しておきたい。それぞれのイラストについて，(1)は女性が何かを食べて

250

いる(かじっている)様子，(2)はベッドと椅子の位置関係やベッドに上にあるもの，(3)は女性4人が食事をしている様子が描写されている。Part 2 からPart 4 までは，解答の選択肢を含めた聞き取りが必要なので，より集中して臨む必要がある。もし放送が1 回のみの場合は，何が問われているか全体を理解することに集中し，聞き取れなかった箇所は前後の文脈から判断して正答できるよう努めよう。放送が2回の場合は，聞き取れなかった箇所を中心に聞き取りつつ，1回目で聞き取った内容が正しいかどうかの確認を同時に行いたい。

【2】(1) ① ウ ② キ ③ ア ④ イ ⑤ オ
(2) ① 対話的 ② 知識 ③ 活用 ④ 判断力 ⑤ 情報 (3) ① (d) ② (e) ③ (a) ④ (g) ⑤ (h)
〈解説〉(1) ① 文部科学省は体罰が社会問題化したことを受け，平成25年3月に「体罰の禁止及び児童生徒理解に基づく指導の徹底について」を通知した。その中で懲戒と体罰の区別について「教員等が児童生徒に対して行った懲戒行為が体罰に当たるかどうかは，当該児童生徒の年齢，健康，心身の発達状況，当該行為が行われた場所的及び時間的環境，懲戒の態様等の諸条件を総合的に考え，個々の事案ごとに判断する必要がある。この際，単に懲戒行為をした教員等や，懲戒行為を受けた児童生徒・保護者の主観のみにより判断するのではなく，諸条件を客観的に考慮して判断すべきである」としたうえで，「その懲戒の内容が身体的性質のもの，すなわち，身体に対する侵害を内容とするもの(殴る，蹴る等)，児童生徒に肉体的苦痛を与えるようなもの(正座・直立等特定の姿勢を長時間にわたって保持させる等)に当たると判断された場合は，体罰に該当する」としている。 ② 「地方教育行政の組織及び運営に関する法律」は昭和31年に制定されたもので，教育委員会の設置，市町村立学校の教職員の身分，学校運営協議会の設置等の地方公共団体の教育行政の基本について定めた法律。平成27年4月1日には大きな制度改正を行うためその一部を改正する法律が施行され，教育委員長と教育長を一本化した新「教育長」の設置，

教育長へのチェックの機能の強化と会議の透明化,「総合教育会議」の全自治体設置, 教育に関する「大綱」の策定が行われた。　③　日本国憲法第94条は, 地方公共団体の権能を定めたものである。なお憲法第92条では「地方公共団体の組織及び運営に関する事項は, 地方自治の本旨に基いて, 法律でこれを定める」とされている。　④　教育基本法が制定された昭和22(1947)年以後, 価値観の多様化, 規範意識の低下, 科学技術の進歩, 国際化, 核家族化等教育を取り巻く環境は大幅に変化した。これを踏まえ, 教育基本法は改正され, 平成18年12月公布・施行された。　⑤　学校教育法施行規則第52条の規定により, 教育課程については, 国が学習指導要領等で学校が編成する教育課程の大綱的な基準を公示し, 学校の設置者たる教育委員会が教育課程等学校の管理運営の基本的事項について規則を制定し, 学校(校長)が学校や地域, 児童生徒の実態等を踏まえて創意工夫した教育課程を編成・実施することになっている。　(2)　中学校学習指導要領総則における「各教科等の指導に当たり配慮する事項」について, 同解説総則編(平成29年7月)では,「知識及び技能が習得されるようにすること, 思考力, 判断力, 表現力等を育成すること, 学びに向かう力, 人間性等を涵養することが偏りなく実現されるよう, 単元や題材等内容や時間のまとまりを見通しながら, 生徒の主体的・対話的で深い学びの実現に向けた授業改善を行うこと, その際, 各教科等の『見方・考え方』を働かせ, 各教科等の学習の過程を重視して充実を図ることを示している」と解説している。　(3)　中学校学習指導要領及び同解説外国語編については, 内容をしっかり理解した上で, 重要な箇所を暗記しておくことが重要である。現行の学習指導要領(平成20年3月告示)とその解説のみならず, 学習評価や学習指導要領改訂案にも目を通しておくことが望ましい。また, (2)のように, 新中学校学習指導要領(平成29年3月告示)からの出題の可能性も高いので, 併せて学習を進めておく必要があるだろう。

【3】(1) ア (2) エ (3) イ (4) ア (5) ウ (6) ア
(7) ア (8) エ (9) イ (10) エ (11) エ (12) エ
(13) エ (14) エ (15) イ (16) イ (17) イ
(18) ウ (19) ウ (20) イ

〈解説〉(1) 前置詞withoutの直後は動名詞の形になる。 (2) 「身分を証明する目的で，いつも名札を身につけなければならない」とすればよいので，identification「身分証明」が適切。なお，identityは「身元，正体」という意味。 (3) 空欄の直前にbe動詞wasがあることから，「司会者が勝者を発表しようとしていた」と考えて，過去進行形にする。 (4) 空欄の直前にeveryoneがあるので，三人称単数現在の形になっているknowsを選ぶ。 (5) 「主に個人の寄付金によって資金の提供を受けている」とすればよい。donation「寄付金」。 (6) 「トムは最も経験がある応募者ではなかったが，その仕事を得た」とすればよい。逆接を表すeven though「～だが，～であるのに」が適切。
(7) praise A for Bは「AをBのことで褒める」という意味の表現。
(8) refrain from Aは「Aを控える」という意味の表現。 (9) due to Aは「Aが原因で，Aのために」，ongoingは「継続している」という意味。
(10) neatは人の性格を表すときは「きれい好きな，きちょうめんな」という意味。 (11) 「ディーン先生は本当に厳しい先生だった。彼は自分の教室でおしゃべりをする生徒を許さなかった」とする。tolerate「許す，大目に見る」。 (12) turn downは「拒否する」，promotionは「出世」という意味。 (13) 「地球温暖化は危険な現象」とすればよい。phenomenon「現象」。 (14) be＋to不定詞は，予定，意図・目的，可能，義務・命令・禁止，運命を表す。ここでは可能の意味である。
(15) 「ケイトはその店を探すのに長い時間を使った。彼女はついにそれを見つけた」となる。eventually「ついに，結局」。 (16) qualify for Aは「Aのための資格を持つ」という意味の表現。 (17) refer to Aは「Aを指す，Aに言及する」という意味の表現。 (18) 「その少年は父親に，友達の前でキスをして自分を恥ずかしがらせないように頼んだ」となる。embarrass「恥ずかしい(きまりが悪い)思いをさせる」。

(19) 「台風に関する警報が午後の間ずっと，沿岸部に出されていた」
となる。in effect「実施されて，発効して」。　(20)　for the benefit of A
は「Aのために」という意味の表現。

【4】(1)　ア　②　　イ　⑤　　(2)　ア　③　　イ　②　　(3)　ア　④
イ　①　　(4)　ア　③　　イ　④　　(5)　ア　⑥　　イ　③
(6)　ア　④　　イ　①　　(7)　ア　⑥　　イ　④　　(8)　ア　④
イ　①　　(9)　ア　④　　イ　②　　(10)　ア　④　　イ　②

〈解説〉(1)　並べ替え後の全文は，You should do as your superior asked.と
なる。superiorは「上司，先輩」という意味の名詞。　(2)　並べ替え
後の全文は，She does not have the time, not to mention the money, to go
anywhere this month.となる。not to mention Aは「Aは言うまでもなく」
という意味の表現。　(3)　並べ替え後の全文は，It goes without saying
that I'm used to hot weather.となる。it goes without saying that ～は「～は
言うまでなく」という意味の表現。　(4)　並べ替え後の全文は，
Sleeping is no less important than learning.となる。A … no less ～ than Bは
「AはBと同様～だ，AはBに劣らないほど～だ」という意味の表現。
(5)　並べ替え後の全文は，What do you think will happen if it snows?と
なる。疑問詞＋do you think…？は疑問詞で始まる疑問文にdo you think
を組み込んだ形。　(6)　並べ替え後の全文は，She takes it for granted
that we will always be there to help her.となる。take it for granted that ～は
「～を当然のことだと考える」という意味の表現。　(7)　並べ替え後
の全文は，She thought that the restaurants and hotels were excellent, but
what she enjoyed most was the galleries.となる。関係代名詞のwhatは「こ
と，もの」という意味を表す。この場合はwhat she enjoyed mostが文の
主語となっている。　(8)　並べ替え後の全文は，Alice drove her car
very slowly so as to avoid having an accident.となる。so as to doは「～す
るために」という意味で，目的を表す。　(9)　並べ替え後の全文は，
Kim's parents objected to his decision to travel alone in Europe and Asia.とな
る。object to Aは「Aに反対する」という意味の表現。toは前置詞であ

ることに注意。 (10) 並べ替え後の全文は，Our boss said that the job called for more experience with computers.となる。call for Aは「Aを必要とする」という意味。

【5】(1) ① イ ② エ ③ ウ ④ ア ⑤ ウ

(2) 史上最も恐ろしく最も危険な兵器の製造に参加した物理学者たちも，罪悪感とは言わないまでも同様の責任感にさいなまれている。

(3) in order to prevent the enemies of mankind from achieving it

(4) 今のところ平和の保証は何も見られず，大西洋憲章が各国に約束したはずの自由は保障されていないから。

〈解説〉(1) ① be known to Aは「Aに知られている」という意味の表現。knownは過去分詞の形容詞的用法で，known up to his timeという形容詞句がexplosiveを修飾している。 ② instituteは動詞で「(制度等を)設ける」という意味。 ③ 空欄の前の文では危険な兵器について言及し，空欄の直後にwarning「(兵器の危険さを訴える)警告」があるので，desist from A「Aを止める」が適切。 ④ 空欄の前の構文を考えてみると，makeの目的語がthe nations of the world，補語が空欄に入る語となる。空欄の直後に「口にするのもはばかられる災害」とあるので，「それを世界各国に気づかせる」と考えてaware ofを選択する。
⑤ 「私たちは，人類全体からの受託者であり平和と自由のために戦う戦士であるアメリカと英国に，この兵器を委ねる」と考える。trustee「受託者，被信託人，保管人」。 (2) 文全体の主語はthe physicists，動詞はare，whoからtimeまではphysicistsを先行詞とする関係代名詞節。forgeは「(金属を)鍛造する」，be harassed by Aは「Aに悩まされる，Aにさいなまれる」という意味の表現。 (3) prevent A from doingは「Aが～するのを妨げる」という意味の表現。「人類の敵がそれ(新しい兵器)を手に入れるのを防ぐために」と考えて並べかえる。 (4) 下線部は「戦争には勝ったが，平和は勝ち取っていない」という意味である。この理由は直前の1文に書かれている。the Atlantic Charterは「大西洋憲章」，guaranteeは「保障」という意味。

【6】(1) ① ウ　② エ　③ イ　④ オ　⑤ ア

(2) One of the best ways of reflecting upon our teaching practice is to become learners ourselves　(3)　・教師が自分を認めてくれることがどれほど重要かということ　・教師の批判に学習者である自分がどれはど敏感かということ　・教師が明確な目標を設定し，いろいろな方法でそこに導いてくれることがどれほど重要かということ

(4)　自分自身がその言語を外国語または第2言語として学んだ教師ならば，その自分の学習経験を覚えているでしょうし，その記憶は非常に生徒の経験に近いものでしょう。

〈解説〉(1)　①　空欄の前後より，「成長」を促進するために，教室世界の外に出る必要があると考える。　②　空欄の前後より，専門的な知識を深め，自分たちの仕事をやりがいのあるものにするのは「実践」だと考える。　③　空欄の前後より，私たち自身が新しい学習経験をすることによって，生徒が「経験」したことへの見方が変わると考える。　④　communicative activitiesで「コミュニケーション活動」。⑤　engaged as professionalsで「専門家として関わる」という意味。(2)　問題文より，主語が「自らの教育実践を振り返る最良の方法」，補語が「教師自身が学習者になること」と考え，これら2つがイコールの関係になるようにbe動詞でつなぐ。reflect upon Aは「Aを振り返る」という意味の表現。　(3)　下線部中の最初のhowからus，2番目のhowからcriticism，3番目のhowからwaysまでを訳出すればよい。　(4)文全体の主語はThose，動詞はhaveで，主語と動詞の間にThoseを先行詞とする関係代名詞節とlanguageを先行詞とする関係代名詞節がある。

【7】(1)　dream　(2)　②　a collection of letters written by people who lost their loved ones in the disaster　⑩　to show how high the tsunami was when it hit the city of Ofunato　(3)　③ イ　④ エ　⑥ ウ　⑦ ア　(4) イ　(5) ウ　(6)　⑧　第2次世界大戦後の復興に肩を並べるような新しい国づくりが思い描かれた。　⑨　原発避難者への心ない言葉や偏見もなくならない。　(7)　日常のありがたさ

とそのもろさを思う。

〈解説〉(1)　空欄の前にあるyouは亡くなった息子を指す。たとえ夢であっても，亡くなった息子に会いたいと考えて空欄にはdreamを入れる。
(2)　②　直前のHiaiの説明文が問われている。「その災害で愛する者を亡くした人々によって書かれた書簡集」と考えて並べかえる。
⑩　大きな垂れ幕が東京の銀座にある建物から吊り下げられている目的が問われている。「津波が大船渡市を直撃した時に，それがどれだけ高かったのかを示すために」と考えて並べかえる。　(3)　③　空欄の直後に，「東日本大震災によって引き起こされた」とあるのでtragedy「悲劇」が適切。　④　lateは「亡くなった，故…」という意味。　⑥　直後に「女性によって書かれた手紙の中の」とあるので，passage「文章」が適切。　⑦　compare A to Bは「AをBに例える」という意味の表現。ここでは受動態となっている。　(5)　問題文は「だから，時にその災害の経験を蘇らせ再考する必要があるのだ」という意味。空欄ウの直前に「震災の経験がますますかすんでいく」という記述があるので，この文の後に入れるのが適切。　(6)　⑧　as to Aは「Aについて」という意味の表現。元々はdramatic processだったものが，原級比較as〜asの使用により，dramaticがasとasの間に移動したと考える。直訳すると「新しい未来が，第2次世界大戦後の廃墟状態からの復興と同じくらい急激な過程を経て，その国のためにどのように作られるべきなのかについて，様々な考えが出された」。　⑨　文全体の主語はEvacuees，動詞はareである。affectedは過去分詞の形容詞的用法でareasを修飾している。　(7)　最終文が解答となる。afreshは「改めて」，uneventfulは「平穏無事な」という意味。

【8】(1)　(名称の読み方，文字が持っている音 の順)　①　evening, eggs　②　ice, ink　③　OK, octopus　④　uniform, umbrella
(2)　・Today we are going to hear speeches on how Japanese schools and American schools are different.　・We have already decided the order of presentations.　・The first, let's listen to Hitomi's speech.　(3)　・I've

been studying English hard since elementary school. 　・I listened to a radio English course every day. 　・I was really glad that I won first prize in the speech contest. 　・Now I'm interested in learning other languages. ・It's not easy, but I'll do my best. 　　(4)　第3文型…I like milk. 　　第4文型…He showed me his album. 　　第5文型…We call him Tom.

〈解説〉(1)　フォニックス(Phonics)は英語のスペルを覚える学習方法で，英語において，綴り字と発音との間に規則性を明示し，正しい読み方の学習を容易にさせる方法の一つである。例えば母音のaはフォニックス読み(文字が持っている音)は「ア」，名前読み(名称の読み方)では「エイ」となる。これを踏まえた上で，示された母音に従って解答すること。　　(2)　問題文にある日本語を，中学3年生が理解できる簡単な英語に訳さなければならない。授業の最初で「今日は～を行います」といったことを伝えるためによく使われる表現は，Today we are going to ～である。「発表」はpresentation，「順番」はorderをそれぞれ用いる。(3)　解答例のように，「小学校からずっと英語を勉強している」，「毎日，ラジオ英語講座を聞いた」，「スピーチコンテストで優勝してうれしかった」，「他の言語に興味がある」，「簡単ではないが，全力を尽くす」といったまとまりがあり，具体的で，中学3年生が理解できる簡単な英語で表現する。　　(4)　第3文型はSVOで動詞は他動詞を用いる。別解としてI have a dog.等も可。第4文型はSVOOで，動詞にはgive, show, teach等を用いる。別解としてMike gave me an apple.等も可。第5文型はSVOCで，callやmake等を用いる。別解でThe news made me sad.等も可。ここでも対象生徒に留意し，簡単な語で英文を作成すること。

【高等学校】

【1】Part 1　(1)　D　　(2)　C　　Part 2　(1)　B　　(2)　B　　(3)　D　　Part 3　C

〈解説〉スクリプトは公表されていないが，一般的なリスニングのポイントとして「数字」，「場所」，「いつ，どこで，だれが何をしたか」を正確に聞き取ることが挙げられる。Part1 はイラストの状況を最も適切に

表す選択肢を選ぶ問題と考えられる。(1)は机の上に書類を出し合い，アイデア等を交換したり，話し合ったりしている様子，(2)はショウルームに車を見に来た客や受付の人，展示されている車の様子である。静物の場合は物の名称・個数・位置関係，人物や動物の場合は動作主の名称・どんな動作をしているか・背景には何があるか等を短時間で把握できるよう，日頃から練習しておく必要がある。Part 2 及びPart 3は，設問も選択肢も聞き取らなければならない。もし放送が1 回のみの場合は，何が問われているか全体を理解することに集中し，聞き取れなかった箇所は前後の文脈から判断して正答できるよう努めよう。放送が2回の場合は，聞き取れなかった箇所を中心に聞き取りつつ，1回目で聞き取った内容が正しいかどうかの確認を同時に行いたい。

【2】※①〜⑤は全員正解とする(解答非公表)。
〈解説〉鳥取県は本問の全て(①〜⑤)を全員正解とし，解答を非公表としている。詳細は各自で自治体に問い合わせられたい。以下は①がウ(学校教育法)，②がキ(地方教育行政の組織及び運営に関する法律)，③がア(日本国憲法)，④がイ(教育基本法)，⑤がオ(学校教育法施行規則)による。

【3】(1)　X　abilities　　Y　communication　　(2)　①　ア　　②　ウ　③　イ　④　ク　⑤　キ
〈解説〉高等学校学習指導要領に関する問題は頻出しており，日本語版，英語版共に目を通しておきたい。その際には各科目の目標，内容，内容の取扱いに留意すること。本問はコミュニケーション英語Ⅰの内容についての空欄補充問題であるが，事前に学習指導要領を読み込んでおけば難しい問題ではない。これに加えて，ヨーロッパ言語共通参照枠(Common European Framework of Reference for Languages; CEF または CEFR)に関する問題も近年よく出題されるので，一読しておくこと。

【4】(1)　①　　(2)　④　　(3)　②　　(4)　①　　(5)　④　　(6)　③
(7)　③

〈解説〉(1)　countは「大切にする」という意味の動詞で，make it countは
直訳で「それを大事する」。ここでは「有意義なものにする」という
意味で考える。　(2)　wishに続く節中では仮定法を用い，wish＋仮定
法過去は，現在の事実とは反対の願望を表す。　(3)　so＋S＋Vは前述
の内容を確認，強調する表現で「全くだ，実際にそうだ」という意味。
(4)　in the sense that～「～という意味において」という表現である。
(5)　名詞節を作るwhateverは「～するものなら何でも」という意味。
provide A with Bは「AにBを与える」という意味の表現である。
(6)　空欄の前後の文の関係は逆接である。よって「にもかかわらず」
という意味のneverthelessが正解。real estateは「不動産」，property value
は「資産価値」という意味。　(7)　「その生徒のチームは先月結成さ
れたばかりであることを考えると，その成績は今のところ，優秀であ
る」とする。exceptional「優秀な，並外れた」。

【5】(1)　that's the way it goes.　　(2)　This will actually help me elevate my
concentration level since I no longer have to deal with all kinds of noise.
(3)　No one can be successful without making an effort.　　(4)　Could you
give her this phone number when you see her at work today?

〈解説〉(1)　解答例のthe way it goesは「世の中そういうもの，仕方ない」
という意味の口語表現。別解としてthe way it isも可。　(2)　下線部
「雑音がなくなり」を「私はあらゆる雑音を聞く必要がなくなったの
で」に，「これで～集中力が増すではないか」を「これが集中力を高
めるでしょう」と読みかえる。解答例のように無生物主語のthisを設
定し，help＋人＋do「人が～するのを助ける，役立つ」を用いるとよ
い。elevate my concentration levelの他に，concentrate more等の表現があ
る。　(3)　第2段落最終文より，初めての挑戦で，必ずしもすべてが
うまくいくわけではないという主旨が読み取れる。さらに最終段落2
文目で，「成功するには努力が欠かせない，たくさん失敗してこそ成

功がある」といったことが述べられている。これらのことを踏まえて簡潔に内容をまとめればよい。　(4)　5文目，6文目より，ミカが会いたがっている可能性があることとジョンの電話番号が提示されていることを踏まえて適切な文を作る。「ミカに電話番号を渡して，彼に電話するように言っていただけませんか」といった解答が考えられる。

【6】(1)　11　　(2)　14　　(3)　5

〈解説〉最初に各targetの共通項を考え，次にそれに合致したロゴを選べばよい。　(1)　目標は，災害等の経済損失を減らし，人々が安心して暮らせる持続可能な環境作り。　(2)　marineとoceanという単語に注目する。目標は，海洋生物を守るためにできることをするということ。(3)　discrimination，women，girlsという単語に注目する。目標は，性差別を無くすということ。

【7】(1)　a　86　　b　130　　(2)　X　polio　　Y　hepatitis B

〈解説〉(1)　空欄aには，2016年の間に世界でDTP3ワクチンを接種した幼児の割合をグラフから読み取って入れる。空欄bには，2016年までに接種率が90％を超えた国が何カ国かをグラフから読み取って入れる。(2)　空欄Xにはポリオ(polio)が入る。ポリオに関する説明の2文目から3文目にかけて「アフガニスタン，パキスタン，ナイジェリアを除くすべての国で，ポリオの感染が止まっている」を参照すること。空欄YにはB型肝炎(hepatitis B)が入る。B型肝炎に関する説明の3文目の「世界で，3回のワクチンの接種率は84％と推定される」を参照すること。

【8】(1)　参加者はジョークに対して5段階の採点をするよう求められる。それぞれのジョークについて，4と5をまとめて「おもしろい」の評価とし，それを読んだ人の何パーセントが「おもしろい」と思ったかでランク付けした。(100字)　(2)　age　　(3)　superiority　　(4)　ウ(5)　ア　little　　イ　playまたはappear

〈解説〉(1)　第1段落1文目から3文目までの内容をまとめる。　　(2)　30分でジグソーパズルを仕上げたことを自慢している男の話である。ジグソーパズルの箱に書かれていたfive to six yearsは「5年から6年完成させるのにかかる」という意味ではなく，「5歳から6歳用」という意味である。　　(3)　第5段落の1文目に「人は自分たちの方が相手より上だと感じた時に笑う」とあるので，同段落3文目にあるsuperiorityを入れて，「おもしろいジョークは読み手の中に優越感を創り出す」という意味にする。　　(4)　哲学者プラトンは，最終段落4文目，5文目より，笑いに対して好意的でなかったことを読み取って解答する。　　(5)　最終段落7文目で，プラトンは「喜劇を見に行く回数を制限すること，喜劇に出演しないこと」と言っている。as little as possibleは「できるだけ少なく」，appear in Aは「Aに出演する」という意味。

【9】(1)　教師と学習者の間のインタラクションは，「現実世界での同種の会話をひどくゆがめたバージョン(もの)」である，という結論。　(2)　例えば，学習者が土台にできるインタラクションの枠組みを提供することで，より知識のある熟達話者が，より知識の少ない初心者を援助するプロセス。　　(3)　イ　　(4)　open questions…可能な答えが複数あって詳述を誘うもの。　　closed questions…可能な答えがひとつに限られ，通常は簡単な1語の答えのもの。　　(5)　open question…Cathy decides not to quit her part-time job at the restaurant. Why do you think she keeps working?　　closed question…・Did Cathy stop working at the French restaurant?　　・What will Cathy make for her family?　から1つ

〈解説〉(1)　Study 6の項の第1段落最終文がThe researchers concludedから始まっていることに注目し，that以下からreal worldまでを解答とする。equivalentは「同等の物，相当物」という意味で，ここではinteractionを指す。　　(2)　Study 7の項の最終文のscaffolding refers to以下が解答となる。なおscaffoldingは「(建築現場等の)足場」という意味だが，近年，英語教育界で頻繁に使われるので知っておきたい概念である。　(3)　「普通，誰が宮殿に住んでいますか」という問いが入る位置を選

ぶ問題であるから，Kingsの前が適切。 (4) closed questionについてはStudy 8の項の2文目，open questionは3文目に詳しい内容が書かれている。 (5) 解答例の他にopen questionの具体例としては，Why do you think the chef has started to teach Cathy how to cook French dishes recently? 等が，closed questionとしては，Who spilled water on a customer's clothes? 等が考えられる。

2018年度　実施問題

【中学校】

【１】放送される指示に従い，答えなさい。

(Part 1)

(1)　　　　　　　　　(2)　　　　　　　　　(3)

(Part 2)

(1)　　　　　　　　　(2)　　　　　　　　　(3)

(Part 3)

(1)　　　　　　　　　(2)　　　　　　　　　(3)

(Part 4)

(1)　　　　　　　　　(2)　　　　　　　　　(3)

(☆☆☆☆◎◎◎◎)

【２】次の(1)～(20)の英文の(　　)にあてはまる最も適切な単語又は語句をそれぞれア～エから選び，記号で答えなさい。

(1)　Mike's boss charged him (　　) planning the office Christmas party.

　　ア　for　　　イ　with　　　ウ　into　　　エ　by

(2)　Rick's finger wouldn't stop (　　) after he cut it when he was chopping meat.

　　ア　bleeding　　イ　pretending　　ウ　figuring　　エ　wasting

(3) Wendy discovered that her daughter (   ) instant noodles every day since she started college.

　ア　is eating　　イ　had been eating　　ウ　will be eating

　エ　will have been eating

(4) During his trip to America, Henry chose not to stay in expensive hotels because his (   ) was quite small.

　ア　budget　　イ　remark　　ウ　shift　　エ　circuit

(5) Having (   ) Tokyo before, Allen knew how to get from the station to his hotel.

　ア　to visit　　イ　visiting　　ウ　been visited　　エ　visited

(6) Annie's boss found some problems in her presentation, so she had to (   ) it.

　ア　revise　　イ　persuade　　ウ　encounter　　エ　accompany

(7) When Tom visited Canada he was (   ) of having conversations with the people there.

　ア　incapable　　イ　ungrateful　　ウ　uninformed　　エ　invisible

(8) Many (   ) arrived in the United States to begin new lives in the 19th century.

　ア　substitutes　　イ　immigrants　　ウ　opponents

　エ　candidates

(9) The man was famous as a (   ) in the study of hydro power.

　ア　citizen　　イ　commuter　　ウ　pioneer　　エ　psychologist

(10) There is a (   ) among universities to move back to the center of the city to increase applicants.

　ア　tendency　　イ　circumstance　　ウ　foundation

　エ　proportion

(11) The (   ) of the enormous company caused thousands of people to lose their jobs.

　ア　necessity　　イ　accuracy　　ウ　compassion　　エ　collapse

(12) In order to determine if the medicine is effective, we have to do some

more (　　).

ア　expectations　　イ　explanations　　ウ　experiments

エ　extinction

(13)　A lot of people are not (　　) of the fact that they kill thousands of small insects when driving on a road.

ア　capable　　イ　deserving　　ウ　found　　エ　aware

(14)　The professor told us that the first student to work (　　) the math problem would be rewarded.

ア　in　　イ　out　　ウ　against　　エ　as

(15)　The manager must make sure that all the employees are (　　) during the disaster drill.

ア　stood up　　イ　accounted for　　ウ　added on

エ　looking after

(16)　We encourage you to (　　) us with any comments or questions about our program.

ア　collect　　イ　coordinate　　ウ　connect　　エ　contact

(17)　Japanese fruit is expensive, nevertheless the (　　) of it has grown in China.

ア　expression　　イ　preservation　　ウ　probability

エ　consumption

(18)　Harrison wants to get some exercise (　　) his stress.

ア　relieving　　イ　relieved　　ウ　to relieve

エ　having relieved

(19)　Bill tried everything he could think of to rebuild his office, but all his efforts were (　　).

ア　in spite　　イ　in charge　　ウ　in vain　　エ　in demand

(20)　Ted took an impressive picture showing the (　　) of Mt. Fuji in the lake.

ア　reflection　　イ　inspiration　　ウ　extinction　　エ　distinction

(☆☆☆○○○○○)

【3】 次の(1)～(10)の〔　　〕内の単語または語句を並べ替えてそれぞれ正しい英文を作るとき，(ア)と(イ)にあてはまる単語または語句をそれぞれ番号で答えなさい。ただし，英文のはじめにくる単語または語句の頭文字も小文字にしてある。

(1) 〔① has　② approved　③ drug　④ been　⑤ by　⑥ this〕
(　　)(　　)(ア)(　　)(イ)(　　) the U.S. Federal Government.

(2) 〔① new　② build　③ nuclear　④ contracted　⑤ a　⑥ to　⑦ plant〕
The construction company (　　)(ア)(　　)(　　)(イ)(　　)(　　).

(3) 〔① distinct　② have　③ his　④ no　⑤ of　⑥ impressions〕
I (　　)(　　)(ア)(　　)(イ)(　　) friend.

(4) 〔① of　② get　③ the shock　④ can't　⑤ over　⑥ their〕
The football team (　　)(　　)(ア)(　　)(イ)(　　) second-round defeat.

(5) 〔① nod　② slight　③ we　④ his　⑤ as　⑥ interpreted　⑦ consent〕
(　　)(ア)(　　)(　　)(イ)(　　)(　　).

(6) 〔① a permit　② obtain　③ must　④ enter　⑤ visitors　⑥ to〕
(　　)(ア)(　　)(　　)(イ)(　　) the school.

(7) 〔① out　② pointed　③ to　④ much　⑤ was　⑥ how　⑦ work　⑧ still〕
He (　　)(ア)(　　)(　　)(イ)(　　)(　　)(　　) be done.

(8) 〔① that　② had　③ made　④ an attack

⑤　reported　　⑥　been　　⑦　was〕

It (ア) ( ) ( ) ( ) ( ) (イ) ( ) on the embassy.

(9)〔①　stand　　②　smoking　　③　around　　④　can't

⑤　people　　⑥　me　　⑦　when〕

I ( ) (ア) ( ) ( ) ( ) ( ) (イ) I'm eating.

(10)〔①　you　　②　a visit　　③　come　　④　why　　⑤　this

⑥　for　　⑦　don't〕

( ) (ア) ( ) ( ) ( ) (イ) ( ) winter?

(☆☆☆☆○○○○)

【4】次の英文を読み，下の(1)～(4)の各問いに答えなさい。

A health checkup for a 500-year-old woman? Of course, no human being can live that long. The checkup is starting for "Mona Lisa," the picture drawn by Leonardo da Vinci early in the 16th century.

Every spring, staff at the Louvre checked the painting, and no big (①) had been found since 1961. The other day, (②), they said that it is in a ㋐'somewhat worrying' condition. The board ㋑(drew / painting / which / da Vinci / on / famous / the) has been warping over the years.

Da Vinci painted directly on a poplar board, not on a canvas, so the painting is easily damaged by the changes in its (③).

(④) the warps still do not seem to be very serious, but such valuable paintings must be protected ㋒at any cost. Imagine that the 'smile' worn by Mona Lisa might become (⑤)!

(朝日新聞「天声人語2004」より)

(1)　本文中の(①)～(⑤)にあてはまる最も適切な単語をそれぞれア～エから選び，記号で答えなさい。

①　ア　posture　　　イ　changes　　　ウ　spoil

　　エ　reserch

②　ア　eventually　　イ　whenever　　ウ　however

エ　actually

③　ア　environment　　イ　inconsistency　　ウ　encounter

　　エ　function

④　ア　Rarely　　　　　イ　Obviously　　　　ウ　Precisely

　　エ　Fortunately

⑤　ア　remade　　　　　イ　invisible　　　　 ウ　distorted

　　エ　managed

(2)　下線部㋐のようになった原因は何ですか。日本語で説明しなさい。

(3)　下線部㋑の(　　)内の単語を正しく並べ替えて書きなさい。

(4)　下線部㋒の英語を日本語にしなさい。

(☆☆☆○○○)

【5】次の英文を読み，あとの(1)〜(4)の各問いに答えなさい。

Peer Teaching, Peer Observation

　　In our teaching lives we are frequently observed by others. It starts on teacher training courses and goes on when academic coordinators, directors of study, or inspectors come into our class as part of some quality control exercise. In all these (　①　) the observed teacher is at a disadvantage since the observers ― however sympathetically they carry out their function ― have power over the teacher's future career.

　　Peer observation and peer teaching, on the other (　②　), involve colleagues ― who are equal ― watching and teaching together so that both may be helped in their understanding and practice.

　　There are various forms of peer teaching. In the first, two teachers hold a dialogue in front of the class about a language point, a text, or an (　③　) of culture. ⒶStudents gain from hearing different views on the same topic, and the participating teachers learn through their public interaction with each other. Sometimes two teachers can take different parts of the same lesson so that at one stage one might be acting as organiser and then observer, while the other plays the roles of prompter, and resource. At other points in the lesson one teacher could explain a grammar point before the other takes over to run a short (　④　) practice session.

　　A more formal way of organising peer teaching and observation is for two teachers to plan a lesson which one of them then teaches. ⑧After the lesson they both describe what happened to their joint plan and detail their experiences of the lesson. They can then discuss how it could be improved. For the next class the position is reversed.

　　As teachers most of us are understandably nervous about having other people observing our lessons. However, when we work with peers this nervousness is (　⑤　), and ⓒ(participant / develop / and / collaboration / each / the result / to / our / as / of / helps / teachers / as / people).

　　　　　　　　　(The Practice of English Language Teaching / Jeremy Harmer)

(1)　本文中の(　①　)〜(　⑤　)にあてはまる最も適切な単語をア〜キから選んで記号で答えなさい。ただし，1つの語は1度しか使えないものとする。

　　ア　controlled　　イ　motivation　　ウ　situations　　エ　aspect
　　オ　dissipated　　カ　financial　　キ　hand

(2)　下線部Ⓐ日本語にしなさい。

(3)　下線部Ⓑを日本語にしなさい。

(4)　下線部Ⓒの(　　)内の単語を，以下の日本語の内容に合うように並べ替えなさい。

　　　『こうした相互の授業観察は，お互いが教師として，また人間として成長することに役に立つでしょう。』

　　　　　　　　　　　　　　　　　　　　(☆☆☆☆○○○○)

【6】次の英文を読み，あとの(1)〜(7)の各問いに答えなさい。(本文には出題の都合上，省略した箇所及び改めた箇所がある。)

　　　[　Ⓐ　]　The last ice age ended 10,000 years ago, and we live in a warm period. That change had nothing to do with human activities. In the 1980s, however, some scientists warned that the Earth might be getting warmer as a result of human activities.

Since the Industrial Revolution in the 18th century, factories, power plants, cars, and farms have been polluting the air with greenhouse gases — carbon dioxide, methane, and so on. Scientists knew that, but the question was whether the Earth was actually getting warmer. [ア]

[Ⓑ] An IPCC (Intergovernmental Panel on Climate Change) report in 2001 says the trend toward a warmer world has begun. The IPCC looked into the data collected during the past 20 years on everything from the air and the sea to wildlife. They say ①(great / this / but / warming / has / slow / had / a / influence / steady) on the Earth.

Glaciers, including the famous snows of Kilimanjaro, are disappearing from the world's highest mountains. Coral reefs are dying off as the seas get too warm for them. Water (②) are common in parts of Asia and Africa. El Niño frequently brings about terrible weather in the eastern Pacific. The Arctic permafrost is starting to melt. Migration patterns for animals like white bears and whales are being (③). Now almost nobody questions the fact that humans are at least partly responsible.

According to the IPCC, worldwide temperatures will have increased between 1.4℃ and 5.8℃ by 2100. [イ] If the rise in temperature is larger, the result would be terrible.

With seas rising as much as 1 meter, vast areas with large (④), such as the Nile Delta and Bangladesh, would disappear under the sea. Agriculture would be badly damaged. [ウ]

Public (⑤) could suffer. Rising seas would pollute fresh water supplies with salt. Hot weather could lead to a rise in deaths from the heat. Warmer temperatures would allow mosquitoes, which carry malaria, to spread to the temperate zones.

Worst of all, this rise in temperature is happening at the fastest rate that the Earth has ever seen in the past 100 million years. Humans will have a hard time, but wildlife will no longer be able to survive. [エ]

In the temperate zones, warmer temperatures and increased CO_2 would make some crops flourish — at first. But beyond a rise of 1.5℃, there would be a dramatic turning point. After that, the U.S. harvest would start to decrease rapidly. Even if temperatures rose only moderately, scientists say, the climate might reach a "tipping point". It is a point at which even a little more increase (6)(into / would / change / throw / the / climate / a / dramatic).

One scientist points out that the CO_2 entering the air today will be there for a century. He says, "Even if we stabilize the amount of CO_2 emissions now, the gas in the air will have reached a fatal amount by the end of the 21st century. Temperatures will rise over the century."

　　　ⓒ　　　 The ongoing disruption of ecosystems and weather patterns is bad enough. But if (⑦) reached the IPCC's worst-case levels and stayed there for as long as 1,000 years, the vast ice fields in Greenland and Antarctica could melt down, raising the sea level more than 9 meters. Every city on the U.S. Eastern coast would be (⑧).

Now is the time to think about global warming seriously. It is too big a problem for one nation to solve. (9)The most important thing is that all nations should work (　) in (　). Without international cooperation, it will be impossible to reduce greenhouse gases in the air. 　オ　

　　　(GLOBAL WARMING IS HAPPENING Based on "LIFE IN THE GREENHOUSE" from *TIME*, April 9, 2001)

(1) 本文中の(②)(③)(④)(⑧)に入る最も適切な単語をそれぞれア～エから選び，記号で答えなさい。

　② ア　sufficiency　　イ　shortages　　　ウ　flaw
　　　エ　flood
　③ ア　disrupted　　　イ　discoursed　　　ウ　disclosed
　　　エ　disabled
　④ ア　disaster　　　　イ　circumstance　ウ　atomosphere
　　　エ　population
　⑧ ア　classic　　　　　イ　geography　　　ウ　history

272

エ　fluid

(2)　①と⑥の(　　)内の単語を，それぞれ正しく並べ替えて書きなさい。

(3)　本文中の(　⑤　)にあてはまる最も適切な単語を答えなさい。

(4)　次のⅠ，Ⅱのそれぞれの文が入るのに最も適切な箇所を本文中の $\boxed{\text{ア}}$ ～ $\boxed{\text{オ}}$ から選び，記号で答えなさい。

　Ⅰ　Hundreds of millions of people would have to move to other places.

　Ⅱ　That may not seem like much, but consider that the last ice age ended as a result of a 5℃ increase.

(5)　(　⑦　)にあてはまる最も適切な単語を本文中から探し，答えなさい。

(6)　下線部⑨の英文の(　　)に単語を入れ，「協力して」という意味を表しなさい。

(7)　以下の3つの英文はパラグラフの先頭である，Ⓐ，Ⓑ，Ⓒのいずれかに入る。本文の内容や前後のつながりを考えて，次のア～ウの中から最も適切なものをそれぞれ選びなさい。

　ア　That is no longer a question.

　イ　The Earth's climate does change.

　ウ　That could be truly terrible

(☆☆☆☆◎◎◎)

【7】次の(1)及び(2)の各問いに答えなさい。

(1)　「中学校学習指導要領」(平成20年3月告示)第2章第9節外国語2内容(1)言語活動ウ読むことの指導事項について，(　①　)～(　⑤　)にあてはまる最も適切な語句をあとのア～コの中から選び，記号で答えなさい。

　(ア)　文字や(　①　)を識別し，正しく読むこと。

　(イ)　書かれた内容を考えながら(　②　)したり，その内容が表現されるように音読すること。

　(ウ)　物語の(　③　)や説明文の大切な部分などを正確に読み取る

こと。

(エ)　伝言や手紙などの文章から書き手の(④)を理解し，適切に応じること。

(オ)　話の内容や書き手の意見などに対して感想を述べたり(⑤)やその理由を示したりなどすることができるよう，書かれた内容や考え方などをとらえること。

ア　賛否　　イ　文法　　　ウ　意向　　エ　反論　　オ　黙読
カ　同意　　キ　あらすじ　ク　符号　　ケ　音声　　コ　人物

(2)　「中学校学習指導要領」(平成20年3月告示)第2章第9節外国語(2)言語活動の取扱いについて，(①)～(⑤)にあてはまる最も適切な語句を下のア～コの中から選び，記号で答えなさい。

イ　生徒の学習段階を考慮して各学年の指導に当たっては，次のような点に配慮するものとする。

(ア)　第1学年における言語活動

小学校における(①)を通じて(②)を中心としたコミュニケーションに対する積極的な(③)などの一定の素地が育成されることを踏まえ，身近な言語の(④)や言語の働きに配慮した言語活動を行わせること。その際，自分の気持ちや身の回りの(⑤)などの中から簡単な表現を用いてコミュニケーションを図れるような話題を取り上げること。

ア　出来事　　イ　態度　　　　ウ　思考　　エ　習得
オ　音声面　　カ　外国語活動　キ　技能　　ク　使用場面
ケ　表理　　　コ　体験

(☆☆☆☆☆○○○○○)

【8】次の文章は鳥取県が平成29年3月に改訂した『鳥取県の「教育に関する大綱」第2編平成29年度重点取組施策』で示している，「学ぶ意欲を高める学校教育の推進」の⑦に記されている内容である。(①)～(⑨)にあてはまる最も適切な語句を答えなさい。(本文には出題の都合上，省略した箇所がある。)

274

（　①　）に対応した英語教育の推進

　（　①　）に対応した教育環境づくりや，次期学習指導要領の全面実施を見据え，（　②　）の充実など小学校の「英語」教科化等に対応する教員の（　③　）向上を図るほか，県内小学校5校に（　④　）を配置し，教員と連携した指導計画の作成や授業研究等にモデル的に取り組みます。

　また，子どもたちの（　⑤　）に対する興味・関心と英語による（　⑥　）を高めるため，海外留学・海外体験への支援のほか，海外（　⑦　）機関との交流を進めるとともに，とっとり（　⑧　）の活動などを通じて（　⑨　）な英語使用の機会の充実に努めます。

(☆☆☆☆◎◎◎◎)

【9】次の(1)～(4)の各問いに答えなさい。

(1)　絵の内容に合う英文になるように，次の（　①　）～（　④　）にあてはまる前置詞をあとの□□□の中から選び，それぞれ書きなさい。

There's a cover (　①　) the cake.
There's a cake (　②　) the table.

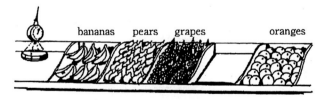

The bananas are (　③　) the pears.

The pears are (　④　) the bananas and the grapes.

in　　on　　beside　　behind　　between　　over　　under
up

(2) 中学校3年生の英語の授業において，「とても…なので〜することができなかった」という言い方の例文を3つ示すこととした。①〜③の語句を用いた例文を1つずつ書きなさい。(必要に応じて時制を変えてもよい。語数は問わない。)

①　can't 〜 because...

②　too...to 〜

③　so...that 〜

(3) 中学校3年生の英語の授業において，「Boxed Lunches or School Lunches?」というテーマでディベートに取り組ませたい。導入としてモデルとなる文例を提示する際，「弁当派」の意見としてどのような文例を提示するか。5文の英語で1つのモデルを書きなさい。(本文前後のあいさつ文は除く。語数は問わない。)

(4) 関係代名詞の2種類の用法(主格，目的格)を説明しようと考えたとき，どのような例文を提示するか，次の書き出しに続けて書きなさい。(語数は問わない。)

【主格(who)】　I (　　　).

【主格(which)】　Our ALT, Mr. Smith (　　　).

【目的格(that)】　This (　　　).

(☆☆☆◎◎◎)

276

【高等学校】

【1】放送される指示に従い，各問いに答えなさい。

(Part 1)

(1)　　　　　　　　　　(2)

(Part 2)

(1)　　　　　　(2)　　　　　　(3)

(Part 3)

(1)　　　　　　(2)　　　　　　(3)

(☆☆☆☆◎◎◎)

【2】次の(1)～(10)の英文の(　　)にあてはまる最も適切な単語又は語句を，それぞれ①～④の中から1つずつ選び，番号で答えなさい。

(1)　It's possible to predict students' success by (　　) from current exam scores.

①　assimilating　②　congregating　③　extrapolating

④　liquidating

(2)　The ABC company offers unique product (　　), easily lasting more than seven years under conditions of normal use.

①　critic　②　establishment　③　facility　④　durability

(3)　I was sure that we still had some eggs, but there are (　　) in the fridge.

①　any　②　no　③　none　④　nothing

(4)　Improvements to automated processes at XX factory made production efficient; (　　), quality was much improved.

① otherwise　　② likewise　　③ despite that

④ on the other hand

(5) We need some volunteers to assist taking children on the excursion next week. (　　) will be given to those who have previous experience and who are physically fit.

① Validity　　② Importance　　③ Priority　　④ Selection

(6) That Italian restaurant is now offering a dessert buffet in (　　) to suggestions from customers.

① order　　② response　　③ proportion　　④ opposition

(7) She cannot work long hours (　　) her children.

① in time for　　② on account of　　③ in keeping with

④ according to

(8) It is said that if local fishermen do not (　　) the number of fish they catch, certain species may disappear completely.

① think over for　　② make up for　　③ drop off on

④ cut back on

(9) As committee chairperson, Jack usually requires that members (　　) the agenda.

① stick to　　② take after　　③ run into　　④ chip in

(10) At the end of the book, it says, "Prices and numbers are (　　) to change without notice."

① emitted　　② adhere　　③ devoted　　④ subject

(☆☆☆◎◎◎◎)

【3】次の(1)～(5)の英文の(　　)内の単語又は語句を並べ替えて意味の通る英文にする場合，(　　)内で3番目と6番目にくる単語又は語句をそれぞれ番号で答えなさい。

(1) The weather forecast says (　① hitting Tokyo　　② no possibility　③ there　　④ the typhoon　　⑤ seems　　⑥ of　　⑦ to be).

Therefore, the international conference will be held as planned.

(2) I saw Kathy get hit by a car while crossing the street at an intersection.
You (① it ② a sight ③ hardly ④ terrible
⑤ imagine ⑥ was ⑦ how ⑧ can).

(3) A : Leave me alone, Dad. I can't (① on ② you ③ work
④ me ⑤ concentrate ⑥ watching ⑦ my
⑧ with).

B : Sorry. I just wanted to see if you needed any help.

(4) Muhammad Yunus once said, "My greatest challenge has been to change
the mindset of people. Mindsets play strange tricks on us. We see things
(① our minds ② instructed ③ way ④ to
⑤ have ⑥ the ⑦ see ⑧ our eyes)."

(5) A : Hey, look at the sign. It says, 'At no (① box ② be
③ this ④ unlocked ⑤ should ⑥ time
⑦ left).' Do you know what's inside?

B : No, but it must be something highly classified, for sure.

(☆☆☆◯◯◯)

【4】次の(1)～(3)の各問いに答えなさい。

(1) 次の文章の下線部①, ②を英語にしなさい。

・イギリス人男性はサッカーのことを驚くくらい率直に語ることが
ある。①奥さんを愛していると公の場で口にしたことがなくても,
サポートしているチームをどれだけ「愛している」かを語ること
はある。

(コリン・ジョイス著／森田浩之訳「*LONDON CALLING*」より抜粋)

・その哲学は, 完全そのものより, 完全を追及する過程により重き
を置くほどダイナミックなものであった。②不完全を完成させた
者のみが, 真の美を見出すことができる。

(岡倉天心著「茶の本」より抜粋)

(2) 次の英文の内容を端的に表現する小見出しを, 英語1文で作成し

279

なさい。

Now, you have no doubt heard the expression. "You are what you eat." A new study takes it one step further, suggesting you are what your mother ate before you were around. British scientists have discovered that higher calorie intake before a woman conceives is likely to produce a boy. A restrictive diet is likely to bring a girl. What's more, the research found women who eat breakfast cereal are more likely to have boys than women who skip the morning meal altogether.

(「やさしいCNN NEWS DIGEST Vol.3」(朝日出版社より抜粋)

(3)　次の指示に従って解答しなさい。

　田中先生は勤務する高校の修学旅行で生徒引率をしています。宿泊先の旅館で生徒と一緒に夕食を取っていると，大学生と思われる外国人の青年グループが少し離れたところで英語で騒々しく話をしています。すると，引率していた生徒Aさんから次のような声をかけられました。田中先生の立場になって，下の英会話中の下線部に次の【要件】を丁寧にお願いする表現を2～3文程度の英語で補いなさい。

> 【要件】ここは共有の場なので少し静かにして周りの人に配慮
> 　　　　してほしい

Student A　　　　: Mr. Tanaka, those people are being rather loud. They are not the only ones here. Please speak to them.

Mr. Tanaka　　　: Okay...Uh, excuse me, but are you foreign tourists?

Foreign guest A : Yes! This is our first experience to stay in a Japanese style *ryokan*. Everything is so gorgeous!

Mr. Tanaka　　　: Glad to hear you are enjoying Japan, but _____.

Foreign guest A : Oh, we are so sorry. We were just so excited to be here!

(「しごとの基礎英語 2017年5月号」NHK出版より抜粋，一部改編)

(☆☆☆◎◎◎)

【5】次の英文を読み，あとの(1)〜(5)の各問いに答えなさい。

One day, while I was playing with my new doll, Miss Sullivan put my big rag doll into my lap, spelled, "d-o-l-l" and tried to make me understand that "d-o-l-l" applied to both. Earlier in the day we had had a tussle over the words "m-u-g" and "w-a-t-e-r." Miss Sullivan had tried to impress upon me that "m-u-g" is *mug* and that "w-a-t-e-r" is *water*, but I persisted in confounding the two. In despair she had dropped the subject for the time, only to renew it at the first opportunity. I became impatient at her repeated attempts and, seizing the new doll, I dashed it upon the floor. I was keenly delighted when I felt the fragments of the broken doll at my feet. Neither sorrow nor regret followed my passionate outburst. I had not loved the doll. In the still, dark world in which I lived there was no strong sentiment or tenderness. I felt my teacher sweep the fragments to one side of the hearth and I had a sense of (①) that the cause of my discomfort was removed.

She brought me my hat, and I knew I was going out into the warm sunshine. This thought, if a wordless sensation may be called a thought, made me hop and skip with pleasure.

We walked down the path to the well-house, attracted by the fragrance of the honeysuckle with which it was covered. Some one was drawing water and my teacher placed my hand under the spout. As the cool stream gushed over one hand she spelled into the other the word *water*, first slowly, then rapidly. I stood still, my whole attention fixed upon the motions of her fingers. ②Suddenly I felt a misty consciousness as of something forgotten - a thrill of returning thought; and somehow the mystery of language was revealed to me. I knew then that "w-a-t-e-r" meant the wonderful cool something that was flowing over my hand. That living word awakened my soul, gave it light, hope, joy, set it free! There were barriers still, it is true, but barriers that could in time be swept away.

I left the well-house eager to learn. Everything had a (③), and each (③) gave birth to a new thought. As we returned to the house every object which I touched seemed to quiver with life. That was because I saw everything with the strange, new sight that had come to me. On entering the door I remembered the doll I had broken. I felt my way to the hearth and picked up the pieces. I tried vainly to put them together. ④Then my eyes filled with tears; for I realized what I had done, and for the first time I felt repentance and sorrow.

(Helen Keller「*The Story of My Life*」より抜粋，一部改編)

(1) この文章に描かれているSullivan先生の人柄を表すのに適切ではないものを，ア～エの中から1つ選び，記号で答えなさい。

　　ア　devoted　　イ　patient　　ウ　irresponsible　　エ　sincere

(2) （　①　）にあてはまる最も適切な語句を，ア～エの中から1つ選び，記号で答えなさい。

　　ア　regret　　イ　satisfaction　　ウ　duty　　エ　guilt

(3) 下線部②を日本語にしなさい。

(4) 本文の趣旨を踏まえて，（　③　）に共通して入る英単語一語を答えなさい。

(5) 筆者が下線部④のようになったのはなぜか。本文の内容に即して100字以内の日本語で具体的に説明しなさい。

(☆☆☆☆○○○)

【6】次の表は，CEFR(ヨーロッパ言語共通参照枠:Common European Framework of Reference for Languages)の共通参照レベルである。

　　あとの(1)，(2)の各問いに答えなさい。

Common Reference Levels : global scale

Proficient User	C2	Can understand with ease virtually everything heard or read. Can （　A　） information from different spoken and written sources, reconstructing arguments and accounts in a coherent presentation. Can express him/herself spontaneously, very fluently and precisely, differentiating finer shades of meaning even in more complex situations.
	C1	Can understand a wide range of demanding, longer texts, and recognise implicit meaning. Can express him/herself fluently and spontaneously without much obvious searching for expressions. Can use language flexibly and effectively （　①　）. Can produce clear, well-structured, detailed text on complex subjects, showing controlled use of organisational patterns, connectors and cohesive devices.

Independent User	B2	Can understand the main ideas of complex text on both concrete and abstract topics, including technical discussions (②). Can interact with a degree of fluency and spontaneity that makes regular interaction with native speakers quite possible without strain for either party. Can produce clear, detailed text on a wide range of subjects and (B) a viewpoint on a topical issue giving the advantages and disadvantages of various options.
	B1	Can understand the main points of clear standard input on familiar matters regularly encountered in work, school, leisure, etc. Can (C) most situations likely to arise whilst travelling in an area where the language is spoken. Can produce simple connected text on topics (③). Can describe experiences and events, dreams, hopes and ambitions and briefly give reasons and explanations for opinions and plans.
Basic User	A2	Can understand sentences and frequently used expressions (④) (e.g. very basic personal and family information, shopping, local geography, employment). Can (D) in simple and routine tasks requiring a simple and direct exchange of information on familiar and routine matters. Can describe in simple terms aspects of his/her background, immediate environment and matters in areas of immediate need.
	A1	Can understand and use familiar everyday expressions and very basic phrases aimed at the satisfaction of needs of a concrete type. Can (E) him/herself and others and can ask and answer questions (⑤) such as where he/she lives, people he/she knows and things he/she has. Can interact in a simple way provided the other person talks slowly and clearly and is prepared to help.

(CAMBRIDGE UNIVERSITY PRESS「*Common European Framework of Reference for Languages: Learning, teaching, assesment*」より抜粋)

(1) (A)～(E)にあてはまる単語又は語句の組み合わせとして最も適切なものを，ア～エの中から1つ選び，記号で答えなさい。

ア　A－deal with　　　　B－summarise
　　C－explain　　　　　D－introduce
　　E－communicate

イ　A－introduce　　　　B－deal with
　　C－explain　　　　　D－communicate
　　E－summarise

ウ　A－communicate　　 B－introduce
　　C－summarise　　　　D－deal with
　　E－explain

エ　A－summarise　　　　B－explain
　　C－deal with　　　　 D－communicate
　　E－introduce

(2) (①)～(⑤)にあてはまる語句の組み合わせとして最も適切なものを，カ～ケの中から1つ選び，記号で答えなさい。

カ　①－about personal details

②－related to areas of most immediate relevance

③－which are familiar or of personal interest

④－in his/her field of specialisation

⑤－for social, academic and professional purposes

キ　①－for social, academic and professional purposes

②－in his/her field of specialisation

③－which are familiar or of personal interest

④－related to areas of most immediate relevance

⑤－about personal details

ク　①－which are familiar or of personal interest

②－in his/her field of specialisation

③－related to areas of most immediate relevance

④－for social, academic and professional purposes

⑤－about personal details

ケ　①－related to areas of most immediate relevance

②－about personal details

③－for social, academic and professional purposes

④－in his/her field of specialisation

⑤－which are familiar or of personal interest

(☆☆☆☆☆○○○○○)

【7】次の英文を読み，あとの各問い答えなさい。

　　Motivation in second language learning is a complex phenomenon. It has been defined in terms of two factors: on the one hand, learners' communicative needs, and on the other, their attitudes towards the second language community. If learners need to speak the second language in a wide range of social situations or to fulfil professional ambitions, they will perceive the communicative value of the second language and are therefore likely to be motivated to acquire proficiency in it. Similarly, if learners have favourable attitudes towards the speakers of the language, they will desire more contact with them. Robert Gardner and Wallace Lambert (1972) coined the terms instrumental motivation (language learning for immediate or practical goals) and integrative motivation (language learning for personal growth and cultural enrichment through contact with speakers of the other language). For a long time integrative motivation was considered to be the stronger predictor of successful learning. In some contexts, however, instrumental motivation was found to be a better predictor. Thus, [①]. However, in some learning environments, it is difficult to distinguish between these two types of orientation to the target language and its community. Furthermore, early research tended to conceptualize motivation as a stable characteristic of the learner. More recent work emphasizes the dynamic nature of motivation and tries to account for the changes that take place over time.

Zoltán Dörnyei (2001a) developed a process-oriented model of motivation that consists of three phases. The first phase. '(X)choice motivation' refers to getting started and to setting goals, the second phase, '(Y)executive motivation', is about carrying out the necessary tasks to maintain motivation, and the third phase, '(Z)motivation retrospection', refers to students' appraisal of and reaction to their performance. An example of how one might cycle through these phases would be: a secondary school learner in Poland is excited about an upcoming trip to Spain and decides to take a Spanish course ([②]). After a few months of grammar lessons he becomes frustrated with the course, stops going to classes ([③]) and finally decides to drop the course. A week later a friend tells him about a great Spanish conversation course she is taking, and his 'choice motivation' is activated again. He decides to register in the conversation course and in just a few weeks he develops some basic Spanish conversational skills and a feeling of accomplishment. His satisfaction level is so positive ([④]) that he decides to enrol in a more advanced Spanish course when he returns from his trip to Spain.

(中略)

In a teacher's mind, motivated students are usually those who participate actively in class, express interest in the subject matter, and study a great deal. Teachers also have more influence on these behaviours and the motivation they represent than on students' reasons for studying the second language or their attitudes toward the language and its speakers. Teachers can make a positive contribution to students' motivation to learn if classrooms are places that students enjoy coming to because the content is interesting and relevant to their age and level of ability, the learning goals are challenging yet manageable and clear, and the atmosphere is supportive. Teachers must also keep in mind that cultural and age differences will determine the most appropriate ways for them to motivate students.

Little research has investigated how pedagogy interacts directly with motivation in second/foreign language classrooms. One exception is (あ)a study by Marie Guilloteaux and Zoltán Dörnyei (2008) who explored the links between teachers' motivational practice and students' motivation for L2 learning. It was a large-scale study with 27 teachers and over 1,300 learners in English as a Foreign Language (EFL) classrooms in Korea. The teachers' motivational strategies were described using a classroom observation scheme ― the Motivation Orientation of Language Teaching (MOLT). MOLT identified 25 motivational practices used by the teachers that were relatively easy to define and to observe. They were divided into four categories that are described below along with examples of the motivational behaviours included within each.

1　(　A　) : arousing curiosity or attention, promoting autonomy, stating communicative purpose/utility of activity.

2　(　B　) : group work/pair work

3　(　C　) : individual competition, team competition, intellectual challenge, tangible task product

4　(　D　) : effective praise, elicitation of self/peer correction session, class applause

In each lesson, the learners' motivation was measured in terms of their level of engagement. The proportion of students who paid attention, who actively participated, and who eagerly volunteered during activities was calculated. A three-level scale was used to measure engagement in each observed lesson: very low (a few students), low (one third to two thirds of the students) and high (more than two thirds of the students). Learners also completed a questionnaire about their motivation levels specifically related to their EFL class.

The researchers found significant positive correlations between the teachers' motivational practices, the learners' engagement behaviours, and the learners' self-reports on the questionnaire. The researchers acknowledge that correlation results do not indicate cause-effect relationships. Nevertheless, the findings are important because this is the first study to provide 'any empirical evidence concerning the concrete, classroom-specific impact of language teachers' motivational strategies' (Guilloteaux and Dörnyei 2008:72).

（Patsy M. Lightbown / Nina Spada「How Languages are Learned」より抜粋）

(1)　 ① にあてはまる最も適切な英文を，ア〜エの中から1つ選び，記号で答えなさい。

　ア　children learn thousands of words in their first language with little observable effort

　イ　children as well as adults are sensitive to social dynamics and power relationships

　ウ　both types of motivation have been found to be related to success in second language learning

　エ　second language learners are not always aware of their individual cognitive or perceptual learning styles

(2)　Zoltán Dörnyei氏の研究内容を参考に，（[　②　]）（[　③　]）（[　④　]）にあてはまる語句を下線部(X)(Y)(Z)から選び，それぞれ記号で答えなさい。

(3)　生徒が積極的に学習しようという気持ちを高める授業とはどのようなものと述べられているか，本文の内容に即して日本語で説明しなさい。

(4)　（　A　）～（　D　）にあてはまる最も適切な語句を，ア～エの中から選び，記号で答えなさい。

ア　Activity design

イ　Teacher discourse

ウ　Participation structure

エ　Encouraging positive retrospective self-evaluation and activity design

(5)　下線部(あ)の研究はどんな点で意義があると述べられているか，本文に即して日本語で説明しなさい。

(☆☆☆◎◎◎◎◎)

【8】アメリカ人の経営思想家が書いた次の英文を読み，あとの各問いに答えなさい。

The Evaluating scale will provide you with important insights into how to give effective performance appraisals and negative feedback in different parts of the world. People from all cultures believe in "constructive criticism." Yet what is considered constructive in one culture may be viewed as destructive in another. Getting negative feedback right can motivate your employees and strengthen your reputation as a fair and professional colleague. Getting it wrong can demoralize an entire team and earn you an undeserved reputation as an unfeeling (あ)tyrant or a hopelessly incompetent manager.

（　A　）

One Thursday in mid-January, I had been (い)holed up for six hours in a dark conference room with twelve people participating in my executive education program. It was a group coaching day, and each executive had thirty minutes to describe in detail a cross-cultural challenge she was experiencing at work and to get feedback and suggestions from the others at the table. The details of each person's situation were steeped in context, and I was beginning to get a headache from concentrating on the ins and outs of each challenge. We had made it through nine people and were just beginning with Willem, number ten.

Willem was a rather shy manager from the Netherlands, and, given his quiet persona, it struck me as unusual that he was a sales director. He had grey, slightly disheveled hair and a very friendly smile that made me think of a lovable St. Bernard. Willem's situation involved an American woman on his team who would call into team meetings while driving her children to school, a necessity given the six-hour time difference between her home in the eastern United States and Rotterdam. When Willem spoke to her about the distraction of screaming kids in the background and asked her to find a better solution, she took offense. "How can I fix this relationship?" Willem asked the group.

Maarten, the other Dutch member from the same company who knew Willem well, quickly jumped in with his perspective. "You are inflexible and can be socially ill-at-ease. That makes it difficult for you to communicate with your team," he reflected. As Willem listened, I could see his ears turning red (with embarrassment or anger? I wasn't sure), but that didn't seem to bother Maarten, who calmly continued to assess Willem's weaknesses in front of the entire group. Meanwhile, the other participants-all Americans-awkwardly stared at their feet. Afterward, several of them came up to me to say how inappropriate they'd found Maarten's comments.

For that evening, we'd planned a group dinner at a (う)<u>cozy</u> restaurant in the French countryside. Entering a little after the others, I (え)<u>was startled</u> to see Willem and Maarten sitting together, eating peanuts, drinking champagne, and laughing like old friends. They waved me over, and it seemed appropriate to comment, "I'm glad to see you together. I was afraid you might not be speaking to each other after the feedback session this afternoon." Willem stared at me in genuine surprise. So I clarified, "You looked upset when Maarten was giving his feedback. But maybe I misread the situation?"

Willem reflected, "Of course, I didn't *enjoy* hearing those things about myself. It doesn't feet good to hear what I have done poorly. But I so much appreciated that Maarten would be transparent enough to give me that feedback honestly. Feedback like that is a gift. Thanks for that, Maarten," he added with an appreciative smile.

I thought to myself, "①<u>This Dutch culture is ... well... *different* from my own</u>."

There has surely been a time when you were on the receiving end of criticism that was just too direct. You finished an important project and after asking a colleague for feedback, she told you it was "totally unprofessional." Or maybe a member of your team critiqued a grant proposal you wrote by calling it "ridiculously ineffective." You probably found this incident extremely painful; you may have felt this colleague was arrogant, and it's likely you rejected the advice offered. You may have developed a strong sense of distaste for this person that lingers to this day.

You may have also experienced the opposite-feedback that was far too indirect at a time when an honest assessment of your work would have been very valuable. Perhaps you asked a colleague for her thoughts about a project and were told, "Overall it's good. Some parts are great, and I particularly liked certain sections." Maybe she then noted that there were just a few very minor details that you might consider adjusting a bit, using phrases like ②<u>"no big deal" and "just a very small thought</u>." that left you thinking your work was nearly perfect.

If you later learned through the office grapevine that this same colleague had ridiculed your project behind your back as "the worst she'd seen in years," you probably were not very pleased. You likely felt a deep sense of betrayal leading to a lasting feeling of mistrust toward your colleague, now exposed in your eyes as a liar or a (a).

Arrogance and dishonesty do exist, of course. There are even times when people give offense deliberately in pursuit of political objectives or in response to personal emotional problems. But ③<u>in some cases, painful incidents like the ones just described are the result of cross-cultural misunderstandings</u>. Managers in different parts of the world are conditioned to give feedback in drastically different ways. The Chinese manager learns never to criticize a colleague openly or in front of others, while the Dutch manager learns always to be honest and to give the message straight. Americans are trained to wrap positive messages around negative ones, while the French are trained to criticize passionately and provide positive feedback (お)<u>sparingly</u>,.

Having a clear understanding of these differences and strategies for navigating them is crucial for leaders of cross-cultural teams.

UPGRADERS, DOWNGRADERS, AND THE ART OF TRANSLATION

One way to begin gauging how a culture handles negative feedback is by listening carefully to the types of words people use. More direct cultures tend to use what linguists call *upgraders*, words preceding or following negative feedback that make it feel stronger, such as *absolutely*, *totally*, or *strongly*: "This is *absolutely* inappropriate," or "This is *totally* unprofessional."

By contrast, more indirect cultures use more *downgraders*, words that soften the criticism, such as *kind of*, *sort of*, *a little*, *a bit*, *maybe*, and *slightly*. Another type of downgrader is a deliberate understatement, a sentence that describes a feeling the speaker experiences strongly in terms that moderate the emotion-for example, saying "We are not quite there yet" when you really mean "This is nowhere close to complete," or "This is just my opinion" when you really mean "Anyone who considers this issue will immediately agree."

(Erin Meyer「THE CULTURE MAP」より抜粋)

(1)　下線部(あ)～(お)の本文中の意味に最も近い語や表現を，それぞれア～エの中から1つずつ選び，記号で答えなさい。

　(あ)　ア　someone who is controlled by someone or something

  イ the person in charge of governing a country that is under the political control

  ウ the person who has the highest position in a company or organization

  エ a ruler who has complete power and uses it in a cruel and unfair way

(い) ア concerned イ discussed ウ pursued

   エ hidden

(う) ア popular and famous イ warm and comfortable

   ウ noisy and crowded エ exclusive or excellent

(え) ア was surprised イ was willing ウ happened

   エ expected

(お) ア very carefully イ very seriously

   ウ in small quantities エ in a discouraging situation

(2) 下線部①について，何と何がどう異なっているのか，具体的に日本語で説明しなさい。

(3) 下線部②は，"upgraders" と "downgraders" のどちらに分類されるか答えなさい。

(4) (a)にあてはまる最も適切な語を，ア～エの中から1つ選び，記号で答えなさい。

  ア hypocrite イ optimist ウ pessimist エ compatriot

(5) なぜ下線部③のようになるのか，本文の内容に即して日本語で説明しなさい。

(6) (A)にあてはまる最も適切な見出しを，ア～エの中から1つ選び，記号で答えなさい。

  ア SPEAKING FRANKLY: A NEEDLE OR A KNIFE IN THE CASE?

  イ SPEAKING FRANKLY: A GIFT OR A SLAP IN THE FACE?

  ウ SPEAKING FRANKLY: TWO STYLES OF REASONING STRATEGIES

  エ SPEAKING FRANKLY: AN AMERICAN APPROACH TO THE

EVALUATING SCALE

(7) 本文の内容と一致するものを，ア～オの中から1つ選び，記号で
答えなさい。

ア　Constructive criticism can make your employees work harder and give
you a good reputation.

イ　When the author heard Willem talk about his cross-cultural challenge,
one of the executives gave very direct feedback and made him angry.

ウ　Giving negative feedback in honest ways always causes awful and
painful incidents in Europe.

エ　To use vocabulary that softens the criticism is the only way people
handle negative feedback well in indirect cultures.

オ　The first simple strategy for giving negative feedback to someone is
that you should give feedback to an individual in front of a group.

(☆☆☆☆○○○○)

解答・解説

【中学校】

【１】Part 1 (1) D　(2) D　(3) A　Part 2 (1) B　(2) A
(3) B　Part 3 (1) A　(2) C　(3) C　Part 4 (1) C
(2) D　(3) C

〈解説〉スクリプトは公表されていない。Part1は提示されている写真に
ついて，適切な説明文を選択する問題と思われる。放送前に写真をよ
く見て，「だれが」「何をしている」情景なのか正確に把握しておきた
い。Part 2 からPart 4までは，解答の選択肢を含めた聞き取りが必要な
ので，より集中して臨む必要がある。特に放送が1回のみの場合は，
聞き取れない箇所があるとあわててしまい，それ以後の放送内容を聞
き逃してしまいがちである。あわてずに放送内容の全体像を把握し，

聞き取れない箇所は前後の文脈から判断して解答できるよう，日頃から市販のリスニング教材などを活用して訓練しておくこと。

【2】(1)　イ　　　(2)　ア　　　(3)　イ　　　(4)　ア　　　(5)　エ　　　(6)　ア
(7)　ア　　　(8)　イ　　　(9)　ウ　　　(10)　ア　　　(11)　エ　　　(12)　ウ
(13)　エ　　　(14)　イ　　　(15)　イ　　　(16)　エ　　　(17)　エ
(18)　ウ　　　(19)　ウ　　　(20)　ア

〈解説〉(1)　charge A with Bは，「AにBを負わせる」という意味の表現。
(2)　bleedは「出血する」という意味の単語。bleedは過去形・過去分詞がbledになることも含めて押さえておこう。　(3)　since she started college (大学に入ってから)と起点を表す表現があることから，継続を表す表現が入ることが推測できる。選択肢のうち，過去のある時点から「ウェンディが発見した(Wendy discovered)」という過去の時点までの継続を表す表現は過去完了を表すイのみである。　(4)　「少ない(small) ために高いホテルに泊まらないと決めた」とあるため，アのbudget「予算，生活費」が適切である。　(5)　分詞構文を用いた過去の表現を扱った問題。分詞になっている部分を普通の文に直すと，"(As/Since) Allen has (　　) Tokyo before"となる。したがって，過去分詞であるエのvisitedが適切である。　(6)　「発表に問題が見つかったため行う必要があるもの」として選択肢のうち適切なのは，アのrevise「修正する，訂正する」である。　(7)　be capable/incapable of doingは「～することができる/できない」という意味の表現である。
(8)　「アメリカにたどり着き新しい生活を始める人」として選択肢のうち適切なのは，イのimmigrants「移民」である。　(9)　水力発電(hydro power) の研究分野にいる人として選択肢のうち適切なのは，ウのpioneer「先駆者」である。　(10)　アのtendencyはto不定詞をとって「～する傾向」という意味の名詞句をつくる。　(11)　「たくさんの人々が職を失うきっかけとなるもの」として選択肢のうち適切なものは，エのcollapse「崩壊，破綻」である。　(12)　「薬が効果のあるものかどうかを決めるために行うもの」として選択肢のうち適切なもの

はウのexperiment(s)「実験」である。 (13) be aware of Aは「Aに気づいている」という意味の表現である。 (14) work outは「(問題など) を解く」という意味の表現である。 (15) account for Aは「Aの行方を確認する，Aの行動を把握している」という意味で使用されている。account自体は自動詞であるため受け身(受動態) にできないが，ここではaccount for全体で目的語をとる句動詞であるため受け身となっている。 (16) contactは「〜と連絡をとる」という意味の表現である。ここでは，「番組に関するコメントや質問とともに私たちに連絡する」→「番組に関するコメントや質問を私たちに寄せる」という意味で用いられている。 (17) 「果物が高いにもかかわらず増加している」という文脈に即しているのは，選択肢のうちエのconsumption「消費」である。 (18) 空欄の箇所は運動(some exercise) をする目的を述べている。したがって，目的を表す用法を有するto不定詞であるウが適切である。 (19) in vainは「(苦労などが) むだな，骨折り損の」という意味の表現である。 (20) 問題文の文意は「湖の中に富士山の何かが写っている写真を撮った」なので，文脈から判断すると，アのreflection「反射，(鏡や水面などに)映った姿」が最も適切である。

【3】(1) ア ① イ ② (2) ア ⑥ イ ① (3) ア ①
イ ⑤ (4) ア ⑤ イ ① (5) ア ⑥ イ ①
(6) ア ③ イ ⑥ (7) ア ① イ ⑦ (8) ア ⑦
イ ⑥ (9) ア ① イ ⑦ (10) ア ⑦ イ ②
〈解説〉(1) 並べ替え後の全文は，This drug has been approved by the U.S. Federal Government.となる。approveは「認可する」という意味の動詞である。「この薬は合衆国連邦政府によって認可されている」。

(2) 並べ替え後の全文は，The construction company contracted to build a new nuclear plant. となる。nuclear plantは「原子力発電所」の意味。plantには「植物」のほかに「装置，(製造) 工場」という意味もあり，要注意である。「その建築会社は新しい原子力発電所を建設する契約を結んだ」。 (3) 並べ替え後の全文は，I have no distinct impressions

of his friend. となる。distinctはdistinguish「はっきり区別する，目立つ」という動詞の形容詞形であり，「はっきりとした，まったく別の」という意味がある。「私は彼の友達についてはっきりとした印象を持っていない」。　(4)　並べ替え後の全文は，The football team can't get over the shock of their second-round defeat. となる。get overは「(困難や障害などから) 回復する，立ち直る」という意味の表現である。footballは，アメリカではアメリカンフットボールを指すが，その他の国では主にサッカーを指すことも併せて押さえておきたい。「そのサッカー [フットボール]チームは，2回戦の敗北のショックから立ち直れない」。

(5)　並べ替え後の全文は，We interpreted his slight nod as consent. となる。「私たちは，彼のかすかなうなずきを承諾の意に解した」の意味。interpret A as Bは「AをBとみなす[理解する]」という意味の表現。類似の表現としては，regard A as B, take A for B, think A B, consider A Bなどがある。それぞれの動詞でとりうる形が異なることも含め押さえておくとよい。　(6)　並べ替え後の全文は，Visitors must obtain a permit to enter the school. となる。enterは「〜へ入る」という意味の他動詞であるため，後ろに直接目的語をとることに注意。permitは名詞として「許可書，免許証」という意味がある。「訪問者は学校に入るために許可書を入手しなければならない」。　(7)　並べ替え後の全文は，He pointed out how much work was still to be done. となる。point outは「指摘する」という意味の表現。be動詞＋to不定詞は，予定や義務，可能，運命，意図を表す。「彼は，するべき仕事がまだどれくらいあるのかを指摘した」。　(8)　並べ替え後の全文は，It was reported that an attack had been made on the embassy. となる。make an attack on Aは「Aに攻撃を加える」という意味の表現で，ここでは過去完了の受動態となっている。「大使館が攻撃を受けているということが報告された」。

(9)　並べ替え後の全文は，I can't stand people around me smoking when I'm eating. となる。standは他動詞として「〜を我慢する」という意味があり，通例否定文や疑問文で用いられる。ここではpeople around meはsmokingの意味上の主語であり，「私の周囲にいる人がタバコを吸う

こと」という名詞句となっている。「私は，自分が食べているときに周りの人がタバコを吸うことが我慢できない」。 (10) 並べ替え後の全文は，Why don't you come for a visit this winter ? となる。why don't you〜は「〜しない？」と相手に提案や勧誘をするときに用いられる定型表現である。親しい間柄の人の間で使い，目上の人には用いないことも併せて押さえておこう。visitは名詞として「訪問」の意味がある。「今度の冬に訪ねて来ない？」。

【4】(1) ① イ ② ウ ③ ア ④ エ ⑤ ウ
(2) ダ・ヴィンチが，キャンバスではなく，ポプラ板に直接モナリザを描いたから。 (3) on which da Vinci drew the famous painting
(4) どんな犠牲を払ってでも

〈解説〉(1) ① 空欄に入る語は，モナ・リザのチェックを行った結果見つからなかったものであるため，選択肢のうちで適切なものは，イのchanges「変化」となる。 ② 空欄のある文ではモナ・リザがやっかいな状態にあると述べられており，前の文の内容とは逆説の関係となっているため，ウのhowever「しかし」が適切である。 ③ 空欄のある文では，モナ・リザがキャンバスではなくポプラ材の板の(poplar board) 上に描かれているという絵の置かれた状況と，それが原因で絵がダメージを受けやすいということが述べられているため，アのenvironment「環境」が適切である。 ④ 空欄のある文で，ゆがみはまだ非常に重大であるようにはみられないが，このような価値ある絵は守られなければならないと述べられており，エのFortunately「幸いにも」が最も適切である。 ⑤ 最後の1文は，このままではモナ・リザのほほえみがゆがんだ(warped) 状態になる可能性を読者に想像させている。したがって，warpedと同じ意味をもつウのdistortedを選べばよい。 (2) Da Vinci paintedから始まる1文で，ポプラ板にモナ・リザを描いたことでダメージを受けやすくなっていることが記述されており，ここが下線部⑦の理由である。 (3) 目的格を表す関係代名詞whichが前置詞onとともに先行詞であるthe boardの後ろに来た形

である。このような文法現象を随伴 (pied piping) という。　(4)　at any costと同様の意味を表す表現としてat all costsやwhatever the costがある。costの単複がそれぞれ異なることに注意。

【5】(1)　①　ウ　　②　キ　　③　エ　　④　ア　　⑤　オ
(2)　生徒は同じ話題に関する異なる意見を聞くことで学ぶことができるし，教師も公開された対話を通してお互いに学びあうことができる。
(3)　授業後，両方の教師が一緒に計画した授業でどのようなことが起こったか，そして授業中に経験したことについて詳述する。
(4)　the result of our collaboration helps each participant to develop as teachers and as people

〈解説〉(1)　①　選択肢のうち，空欄より前に取り上げられている事柄をまとめて指しうる語はウのsituations「状況」しかない。　②　on the other handは「他方では」という意味の表現。　③　選択肢のうち，文化に関してクラスの前で扱うことができるのは文化の側面 (aspect) である。また，空欄の前の不定冠詞がanであることから，空欄には母音で始まる語，つまりaspectが入ることがわかる。　④　空欄は，一方の教師が文法の説明をした後に他の教師が引き継いで行う練習の時間を説明する語が入る。選択肢のうち，この文脈で最も適切なものはアのcontrolled「管理された，統制された」である。　⑤　他の教師に授業を見せることで生じる緊張がピア(同僚) による観察の場合はどのようになるかが空欄に入る。選択肢のうち最も適切なのは，オのdissipated「(気持ちなどが) 晴れた」である。dissipateには，「(霧や気持ちなどを)晴らす」という意味がある。　(2)　当該の文を構成する単語や文法は複雑ではないため，"different views on the same topic"「同じ話題に関する異なる意見」や"learn through their public interaction with each other"「公開されたやり取りを通してお互いに学ぶ」といった名詞句や副詞句の意味を丁寧に日本語訳に反映させることが重要である。　(3)　(2)と同様に，使用される単語や文法は難しくないため，文法関係や修飾関係をしっかり日本語訳に反映させることが重要であ

る。detailには，「詳細な」という形容詞としての用法のほかに，「詳細に述べる」という動詞の用法もあることは押さえておくとよい。

(4) このような並べ替えの和文英訳問題は日本語訳を逐一反映させようとすると解くのが難しいため，英単語同士で句を作り，意訳をしていくとよい。たとえば，the resultはofと共起しやすい単語であるため，the result of our collaborationという名詞句を作ったり，helpに3人称単数のsが付いていることから文の中心的な構造をhelp A do「Aが〜するのを助ける」であると推察したりすることから始めるとスムーズに並べ替えられる。

【6】(1) ②　イ　　③　ア　　④　エ　　⑧　ウ　　(2) ①　this slow but steady warming has had a great influence　　⑥　would throw the climate into a dramatic change　　(3) ⑤　health　　(4) Ⅰ　ウ　　Ⅱ　イ　　(5) ⑦　temperatures　　(6) ⑨　(　hand　) in (　hand　)　　(7) Ⓐ　イ　　Ⓑ　ア　　Ⓒ　ウ

〈解説〉(1) ②　第4段落では，温暖化によって引き起こされている世界各地の現象が述べられている。選択肢の中でアジアやアフリカで起こっており，かつwaterと共起した現象を表すのはイのshortagesである。water shortageは「水不足」の意味。　③　空欄がある文は，②と同じく温暖化による現象の1つを述べている。動物の移動の型の変化を表すものとして選択肢のうち適切なものは，アのdisrupted「崩壊した，乱された」である。　④　空欄を含む "vast areas with large (　　)" の具体例としてナイル川デルタやバングラデシュといった河口付近の地域を挙げている。したがって，選択肢のうち適切なものは，エのpopulations「人口」である。　⑧　空欄は，もし海面が9メートル以上上昇した場合にアメリカの東海岸の街が陥る状態を述べている。選択肢のうち適切なものは，ウのhistory「歴史，過去のもの」である。

(2) ①　butは対立する語や句，節などを結び付ける等位接続詞である。並べ替える単語のうち，動詞が1つであることやwarmingとinfluenceが対立する概念でないことから，対立する語は形容詞である

ことがわかる。influenceは通常不可算名詞扱いであるため不定冠詞はつかないが，greatやenormousといった形容詞に修飾されると不定冠詞がつく。have influence on Aは「Aに影響を与える」という意味の表現である。以上のことを踏まえて並べ替えると解答が得られる。

⑥　throw A into Bは「AをBに陥れる」という意味の表現である。

(3)　空欄⑤を含む文の段落では，海面の上昇により真水が塩害を受けること，高温のため死者が増加すること，マラリアを媒介する蚊が広く繁殖することなど，公衆衛生に関して述べられている。このことから，空欄に入る単語として最も適切なものは，healthである。public healthは「公衆衛生」を意味する。　(4)　Ⅰの意味は「数百万人が他の地域に引っ越さなければならないだろう」。空欄ウを含む第6段落ではWith seas rising以下で，「海面の上昇によって人口の多い河口地域が海に沈む」と述べている。よって，Ⅰはウが適切であるといえる。また，Ⅱの意味は「たいした差ではないように思えるだろうが，気温が5℃上昇しただけで氷河期が終わったことに注意しなければならない」。具体的に上昇している気温の程度に触れているのは，第5段落のAccording to the IPCC以下である。このため，Ⅱはイが適切であるといえる。　(5)　第3段落の2文目The IPCC looked into以下，「IPCCが大気と海から，あるもののデータを収集している」こと，また第11段落では「あるものが，もしIPCCの想定する最悪レベルの状態で1000年間続いた場合，グリーンランドや南極大陸の氷が溶けてしまう」と述べていることから，空欄に入る単語として最も適切なものは，temperaturesである。　(6)　hand in handには，お互いが手を取り合って何かを行うという意味がある。hand in handと同様に同じ単語を繰り返し用いて「協力して」という意味になる表現としてshoulder to shoulderがある。

(7)　Ⓐ　空欄に続く文で，「1万年前に氷河期が終わり温暖な時期に変わった」ことが述べられている。またこの段落全体を通して，気候の変化(温暖化)が取り上げられている。これらのことから，選択肢のうち適切なものはイの"The Earth's climate does change"「地球の気候は変化する」であるといえる。　Ⓑ　第2段落2文目のbut the question was以

下で提示された問い (地球は暖かくなっているのか？) の答えが，続く
第3段落では前提とされており，いつ暖かくなり始めたかについて述
べられている。このことから，選択肢のうち適切なものはアの "That
is no longer a question." 「それは疑問の余地がない」であるといえる。
ⓒ　第10段落では，「今日大気中に放出された二酸化炭素は，今後1世
紀の間大気中に留まり続ける」というある科学者の言葉を取り上げて
いる。続く第11段落では，「現在進行している生態系と気候の崩壊が
十分深刻なのに，さらに悪い状況が1000年ほど続いたらどのようなこ
とが起こるか」について述べてられている。このことを踏まえると，
選択肢のうち適切なものはウの "That could be truly terrible." 「それは
非常に恐ろしいことになるだろう」であるといえる。

【7】(1)　①　ク　　②　オ　　③　キ　　④　ウ　　⑤　ア
(2)　①　カ　　②　オ　　③　イ　　④　ク　　⑤　ア
〈解説〉中学校学習指導要領および同解説外国語編については，内容をし
っかり理解した上で暗記しておくことが重要である。また，現行の学
習指導要領とその解説のみならず，学習評価や平成29年3月告示の新
学習指導要領，新旧対応表にも目を通しておくことが望ましい。

【8】①　グローバル化　　②　教員研修　　③　指導力　　④　外国語
指導助手(ALT)　　⑤　外国　　⑥　コミュニケーション能力
⑦　高等教育　　⑧　イングリッシュクラブ　　⑨　実践的
〈解説〉「鳥取県の『教育に関する大綱』」とは，鳥取県の教育や学術，文
化の振興に関する総合的な施策の目標と方針を明らかにするために定
められたものである。次期学習指導要領の内容を踏まえ，平成29年3
月に改訂された。鳥取県の教職員を目指すのであるから，国の施策だ
けでなく県独自の教育施策等についても理解しておく必要がある。日
頃から県のホームページ等を確認し，どのような動きがあるのか把握
しておくこと。

【9】(1)　①　over　　②　on　　③　beside　　④　between

(2)　①　I couldn't buy these shoes because they were too expensive.
②　It's too cold to go swimming.　　③　She was so tired that she couldn't study at all last night.　　(3)　・I believe that boxed lunches are better for us Jr. high school students.　・Let me explain two reasons.　・First, we don't have to eat things we don't like.　　・Second, we can eat as much as we want.　　・So, if we have boxed lunches, we are able to enjoy lunch more.　　(4)　【主格(who)】　I (have a friend who lives in Okinawa).　【主格(which)】　Our ALT, Mr. Smith (visited a temple which was built a long time ago).　　【目的格(that)】　This (is the bag that my mother gave me on my birthday).

〈解説〉(1)　4問とも基本的な前置詞の違いを問うている。基礎的な部分であるがゆえに使い分けについてあいまいにしたままになっている場合があるため，文法書や辞書等で前置詞のコアとなるイメージを確認することをおすすめする。　(2)　生徒への指導を意識した例文作成を心がけよう。具体的には，中学3年生までに既習であろう語彙のみを用いること，生徒にとって身近な状況を描写すること，教科書や辞書を調べずとも目標とする表現の意味を分かりやすくすることなどが挙げられる。　(3)　ディベートのスピーチは，最初に自分の主張を述べ，その後に主張をサポートする理由を述べるのが基本である。したがって，最初に弁当の方がいい理由を述べた後に，その理由を述べる流れを展開するとよい。　(4)　whoとwhichの場合は，人か物かによって使い分ける必要があることを生徒に理解してもらう必要がある。そのため，whichを使った文では，先行詞を建物や道具などのような無生物にするといった工夫が考えられる。

【高等学校】

【1】Part 1　(1)　A　　(2)　C　　Part 2　(1)　D　　(2)　C　　(3)　B
Part 3　(1)　B　　(2)　D　　(3)　B
〈解説〉スクリプトは公表されていないが，一般的なリスニングのポイン

トとして「数字」,「場所」,「だれが何をしたか」を正確に聞き取ることが挙げられる。Part1は写真の状況を最も適切に表す選択肢を選ぶ問題と考えられる。(1)は食器棚に収納された食器類であり,(2)は浜辺を走っている4人家族である。静物の場合は物の名称・個数・位置関係,人物や動物の場合は動作主の名称・どんな動作をしているか・背景には何があるかなどを短時間で把握できるよう,日頃から練習しておく必要がある。Part 2 およびPart 3は,設問も選択肢も聞き取らなければならない。もし放送が1回のみの場合は,何が問われているか全体を理解することに集中し,聞き取れなかった箇所は前後の文脈から判断して正答できるよう努めよう。聞き取れなかった箇所にこだわるあまり,それ以後の放送内容を聞き逃してしまうことは避けたい。

【2】(1) ③ (2) ④ (3) ③ (4) ② (5) ③ (6) ②
(7) ② (8) ④ (9) ① (10) ④
〈解説〉(1) 「生徒の成績をもとに生徒の成功を予測するために行うこと」として選択肢のうち適切なものは,③のextrapolating (extrapolate)「(未知の事柄を) 既知の事柄から推定する」である。 (2) 「普通に使えば7年以上も長続きするもの」という文脈において選択肢のうち適切なものは,④durability「耐久性」である。"The ABC company offers unique product durability" は「ABC社は他に類を見ない製品の耐久性を提供する」ということ。 (3) 選択肢のうち,1語で「少しもない」ことを表せるのは③のnoneのみである。②のnoは,no＋名詞の形であれば適切。 (4) 文の前半と後半の両方で,生産が良くなったことを述べている。選択肢のうち先行する文や節を受けて同じであることを表すのは,②のlikewise「同様に」である。 (5) 「子どもたちの遠足の引率を補助するボランティアの募集で,経験者や身体健康な者に与えられるもの」として選択肢のうち適切なものは,③のPriority「優先(権)」である。give priority to Aは「Aを優先する」という意味の表現である。 (6) in response to Aは「Aに応じて」という意味の表現である。他の選択肢に関して,①はin order to doで「～するために」,③はin

proportion to Aで「Aと釣り合って」，④はopposition to Aで「Aに反対して」という意味の表現となる。　(7)　on account of Aは「Aの理由で」という意味の表現である。　(8)　「もし魚の数に対して空欄のことを行わなければ，特定の種が完全に絶滅してしまう」という文脈において選択肢のうち適切なものは，④のcut back on「～の量を減らす」。(9)　議長がメンバーに対して予定表(agenda) について求めることとして選択肢のうち適切なものは，①のstick to「(規則などを) 守る，執着する」である。　(10)　be subject to Aは「Aに従う，A(の影響) を受けやすい」という意味の表現。本の巻末に書かれていることは，「価格等は予告なく変更する場合があります」ということ。

【３】(1)　3番目…⑦　　6番目…④　　(2)　3番目…⑤　　6番目…②
(3)　3番目…⑦　　6番目…②　　(4)　3番目…①　　6番目…⑧
(5)　3番目…③　　6番目…⑦

〈解説〉(1)　並べ替え後の全文は，The weather forecast says there seems to be no possibility of the typhoon hitting Tokyo.となる。動名詞の前に(代)名詞(の所有格/目的格)を置くことで，動作の動作主を表す。　(2)　並べ替え後の全文は，You can hardly imagine how terrible a sight it was.となる。"how 形容詞a(n) 名詞 SV" という語順は特殊ではあるが，見られなくはない表現である。この場合のhow節はwhat a terrible sight it wasに言い換えが可能である。　(3)　並べ替え後の全文は，I can't concentrate on my work with you watching me. となる。withは付帯状況を表す句を導いて「～しながら，～という状況で，～なのだから」といった意味で用いられる。また，動名詞の前に(代)名詞の所有格/目的格を置くことで，動作の動作主を表す。この場合は，「あなたが私を見ている(という状況なのだ)から，仕事に集中できない」という意味である。　(4)　並べ替え後の全文は，We see things the way our minds have instructed our eyes to see.となる。the wayは後ろに文が続いて，「…が～するように」と接続詞的に用いられる。instruct A to doは「Aに～するように命じる/指示する」という表現。　(5)　並べ替え後の全文

は，At no time should this box be left unlocked.となる。 at no timeはnever
と同義で「決して～することはない」という表現。hardly, scarcely,
seldomと同様，否定を表す副詞(句)が文頭に来ると倒置が起こる。こ
こでは，主語であるthis boxと助動詞であるshouldが倒置されている。
主語の前に移動するのは本動詞または助動詞のみであり，そのほかの
述語の要素は主語の後ろにとどまることに注意。

【4】 (1) ① Englishmen sometimes talk about how much they "love" their
team, whereas they might never publicly admit to loving their wives.
② True beauty could be discovered only by one who mentally completed
the incomplete. (2) Diet affects gender of child. (3) could you
keep it down just a bit? This is a shared space, so please be thoughtful of
everyone else.

〈解説〉(1) ① 下線部には主語が明示されていないが，その前の文に
ある「イギリス人男性」であることを把握して作文する必要がある。
対立する2つの文の状況を表現する方法としては，解答例の"…,
whereas ～"のほかに，"…though/although ～"や"Even though …,～"な
どがある。 ② 解答例では，真の美(true beauty) を主語に文が作られ
ているが，"Only one who has completed…"のように人を主語に文を書
くことも可能である。「不完全」は解答例にあるthe incompleteのほかに，
名詞のincompletionを用いてもよい。 (2) "what you eat"や"what your
mother ate"ということから，日常的な摂取物(diet) の話をしていること
がわかる。また，後半の2文では，女性の摂取物によって子どもの性
別(sex/gender)が変わることが述べられている。これらのことを踏まえ
て簡潔に内容をまとめればよい。 (3) ここでは，①相手にしてほし
いこと，②なぜそうしてほしいのかの2点を相手に丁寧に伝えること
が重要である。相手に丁寧にお願いをするときの基本的な表現には
"Could/Would you ～"や"I would be glad if you would ～"がある。

【5】(1)　ウ　　(2)　イ　　(3)　突然，私は何か忘れていたものを思い出すような漠然とした感覚に襲われました。頭の中に何かがよみがえってくるような，ぞくぞくする感じでした。そして，どういう拍子か，言葉という神秘が姿を現したのです。　　(4)　name　　(5)　音も光も言葉も存在しない世界に住んでいたヘレンがすべての物には名前がありそれを表すのが単語なのだと知ったとたん，新たな感情が芽生え，かんしゃくのあまり壊した人形に対する愛しさや罪悪感を覚えたため。(98字)

〈解説〉本問を解くにあたって，この文章の筆者であるHelen Kellerが視覚と聴覚の重複障害者(＝盲ろう者) であることを念頭に置く必要がある。　　(1)　筆者に何度も物の綴りを教えようとしていたSullivan先生の行動から，先生は筆者に綴りを教えることに熱心であり(devoted)，筆者が理解しなくても何回も教え続けるくらい根気強く(patient)，行動のすべてがうそ偽りなく誠実である(sincere) ことがわかる。しかし，Sullivan先生の描写に無責任である(irresponsible) と捉えられる箇所はない。　　(2)　空欄の後ろに続く "the cause of my discomfort was removed"「私の不快感の原因がなくなった」という気持ちを一番表しているのは，選択肢のうちイのsatisfaction「満足(感)，喜び」である。　　(3)　下線部で使用されている単語や文法自体は難しくないため，各語の意味していること(特に名詞句) を自然な日本語に反映させられるように丁寧に訳するとよい。　　(4)　第1段落で，筆者は物とその名前(綴り) の関係がわからず混乱していた(confounding the two) ということが述べられている。その後，Sullivan先生の "water" の指導によって，ものにはそれを表す名前があることに気づかされる。このことから，筆者が感じたことは，すべてのものには名前があるということであると推察できる。　　(5)　下線部のある文の最後で，はじめて後悔と悲しみを覚えた(for the first time I felt repentance and sorrow) とある。これは，第1段落7〜9文目の，人形を壊した後の記述である「sorrowやregret, strong sentiment, tendernessといった感情を筆者は覚えることがなかった」に対応している。Sullivan先生の指導により，すべてのものに名前がある

と気づいたことで，これらの感情を覚えるようになったという変化に焦点を当ててまとめればよい。

【6】(1) エ　　(2) キ

〈解説〉ヨーロッパ言語共通参照枠(Common European Framework of Reference for Languages; CEFまたはCEFR)とは，第二言語/外国語学習者の言語運用能力を客観的に評価するための国際指標である。各種の資格・検定試験で測定された言語能力のレベルを，試験間で比較するためにも用いられている。CEFRの最も大きな特徴は，「〜ができる」という「CAN-DOディスクリプタ」によって，各レベルが定義されていることである。

【7】(1) ウ　　(2) ② X　　③ Y　　④ Z　　(3) 授業内容がおもしろくて，生徒の年齢と能力レベルに合っていて，学習目標は簡単ではないにしろ，達成可能かつ明確で，元気づけるような雰囲気だという理由で生徒が喜んで受けにくるような授業。　　(4) A　イ　B　ウ　C　ア　D　エ　　(5) この研究は，語学教師の動機づけストラテジーには具体的な，教室に特化した影響力があるという実証的な証拠を初めて提供した点。

〈解説〉(1)　空欄の前までに，従来は統合的動機づけ(integrative motivation) が，そして近年では道具的動機づけ(instrumental motivation) が学習の成功の強い指標となるということが述べられている。したがって，どちらも第二言語学習の成功に結びついていることがわかったと述べているウが正解である。　　(2)　(X) choice motivationとは，開始しゴールを決めることを指す「選択的動機づけ」。(Y) executive motivationとは，モチベーションを維持するために必要なタスクをこなすことを指す「実行動機づけ」。(Z) motivation retrospectionとは，生徒が自身のパフォーマンスを振り返って評価することを指す「動機づけを高める追観」。②③④はそれぞれ，これらの具体例として取り上げられている。　　(3)　第3段落3文目Teachers can make以下に述べられて

いるので，ここをまとめればよい。　（4）　Aは好奇心や注意をひきつけたり，自律性を高めたり，コミュニケーションの目的をまとめたりすることとある。これは教師が生徒に会話などを通じて行うことであり，選択肢の中ではイが最も適切である。　Bは生徒がグループワークかペアワークかのどちらに参加するかということであり，ウが適切である。　Cは個人間の競争，グループ間の競争，知的困難度，達成可能なタスクの成果物など，どのような活動を行うかということが述べられており，アが適切である。　Dは効果的なほめ方や，自身や仲間たちの誤りを修正する会，クラスでの称賛といった振り返り活動の説明をしており，エが適切である。　（5）　下線部の研究で研究者らが重要であると考えている理由は，第6段落3文目Nevertheless以下に述べられている。

【8】（1）　（あ）　エ　　（い）　エ　　（う）　イ　　（え）　ア　　（お）　ウ
（2）　否定的なフィードバックを正直に率直に伝えるオランダ文化は，否定的なフィードバックを肯定的な評価で包み込んで遠まわしに伝えるというアメリカ文化とは異なるということ。　　（3）　downgraders
（4）　ア　　（5）　フィードバックを行う方法が，国や文化によって様々であるから。　　（6）　イ　　（7）　ア
〈解説〉（1）　（あ）　tyrantは「暴君」を意味する単語。　（い）　hole upは「隠れる」という意味の表現。　（う）　cozyは「温かみがあり居心地がいい」を意味する単語。　（え）　be startledは「びっくりする」という意味の表現。　（お）　sparinglyは「控えめに，節約して」という意味の表現。　（2）　第4段落1文目Maarten, the other以下に，Willemに対して否定的なコメントを会議のメンバーの前で述べていたことが書かれている。それに対し，You may haveから始まる段落では，肯定的な評価を述べてから最後に少しだけ直すべきところを述べる，ということが読み手の経験としてあるだろうということが述べられている。下線部の文言に沿って解釈すると，前者がオランダの文化，後者が筆者（アメリカ）の文化ということになる。したがって，上記の違いをまとめれ

ばよい。　(3)　UPGRADERS, DOWNGRADERS…という見出しの項では「upgradersとは否定的フィードバックの前後にある語でその内容を強めるものである」と述べられており，例としてabsolutely, totallyなどが挙げられる。一方，「downgradersとは，批判や感情を和らげる言葉づかいのことであり，kind ofを挿入して語調を和らげたり，"This is nowhere close to complete" の代わりに "We are not quite there yet" とやんわり述べたりすることがその例である」と述べられている。したがって，②の傍線部の表現は，フィードバックを和らげているため，downgradersの例であることがわかる。　(4)　第9段落では，「自分が言われたことと裏で言われていることが異なる場合，裏切られたと感じて同僚への疑いの念を抱き，嘘つきや空欄のように目に映る」ということが述べられている。この文脈において選択肢のうち適切なものは，アのhypocrite「偽善者」である。　(5)　下線部③の次の文では，各国の管理者がどのようにフィードバックを与えるのかについて述べている。この内容から，各国によってフィードバックの方法が異なることがわかる。そのことをまとめればよい。　(6)　Aの見出しが入る項では，「文化によって，否定的なフィードバックを直接的に言うことが誠実さを表し，Willemの言葉を借りれば "gift" であると考えられる国や文化もあれば，painfulであると感じられる文化もある」と述べられている。このことを踏まえると，選択肢のうち適切なものはイである。(7)　建設的な批判(constructive criticism)とは，否定的なフィードバックをもらうことである。第1段落4文目のGetting negative feedback以下に，「否定的なフィードバックを得ることで社員の動機づけを高め，公正であるとの評判が高まる」と述べられている。したがって，アが正解である。

2017年度　実施問題

【中学校】

【１】放送される指示に従い，答えなさい。

(Part　1)

(1)　　　　　　　　　　(2)　　　　　　　　　　(3)

(Part　2)

(1)　　　　　　　　　　(2)　　　　　　　　　　(3)

(Part　3)

(1)　　　　　　　　　　(2)　　　　　　　　　　(3)

(Part　4)

(1)　　　　　　　　　　(2)　　　　　　　　　　(3)

(☆☆☆☆◎◎◎)

【２】次の(1)〜(20)の英文の(　　)に入る最も適切な単語又は語句を選び，記号で答えなさい。

(1)　Thomas and Bill (　　) cheap bars every week.

　　ア　seldom　　イ　frequent　　ウ　often　　エ　frequently

(2)　All the people in the world should wish for the (　　) of peace.

　　ア　restoration　　イ　respective　　ウ　respiration　　エ　response

(3)　She finally succeeded (　　) her persistence.

　　ア　to the contrary　　イ　in case of　　ウ　instead of　　エ　due to

(4)　The park is (　　) three miles of our house.

ア　forward　　イ　within　　ウ　until　　エ　behind

(5)　It is (　　) to resist him.

　　ア　usually　　イ　rarely　　ウ　terminal　　エ　useless

(6)　This is (　　) we first met about ten years ago.

　　ア　whose　　イ　up　　ウ　where　　エ　whenever

(7)　The government (　　) a statement condemning the dispute.

　　ア　issued　　イ　played　　ウ　tasted　　エ　traveled

(8)　Cindy (　　) that it would take two weeks to finish this work.

　　ア　continues　　イ　estimates　　ウ　praises　　エ　resumes

(9)　Mr. Chan was (　　) in his room nor in the garden when his daughter visited his house.

　　ア　between　　イ　when　　ウ　not only　　エ　neither

(10)　Bob was confused because he knew nothing (　　) the matter which his superior talked to him about.

　　ア　regarding　　イ　refuge　　ウ　to　　エ　except

(11)　They will (　　) various materials on the attitudes of everyone in the country into a magazine.

　　ア　bargain　　イ　urge　　ウ　compile　　エ　simulate

(12)　Attendance at elementary school is (　　) for children in Japan.

　　ア　each　　イ　pointed　　ウ　intact　　エ　compulsory

(13)　I am not accustomed to attending (　　) functions.

　　ア　public　　イ　correction　　ウ　eminence　　エ　consent

(14)　She (　　) the crying child by giving him a piece of candy.

　　ア　notorious　　イ　soothed　　ウ　completed　　エ　polite

(15)　Paul was (　　) to painting in those days.

　　ア　agreed　　イ　arranged　　ウ　addicted　　エ　assorted

(16)　Though he's gained more experience and technical knowledge, I doubt his (　　) for such a post.

　　ア　distress　　イ　prejudice　　ウ　fund　　エ　competence

(17)　Most of people are hoping that the good weather will (　　) for the holidays.

ア　persist　　イ　resist　　ウ　remind　　エ　index

(18) Kevin (　) himself with his job.

ア　alternated　　イ　accelerated　　ウ　acquainted

エ　accumulated

(19)　A great poet sometimes (　) an unusual implication upon a word.

ア　objects　　イ　imposes　　ウ　interferes　　エ　translates

(20)　A man (　) a million dollars for the old book in the auction.

ア　impeded　　イ　applauded　　ウ　bid　　エ　crushed

(☆☆☆○○○○○)

【３】次の(1)～(10)の〔　　〕内の単語又は語句を並べ替えてそれぞれ正
しい英文を作るとき，(　ア 　)と(　イ 　)に入る単語又は語句をそれぞ
れ番号で答えなさい。ただし，英文のはじめにくる単語又は語句の頭
文字も小文字にしてある。

(1)〔　①　action　　②　with　　③　such　　④　spirit
　　⑤　inconsistent　　⑥　an　　⑦　the　　⑧　is　〕
　　(　) (　) (　ア 　) (　) (　) (　イ 　) (　) (　) of
autonomy.

(2)〔　①　chemistry　　②　contributed　　③　to　　④　of
　　⑤　development　　⑥　the　　⑦　immensely　〕
　　He (　) (　) (　ア 　) (　) (　イ 　) (　) (　).

(3)〔　①　up　　②　a　　③　scholarly　　④　he　　⑤　in　　⑥
was　　⑦　brought　〕
　　I think (　) (　ア 　) (　) (　) (　イ 　) (　) (　)
atmosphere.

(4)〔　①　catering　　②　with　　③　to　　④　other　　⑤　in
　　⑥　compete　　⑦　each　〕
　　These hotels (　) (　ア 　) (　) (　) (　) (　イ 　) (　) the
comfort of their guests.

(5) 〔 ① snake ② sight ③ him ④ a ⑤ mere
⑥ makes ⑦ of 〕
The (ア)( )( )( )(イ)( )( ) shudder.

(6) 〔 ① to ② the ③ birth ④ is ⑤ fall
⑥ rate ⑦ apt 〕
( )( )(ア)( )(イ)( )( ) in advanced
countries.

(7) 〔 ① reproach ② me ③ behavior ④ his
⑤ toward ⑥ was ⑦ above 〕
( )( )(ア)( )( )(イ)( ).

(8) 〔 ① could ② that ③ not ④ was ⑤ the
stone ⑥ it ⑦ heavy ⑧ move ⑨ we 〕
So ( )(ア)( )( )( )(イ)( )( )
( ).

(9) 〔 ① notable ② been ③ has ④ his
⑤ there ⑥ a ⑦ condition ⑧ improvement
⑨ in 〕
( )(ア)( )( )( )(イ)( )( )( ).

(10) 〔 ① than ② rude ③ take ④ his
⑤ words ⑥ I ⑦ were ⑧ more ⑨ could 〕
( )(ア)( )( )( )( )(イ)( ).

(☆☆☆☆○○○○○)

【4】次の英文を読み，あとの(1)～(4)の各問いに答えなさい，

Many people claim they are mechanically challenged, but I think a lot of them are that way by (①). An old acquaintance of mine once groused, "I suspect engineers believe it's progress when they build a tiny device that's crammed with many (②)."

Recalling an over-the-top, high-tech wristwatch he bought when he was young, my friend said it ended up in his desk drawer, ⓐnever worn, because he just couldn't be bothered to figure out its numerous functions.

I suppose I could call him an old dork of the Showa Era (1926-1989), but when I met him recently after many years, he declared ⑧(smartphone / he / longer / his / live / no / without / could). I (③) him about his change of heart, but he kept thumbing the gadget expertly. And he even pitied me for falling way (④) the times.

Essentially a wristwatch-style smartphone, the product went on sale recently amid media fanfare. Come to think of it, what is happenning is a cellphone evolution (⑤) to how wristwatches replaced pocket watches in the past. ⓒWearing one's smartphone on the wrist should reduce chances of misplacing or losing it. But wouldn't that also make one feel constrained? Or is this just my prejudice as an "analog person?"

(原書房「天声人語2015夏」より)

(1) 本文中の(①)～(⑤)に入る最も適切な語をそれぞれア～エから選び，記号で答えなさい。

① ア　luck　　　イ　post　　　ウ　choice
　　エ　means

② ア　functions　イ　people　　ウ　engagements
　　エ　population

③ ア　praised　　イ　flattered　ウ　treated
　　エ　teased

④ ア　remember　イ　behind　　ウ　remark
　　エ　belong

⑤ ア　different　イ　fade　　　ウ　similar
　　エ　handy

(2) 下線部Ⓐの理由について，日本語で説明しなさい。

(3) 下線部Ⓑの( )内の単語を正しく並べ替えて書きなさい。

(4) 下線部Ⓒを日本語にしなさい。

(☆☆☆○○○○)

【5】次の英文を読み，あとの(1)〜(4)の各問いに答えなさい。

At its most basic level, motivation is some kind of internal (①) which pushes someone to do things in order to achieve something. As H Douglas Brown points out, a cognitive view of motivation includes factors such as the need for exploration, activity, stimulation, new knowledge, and ego enhancement. The adult who starts going to a gym, for example, may hope that a new body image will aid ego enhancement and be (②) by the active nature of this new undertaking.

Marion Williams and Richard Burden suggest that motivation is a ⓐ (which / a decision / cognitive / of / state / to / provokes / arousal / act) as a result of which there is sustained intellectual and /or physical effort so that the person can achieve some previously set goal. They go on to point out that ⓑ the strength of that motivation will depend on how much value the individual places on the outcomee he or she wishes to achieve. Adults may have clearly defined or vague goals. Children's goals, on the other hand, are often more amorphous and less easy to describe, but they can still be very powerful.

In discussions of motivation an accepted (③) is made between extrinsic and intrinsic motivation, that is motivation which comes from outside and from inside.

Extrinsic motivation is caused by any number of outside factors, for example, the need to pass an exam, the hope of financial (④), or the possibility of future travel. Intrinsic motivation, by contrast, comes from within the individual. Thus a person might be motivated by the enjoyment of the learning (⑤) itself or by a desire to make themselves feel better.

Most researchers and methodologists have come to the view that intrinsic motivation is especially important for encouraging success. Even where the original reason for taking up a language course, for example, is extrinsic, the chances of success will be greatly enhanced if the students come to love the learning process.

(THE PRACTICE OF ENGLISH LANGUAGE TEACHING / Jeremy Harmer)

(1) 本文中の(①), (②), (③), (④), (⑤)に入る最も適切な単語をア〜キから選んで記号で答えなさい。ただし, 1つの語は1度しか使えないものとする。

　ア　declined　　イ　reward　　ウ　distinction　　エ　stimulated
　オ　discourse　　カ　drive　　キ　process

(2) 下線部Ⓐの(　　)内の単語を正しく並べ替えて書きなさい。

(3) 下線部Ⓑを日本語にしなさい。

(4) 本文中に示されている多くの研究者や方法論学者の見解を日本語で簡潔に書きなさい。

(☆☆☆☆○○○○○)

【6】次の英文を読み, あとの(1)〜(6)の各問いに答えなさい。(本文には出題の都合上, 省略した箇所がある)

　　Over the centuries, many American presidents and other statesmen have been renowned for their great public speaking skills. Abraham Lincoln, Martin Luther King Jr., Ronald Reagan, John F. Kennedy, and Barack Obama all come to mind. Were they all natural public speakers? That is doubtful. Although it is true that Americans as a whole tend to be outgoing, cheerful and definitely not shy, public speaking itself is a skill that takes practice and training.

　　The process often begins at a very early age, even in elementary school. I can remember the first time it was my turn for "Show and Tell". I think I talked about my father's old baseball glove, a Ted Williams model from 1955. I carried the old brown glove to the front of the room, lifted it up and started to speak. But before I could (①) a word, my mouth went dry and my mind went blank. I started at my classmates and they all stared back at me: A disaster in the making? Not at all. Our teacher was prepared for just such a situation. She smoothly stepped in, asked me a few questions...and I was fine.

It happened that way for many of my classmates. 〔 ア 〕

The process continues into Jr. and Sr. high school with speech contests. There are other (②) to everyday life and school life that encourage freedom to speak out and creativity. Besides this, many American kids have part-time jobs where they learn to deal with problems and communicate with adults. Finally, American kids often go with their parents to work. Many American corporations sponsor "Family Day" where family members ③(where / invited / and / into / the / to / are / see / office) how their moms and dads work. While there, they are encouraged to ask lots of questions. I often accompanied my dad to work when he was the manager of a large department store, Woolworth's. 〔 イ 〕

As we get older, Americans become used to (④) their opinions on just about any topic —— often controversial —— in just about any environment. Young people are encouraged to say what they think, and to engage in informal debate. There is nothing wrong with disagreeing with someone else's opinion (even your parents' or the teacher's), as long as you are polite and well-mannered in the way you express yourself. 〔 ウ 〕

But that is not enough. Nowadays, public speaking clubs like Toastmasters International, and seminars like the Dale Carnegie Public Speaking Course proliferate. Why? ⑤(ironic / that / you / here / quite / might / is / surprise / something):In Gallup's yearly "FEAR POLL" that asks American adults what they are most afraid of in life, the fear of public speaking (despite all the practice we get when we are young) is often listed among the Top 5 Fears, along with other horrific concerns like spiders and snakes, and high places. It seems that there is a big difference between actual "speech making" and just "speaking".

The difference, of course, is the (⑥) in front of you. ⑦Americans still tend to clam up when called upon to speak in front of formal gatherings, large or small! Even Mark Twain, who at one time was known as the funniest man alive, was apparently (at first) terrified to speak in public. So what then is the

317

secret to overcoming that sickening feeling in the pit of your stomach? Experience; as much experience as possible! | エ |

I think ⑧the American attitude and approach towards public speaking makes sense: Start young and continue as an adult. Don't be afraid to speak up. Say what's on your mind. Because — you never know — each and every one of us might have the (⑨) to become the next Barack Obama!

(*"Larry's Americana"* Public Speaking / Larry Knipfing)

(1) 本文中の(①)(②)(④)(⑨)に入る最も適切な単語をそれぞれア～エから選び，記号で答えなさい。

① ア consult 　　イ utmost 　　ウ utter
　 エ exceed

② ア aspects 　　イ secure 　　ウ image
　 エ significance

④ ア express 　　イ expressed 　　ウ expression
　 エ expressing

⑨ ア issue 　　イ positive 　　ウ coupon
　 エ potential

(2) 下線部③と⑤の(　　)内の単語を，それぞれ正しく並べ替えて書きなさい。

(3) 本文中の(⑥)に入る最も適切な単語を答えなさい。

(4) 次の1文が入るのに最も適する部分を本文中の| ア |～| エ |から選び，記号で答えなさい。

It was a great experience and helped me overcome my shyness.

(5) 下線部⑦を日本語にしなさい。

(6) 下線部⑧について，その具体的内容を3つ日本語で答えなさい。

(☆☆☆◎◎◎)

【７】次の各問いに答えなさい。

(1) 「中学校学習指導要領」(平成20年3月告示)第2章第9節外国語における，言語活動「話すこと」の指導事項について，(ア)～(オ)の

（　　）に入る最も適切な語句を答えなさい。

（ア）　強勢，（　　），区切りなど基本的な英語の音声の特徴をとらえ，正しく発音すること。

（イ）　自分の考えや気持ち，（　　）などを聞き手に正しく伝えること。

（ウ）　聞いたり読んだりしたことなどについて，（　　）したり意見を述べ合ったりなどすること。

（エ）　（　　）を用いるなどのいろいろな工夫をして話を続けること。

（オ）　与えられたテーマについて簡単な（　　）をすること。

(2)　「中学校学習指導要領」(平成20年3月告示)第2章第9節外国語における，教材選定の観点について，（　①　）～（　⑤　）に入る最も適切な語句を答えなさい。

　教材は，聞くこと，話すこと，読むこと，書くことなどのコミュニケーション能力を総合的に育成するため，実際の言語の使用場面や言語の（　①　）に十分配慮したものを取り上げるものとする。その際，英語を使用している人々を中心とする世界の人々及び日本人の日常生活，風俗風習，物語，地理，歴史，伝統文化や自然科学などに関するものの中から，生徒の（　②　）及び興味・関心に即して適切な題材を変化をもたせて取り上げるものとし，次の観点に配慮する必要がある。

ア　多様なものの見方や考え方を理解し，公正な（　③　）を養い豊かな心情を育てるのに役立つこと。

イ　外国や我が国の生活や文化についての理解を深めるとともに，言語や文化に対する関心を高め，これらを（　④　）する態度を育てるのに役立つこと。

ウ　広い視野から国際理解を深め，国際社会に生きる日本人としての自覚を高めるとともに，（　⑤　）の精神を養うのに役立つこと。

(☆☆☆☆☆○○○○○)

【8】次は，文部科学省が『各中・高等学校の外国語教育における「CAN-DOリスト」の形での学習到達目標設定のための手引』(平成25年3月)で示している「CAN-DOリスト」の形で学習到達目標を設定する目的である。(①)～(⑩)に入る最も適切な語句を答えなさい。

○　学習指導要領に基づき，外国語科の(①)学習状況の評価における「(②)の能力」と「(③)の能力」について，生徒が身に付ける能力を各学校が明確化し，主に教員が生徒の指導と評価の改善に活用すること

○　学習指導要領を踏まえた，「聞くこと」，「話すこと」，「読むこと」及び「書くこと」の4技能を(④)的に育成し，外国語による(⑤)能力，相手の文化的，社会的背景を踏まえた上で自らの考えを適切に伝える能力並びに(⑥)力・(⑦)力・表現力を養う指導につなげること

○　(⑧)の観点から，教員が生徒と目標を共有することにより，言語習得に必要な(⑨)的学習者として(⑩)的に学習する態度・姿勢を生徒が身に付けること

(☆☆☆☆◎◎◎◎)

【9】次の問いに答えなさい。

(1)　次の数字や数式の読み方を英語で書きなさい。

①　3.14

②　1,000,000,000

③　4分の3

④　24×6＝144

(2)　中学校3年生の英語の授業において，いっしょにテニスをしようと相手を誘ったり，相手に提案したりする言い方の例文を複数示すこととした。それぞれ次の書き出しで始まる疑問文を一つずつ書きなさい。ただし，( )内は5語以上とすること。

○　Why (　　　　　　　　　　　　　　　)?

○　Do (　　　　　　　　　　　　　　　)?

○　How (　　　　　　　　　　　　　　　　)?

(3)　中学校3年生の英語の授業において，「修学旅行の思い出」という
　　　タイトルの作文および発表に取り組ませたい。導入としてモデルを
　　　提示する際に，どのようなモデルを提示するか，5文の英語で1つの
　　　モデルを書きなさい。(本文前後のあいさつ文は除く。語数は問わ
　　　ない。)

(4)　現在完了形(継続・経験・完了)の3種類の文の用法を説明しようと
　　　考えたとき，どのような例文を提示するか，次の書き出しに続けて
　　　書きなさい。

【継続】　I (　　　　　　　　　　　　　　　　　　　　　　　).

【経験】　Our ALT, Mr.Clapton (　　　　　　　　　　　　　).

【完了】　My father and sister (　　　　　　　　　　　　　).

(☆☆☆◎◎◎)

【高等学校】

【1】放送される指示に従い，答えなさい。

(Part 1)

(1)　　　　　　　　　　　　　　　　　(2)

(Part 2)

(1)　　　　　　　　(2)　　　　　　　　(3)

(Part 3)

(1)　　　　　　　　(2)　　　　　　　　(3)

(☆☆☆☆◎◎◎◎)

【2】次の(1)〜(10)の英文の(　　　)に当てはまる最も適切な単語又は語句を，下の①〜④の中から選び，番号で答えなさい。

(1) In order to promote the sale, the new car will be (　　) displayed in the driveway.

① pessimistically　② predictably　③ prominently

④ practically

(2) The city has many hotels that (　　) to the increasing number of foreign tourists.

① cater　② concede　③ convey　④ transmit

(3) Heart disease is one of the most (　　) causes of death.

① common　② normal　③ regular　④ average

(4) According to the latest (　　), approximately 85％ of Americans have health insurance.

① purchase　② surplus　③ revenge　④ census

(5) Diligence and perseverance will (　　) in the long run.

① stand for　② make for　③ pay off　④ hit on

(6) His weight has (　　) massively and his body has ballooned.

① risen　② gained　③ lifted　④ given

(7) Mr.Selby is seriously ill and has been transferred to (　　) care.

① invisible　② inevitable　③ intensive　④ insensitive

(8) Cyber-bullying through the Internet is much more difficult for teachers and parents to (　　) than physical bullying.

① spread　② promote　③ generate　④ identify

(9) (　　) that knob to the right and the box will open.

① Select　② Twist　③ Squeeze　④ Express

(10) In British English, 'little' is unusual in the (　　) position, and comparative and superlative forms are not normally used.

① predicative　② predictive　③ prescriptive

④ preclusive

(☆☆☆○○○○)

322

【3】次の(1)～(5)の英文の(　　)内の単語又は語句を並べ替え，意味の通る英文にする場合，(　　)内で3番目と6番目にくる単語又は語句を番号で答えなさい。

(1)　A: What will it cost me to send this package to Singapore?
　　　B: That (① depends　② to arrive　③ want　④ how
　　　⑤ soon　⑥ on　⑦ you　⑧ it).

(2)　A: Could (① have　② all night　③ you　④ left
　　　⑤ lights　⑥ the office　⑦ on)?
　　　B: It wasn't me! Frank was still here when I left last night.

(3)　A: When will you have time to interview the candidates for the job?
　　　B: I (① clear　② toward　③ my schedule　④ could
　　　⑤ do　⑥ to　⑦ it) the end of the week.

(4)　A: Hello. I need to get my bike repaired for a trip this weekend. Is it possible to have it ready by Thursday?
　　　B: I'm afraid not. We will (① order　② and that　③ take
　　　④ need　⑤ spare parts　⑥ to　⑦ will) two weeks.

(5)　A: I have a question regarding the tuition for my classes next year. Do I have to pay it at once?
　　　B: We also have an alternative payment plan. Instead of paying all of your tuition at once, you (① scheduled payments　② to
　　　③ every month　④ for　⑤ opt　⑥ make
　　　⑦ can) a period of 10 months beginning on July 15th.

(☆☆☆◎◎◎)

【4】次の文の下線部(1)～(3)を英語にしなさい。

竹はとても軽く，細く，強く，曲がりやすいものです。軽くて，しなやかで，強靭な人のことをGRACEFULと表現します。(1)gracefulnessとは，「力の効率的使用」，すなわち，体重を最適にして最大の力を発揮できることを意味します。

…(略)…

鳥と蝙蝠のちがいは何でしょうか。(2)蝙蝠には地肌で覆われている翼があり，体は柔毛で覆われています。しかし，鳥の体は，羽毛で覆われています。

（弦書房「ラフカディオ・ハーンの英語教育」の一部より）

(3)礼儀を行うのに，真実と誠実の心が欠けていたならば，それは茶番になりお芝居となってしまう。伊達政宗は「礼儀も過ぎれば，へつらいとなる」と言っている。

（新渡戸稲造　著「武士道」の一部より）

（☆☆☆◎◎◎）

【５】次の英文を読み，あとの(1)～(5)の各問いに答えなさい。

Take a look at the following dialogue.

DIALOGUE Ⅰ

A) I would really appreciate it if you could take up this project for consideration.

B) Hmm. What do you think, C?

C) Well, (①).

A) Isn't there something you can do? We would even consider covering part of the expenses.

B) Okay. I'll think it over.

A is visiting the company where B and C work (B is obviously the boss) to give a sales pitch for a project, and we can see that B and C are ready to turn it down.

This dialogue is chock-full of (②) Japanese expressions.

First, instead of issuing a direct rejection, B hopes to politely turn down the project by asking C's opinion and incorporating C's thinking in his own. Falling in with B's thinking, C uses the phrase "(①)" to convey to A that the project will not be considered. A tries to have this decision reconsidered by making an additional proposal, but C politely turns down the project again with the phrase "I'll think it over." It is worth noting that nowhere in the dialogue does the word "(③)" appear.

Americans are likely to misunderstand this and think. "If there is a problem, then we can fix it and everything will be all right." Then again, B's response, following up on C's comment, is puzzling. If it is not going to work, why doesn't B tell A that straight out? If A is an American, he might think that there is some (④) reason for not doing so. And hearing B's final comment, A might think. "What do you mean, 'I'll think it over'? What are you going to think over? If there is some reference material you need to think over. I'd like to hear what it is."

Well then, how could these conversations be changed to improve them? The dialogue would go something like the following:

DIALOGUE Ⅱ

A) I would really appreciate it if you could take up this project for consideration.

B) I see. As it happens, though, (⑤). We would like to pass this time around. C, do you have any comments?

C) Well, to be realistic, if costs could be brought down another 30 percent, we do have a need for this type of project.

A) I see your point. We should think about covering part of the cost, then. I will take it back to my office for discussion.

B) I'd appreciate that. But keep in mind that we still may not be able to meet your expectations.

C) Contact my office if there is anything you need. I can give you (⑥) information about our requirements. B, is that all right with you?

B) Of course.

Wouldn't this be much (⑦)? If the matter is not an absolute impossibility, a dialogue like this often leads to an (⑧) brainstorming ⑨that turns the impossible into the possible.

(IBCパブリッシング　「完璧すぎる日本人」の一部より改変)

(1) （　①　）に入る適切な文を次のア～エから選び，記号で答えなさい。

ア　that might be true

イ　I see what you mean

ウ　I have high hopes for you

エ　that might be a little difficult

(2) （　②　）（　④　）（　⑥　）（　⑦　）（　⑧　）に入る最も適切な単語を次のア～キから選び，記号で答えなさい。

ア　instantaneous　　イ　worse　　ウ　detailed　　エ　vague

オ　hidden　　カ　clearer　　キ　positive

(3) （　③　）に入る適切な語句を答えなさい。

(4) （　⑤　）に入る適切な文を答えなさい。

(5) 下線部⑨について，| DIALOGUE Ⅱ | では具体的にどういうことなのか，日本語で答えなさい。

(☆☆☆☆○○○)

【６】次の英文を読み，以下の各問いに答えなさい。

<English Communication Ⅰ>

1. Objective

To develop students' basic abilities such as accurately understanding and appropriately （　①　） information, ideas, etc., while fostering （　②　） toward communication through the English language.

2. Contents

(1) The following language activities, designed for specific language-use situations in order to encourage students to apply their abilities to understand and convey information, ideas, etc., should be conducted in English.

A.　Understanding information, ideas, etc., and （　③　） the outline and the main points by listening to introductions to specified topics, dialogues, etc.

 B. Understanding information, ideas, etc., and (③) the outline and the main points by reading explanations, stories, etc. Reading passages aloud so that the meaning of the content is expressed.

 C. (④) opinions on information, ideas, etc., based on what one has heard, read, learned and experienced.

 D. Writing brief passages on information, ideas, etc., based on what one has heard, read, learned and experienced.

(2) To effectively conduct the language activities stated in (1), consideration should be given to the following instructional points.

 A. Listening and speaking with due attention to the characteristics of English sounds, such as rhythm and intonation, speed, volume, etc.

 B. Reading and writing with due attention to phrases and sentences indicating the main points, connecting phrases, etc.

 C. Understanding and (①) matters, distinguishing facts, opinions, etc.

3. Treatment of the Contents

(1) Based on general instruction to develop basic communication abilities given in lower secondary schools, the four areas of language activities should be (⑤) for comprehensive learning, while incorporating appropriate language activities involving speaking and writing about content heard or read.

(2) Consideration should be given so that students master the items introduced in lower secondary schools and upper secondary schools through repeated instruction in accordance with students' circumstances, while experiencing various situational language activities.

<English Expression Ⅰ>

1. Objective

 To develop students' abilities to evaluate (⑥), opinions, etc. from multiple perspectives and communicate through reasoning and a range of expression, while fostering (　②　) toward communication through the English language.

2.　Contents

(1)　The following language activities, designed for specific language-use situations in order to encourage students to apply their abilities to understand and convey information, ideas, etc., should be conducted in English.

A.　(　⑦　) speaking on a given topic. Speaking concisely in a style suitable for the audience and purpose.

B.　Writing brief passages in a style suitable for the audience and purpose.

C.　(　⑧　) and presenting information, ideas, etc., based on what one has heard, read, learned and experienced.

(2)　To effectively conduct the language activities stated in (1), consideration should be given to the following instructional points.

A.　Speaking with due attention to the characteristics of English sounds such as rhythm and intonation, speed, volume, etc.

B.　Writing with due attention to phrases and sentences indicating the main points, connecting phrases, etc. and reviewing one's own writing.

C.　Learning presentation methods, expressions used in presentations, etc. and applying them to (　⑨　) situations.

D.　Forming one's own opinion by comparing what one has heard or read with opinions from other sources, and identifying similarities and differences.

3.　Treatment of the Contents

(1)　Based on general instruction to develop basic communication abilities given in lower secondary schools, students should be instructed so as to improve their abilities to convey information, ideas, etc., while focusing on language activities involving speaking and writing.

(2)　Instruction on speaking and writing should be conducted more effectively through (　⑩　) with listening and reading activities.

(3)　Consideration should be given so that students master the items introduced in lower secondary schools and upper secondary schools through repeated instruction in accordance with students' circumstances, while experiencing various situational language activities.

　　高等学校学習指導要領(平成21年3月告示)英語版(仮訳)の一部より

(1)　(　①　)~(　⑤　)に入る最も適切な単語又は語句を，次のア~オから選び，記号で答えなさい。(文頭に来る場合も小文字にしてある。)

ア　interlinked　　イ　discussing and exchanging　　ウ　conveying
エ　grasping　　　オ　a positive attitude

(2)　(　⑥　)~(　⑩　)に入る最も適切な単語又は語句を，次のア~オから選び，記号で答えなさい。(文頭に来る場合も小文字にしてある。)

ア　impromptu　　イ　summarizing　　ウ　real-life
エ　integration　　オ　facts

　　　　　　　　　　　　　　　　　(☆☆☆☆☆○○○○)

【7】次の英文を読み，あとの(1)~(6)の各問いに答えなさい。

　　Many theories have been proposed for the best way to learn a second language in the classroom. Even more teaching methods and materials have been developed to implement these theories. But the only way to answer the question 'What is the best way to promote language learning in classrooms?' is through research that specifically investigates relationships between teaching and learning.

　　In this chapter, we examine six proposals for second and foreign language teaching, provide examples from classroom interaction to illustrate how the proposals get translated into classroom practice, and discuss research findings that help to assess their effectiveness. The labels we have given these proposals are:

1　Get it right from the beginning

2　Just listen...and read

3　Let's talk

4　Two for one

5　Teach what is teachable

6　Get it right in the end

〜中略〜

Proponents of the 'Get it right in the end' position recognize an important role for form-focused instruction*, but ①they do not assume that everything has to be taught. Like advocates of the 'Let's talk', 'Two for one', and the 'Just listen...and read' positions, they have concluded that many language features —from pronunciation to vocabulary and grammar—will be acquired naturally if learners have adequate exposure to the language and a motivation to learn. Thus, while they view comprehension-based, content-based, task-based, or other types of essentially meaning-focused instruction as crucial for language learning, they hypothesize that learners will do better if they also have access to some form-focused instruction. They argue that learners will benefit in terms of both (　②　) of their learning and the level of (　③　) they will eventually reach.

④Proponents of this position also agree with advocates of the 'Teach what is teachable' position that some things cannot be taught if the teaching fails to take the student's readiness (stage of development) into account. This proposal differs from the 'Teach what is teachable' proposal, however, in that it emphasizes the idea that some aspects of language must be taught and may need to be taught quite explicitly. There are a number of situations in which ⑤ For example, when learners in a class share the same first language, they will make errors that are partly the result of transfer from that shared language. Because the errors are not likely to lead to any kind of communication breakdown, it will be virtually impossible for learners to discover the errors on their own.

〜中略〜

Proponents of 'Get it right in the end' argue that what learners focus on can eventually lead to changes in their interlanguage systems, not just to an appearance of change. However, the supporters of this proposal do not claim that focusing on particular language points will prevent learners from making errors or that they will begin using a form as soon as it is taught. Rather, they suggest that the focused instruction will allow learners to notice the target features in subsequent input and interaction. Form-focused instruction as it is understood in this position does not always involve metalinguistic explanations, nor are learners expected to be able to explain why something is right or wrong. They claim simply that the learners need to notice how their language use differs from that of a more proficient speaker. As we will see in the examples below, teachers who work in this approach look for the right moment to create increased awareness on the part of the learner—ideally, at a time when the learner is motivated to say something and wants to say it as clearly and correctly as possible.

⑥

〜中略〜

Proponents of 'Get it right in the end' argue that it is sometimes necessary to draw learners' attention to their errors and to focus on certain linguistic (vocabulary or grammar) points. However, it is different from the 'Get it right from the beginning' proposal in acknowledging that it is appropriate for learners to engage in meaningful language use from the very beginning of their exposure to the second language. They assume that much of language acquisition will develop naturally out of such language use, without formal instruction that focuses on the language itself.

(Patsy M. Lightbown / Nina Spada, *How Languages are Learned*の一部より)

(注)

form-focused instruction* : Instruction that draws attention to the forms and structures of the language within the context of communicative interaction. This may be done by giving metalinguistic information, simply highlighting the form in question, or by providing corrective feedback.

(1)　下線部①について，学習者はどのような場合にすべてを教えられなくとも学ぶ可能性があるか，本文の内容に即して日本語で説明しなさい。

(2)　(②)(③)に入る最も適切な単語を次のア～エから選び，記号で答えなさい。

　ア　bilingualism　　イ　efficiency　　ウ　conclusion
　エ　proficiency

(3)　下線部④の両者の意見が対立している点を日本語で説明しなさい。

(4)　［　⑤　］に入る最も適切なものを次のア～エから選び，記号で答えなさい。

　ア　guidance—form-focused instruction or corrective feedback—is expected to be especially important.

　イ　it is better not to allow learners to make errors, because the errors could become bad habits.

　ウ　learners are exposed to comprehensible input through listening or reading.

　エ　the level of language the teacher is offering them is beyond their current stage of development.

(5)　［　⑥　］に入る最も適切な事例を次のア～ウから選び，記号で答えなさい。

ア　(A group of twelve-year-old ESL students are discussing a questionnaire about pets with their teacher.)

Student : And what is 'feed' ?

Teacher : Feed? To feed the dog?

Student : Yes, but when I don't have a ...

Teacher : If you don't have a dog, you skip the question.

イ　(A group of twelve-year-old learners of English as a foreign language.)

Teacher : Repeat after me. Is there any butter in the refrigerator?

Class 　: Is there any butter in the refrigerator?

Teacher : There's very little, Mom.

Class 　: There's very little, Mom.

Teacher : Are there any tomatoes in the refrigerator?

Class 　: Are there any tomatoes in the refrigerator?

ウ　(The students are playing 'hide and seek' with a doll in a doll's house, asking questions until they find out where 'George' is hiding. Although a model for correct questions has been written on the board, the game becomes quite lively and students spontaneously ask questions that reflect their interlanguage stage.)

Student : Is George is in the living room?

Teacher : You said 'is' two times dear. Listen to you—you said 'Is George is in?' Look on the board. 'Is George in the' and then you say the name of the room.

Student : Is George in the living room?

Teacher : Yeah.

(6)　'Get it right in the end'の考え方に合うものにはTを，合わないものにはFを記入しなさい，

ア　Learners will make errors even if they are given particular language points.

イ　Giving students the correct answer from the beginning is the best way to acquire the language.

ウ　Teachers should teach focusing on the language itself.

エ　The best moment to draw students' attention to their errors is when they want to say something as clearly and correctly as possible.

オ　Learners should be engaged in meaningful language use at the very end of their exposure to the second language.

(☆☆☆○○○○○)

【8】次の英文を読み，あとの(1)～(6)の各問いに答えなさい。

Japan's welfare rolls rose to a record high in July, (　①　) the need for the government to devise a cash assistance program that can effectively move people from welfare to work.

The number of people seeking welfare benefits hit 2.05 million that month, (　②　) levels seen in the aftermath of World War Ⅱ, according to the Health, Labor and Welfare Ministry. Especially noteworthy was an increase in welfare recipients who belonged to the working population who could have earned their livelihoods if they had jobs.

Launched in 1950, the welfare program is designed to ensure minimum livelihood for people in poverty. The recipients exceeded 2.04 million in fiscal 1951, but the rolls shrank steadily as Japan grew economically. The figure dipped below 900,000 in fiscal 1995.

But the number of recipients began to rise again after that, and has been increasing at an annual pace of 150,000 to 200,000 since the global financial crisis (　③　) in 2008. The sharp rise reflects people's (　④　) reluctance to apply for welfare and increasing ease (　⑤　) which the applicants are put on the welfare rolls by the government. (　⑥　), the cash assistance program will cost the central and regional governments a combined ￥3.4 trillion this fiscal year, as measured by fiscal 2011 initial budget allocations, up sharply from ￥1.9 trillion in fiscal 2000.

Elderly households account (　⑦　) more than 40％ of all welfare recipients, showing that an aging population is a major reason for the expanding rolls. But what is more noteworthy is a sharp increase in recipient households that belong to other categories, excluding those headed by the injured, the physically handicapped and single mothers. This "other category" household accounted (⑦   ) 16.1% of all welfare households in fiscal 2010, up from 10.6% in fiscal 2008.

A fair number of these "other category" recipients could work if they had jobs. A new social security program was launched in October, in which those who cannot receive unemployment benefits are given job training while also receiving cash assistance. The government must ensure that the job training under this program is effective enough to quickly put trainees to work.

As many critics point out, a growing number of those capable of earning their livelihoods are joining the welfare rolls, and ⑧those already on welfare are reluctant to come off it. (⑨   ) light of these criticisms, the government must strictly implement the welfare program, providing both support and incentives to quickly move people from welfare to work.

The welfare program is run with taxpayer money. Cash assistance should be given only to those (⑩   ) need. (⑪   ), the program would lose its legitimacy. ⑫The government, for example, should require welfare recipients to report how they spend the money they receive, or limit the period when those deemed capable of working can receive cash handouts on condition that they also receive adequate job training and support. (⑬   ) about half of all welfare benefits are spent on health-care, some ways must be devised to develop cost consciousness among the recipients who need such care.

(THE NIKKEI WEEKLY, December 5, 2011の一部より)

(1)　本文の内容と一致するものとして最も適切なものを二つ選び記号で答えなさい。

　　ア　厚生労働省によると生活保護費の受給額が過去最高を記録した。

　　イ　国と地方の負担額は2000年度から2011年度の間で1兆5千億円増

加した。

ウ　生活保護受給者は1950年以降，年間15万～20万人規模で増加している。

エ　受給者増加の一因は傷病・障がい，母子などの世帯の増加である。

オ　医療補助の無駄を減らすには，患者のコスト意識を培う工夫も必要だ。

カ　10月から，失業給付を受けながら職業訓練を受ける新制度が始まった。

(2)　(　①　)～(　④　)に入る最も適切な単語を，次の語群から選び，適当な形に変えて答えなさい。

語群　[　recede　　exceed　　underscore　　erupt　]

(3)　(　⑤　)，(　⑦　)，(　⑨　)，(　⑩　)に入る最も適切な単語を答えなさい。

(4)　(　⑥　)，(　⑪　)に入る最も適切な単語又は語句を，次のア～エから選び，記号で答えなさい。

ア　On the whole　　イ　Otherwise　　ウ　On the other hand

エ　As a result

(5)　下線部⑧，⑫を日本語にしなさい。

(6)　(　⑬　)に入る最も適切な語句を，次のア～エから選び，記号で答えなさい。

ア　Given that　　イ　In order that　　ウ　By the time

エ　Except that

(☆☆☆◎◎◎)

解答・解説

【中学校】

【1】 Part1 (1) B (2) D (3) A Part2 (1) C (2) B
(3) A Part3 (1) D (2) B (3) C Part4 (1) C
(2) B (3) B

〈解説〉スクリプトが公表されていないので、一般的な注意を述べておく。
Part1は写真が出ているので、説明文が読まれ、適切なものを表してい
るものを選択する問題だと考えられる。Part2から4までは英文が読ま
れ、適切な答えを選択する内容と類推できる。2回読まれる場合は1回
目で数字や名詞などに注意して聞き、2回目で内容チェックをすれば
よい。1回しか読まれない場合には、最初から集中して聞く必要があ
るので、かなりの集中力が必要である。

【2】 (1) イ (2) ア (3) エ (4) イ (5) エ (6) ウ
(7) ア (8) イ (9) エ (10) ア (11) ウ (12) エ
(13) ア (14) イ (15) ウ (16) エ (17) ア
(18) ウ (19) イ (20) ウ

〈解説〉(1) frequentには「頻繁に通う」という動詞の意味がある。
(2) 空欄部分は「平和の回復」(元の姿に修復する)という意味で考え
ればよい。 (3) 空欄は「彼女の根気のゆえに」という意味で、直接
の原因を表している。 (4) 空欄は「3マイル以内の距離に」の意味
で考える。 (5) 空欄は「無駄である、益が無い」の意味である。
(6) 文章は「ここは約10年前に会った場所」といった意味で考える。
whereの前にthe placeが省略されている。 (7) 「政府は声明を出した」
の意味である。なお、issueは名詞で「問題」の意味もあるので注意す
ること。 (8) 「見積もる」の意味であり、that以下は形式主語の構文
である。 (9) neither A nor B で、「AでもBでもない」の意味である。
(10) 空欄は「その問題に関して」という意味であり、superiorは「上

司，上官」である。　　(11)　空欄は「さまざまな素材を編集する」という意味である。　　(12)　空欄は「義務の」という意味である。

(13)　空欄は「公共の役目，任務」の意味である。なお，be accustomed to …で「…に慣れている」という意味である。　　(14)　空欄は「泣きわめく子をなだめた」という意味である。　　(15)　空欄は「絵を描くことに没頭する」という意味になる。なお，in those daysは「当時は」という意味である。　　(16)　doubtは「…でないと思う」の意味であり，suspectは「…であると思う」の意味であることに注意する。

(17)　空欄は「持続する」という意味で，persistの形容詞形はpersistentである。　　(18)　空欄は「…に精通する」という意味である。

(19)　空欄は「言外の意味をことばにもたせる」という意味である。

(20)　空欄は「100万ドルの値を付けた」という意味である。

【3】(ア・イの順)　(1)　1・2　　(2)　3・5　　(3)　6・5　　(4)　2・1
(5)　5・1　　(6)　6・7　　(7)　5・7　　(8)　4・1　　(9)　3・8
(10)　2・9

〈解説〉それぞれの全文を以下に示す。　　(1)　Such an action is inconsistent with the spirit of autonomy.　　(2)　He immensely contributed to the development of chemistry.　　(3)　I think he was brought up in a scholarly atmosphere.　　(4)　These hotels compete with each other in catering to the comfort of their guests.　　(5)　The mere sight of a snake makes him shudder. (6)　The birth rate is apt to fall in advanced countries.　　(7)　His behavior toward me was above reproach.　　(8)　So heavy was the stone that we could not move it.　　(9)　There has been a notable improvement in his condition. (10)　His rude words were more than I could take.　なお，(8)は強調のために倒置が起きている構文であり，本来の語順は，The stone was so heavy …である。

【4】(1)　①　ウ　　②　ア　　③　エ　　④　イ　　⑤　ウ
(2)　機能が多すぎて，どのつまみを押せば何が動くのか分からず面倒

になった。　(3)　he could no longer live without his smartphone

(4)　手首にスマートフォンを巻けば，置き忘れや紛失は減るかもしれない。

〈解説〉(1)　①　空欄の部分は「多くの者が自ら好んでそんな風になっている」という意味になる。　②　空欄の部分は「多くの機能を詰め込んだ小さな道具」という意味になる。　③　第1段落2文目のI suspect以下のことを言った者が，下線部Bのようなことを言ったので，「からかった」のである。　④　空欄は「時代遅れ」という意味になる。　⑤　携帯電話の革命的な状況と懐中時計が腕時計に変わった状況とを比較している。　(2)　第1段落にあるa tiny以下がヒントになる。つまみと機能との関係が把握できなかったからである。　(3)　二重否定の構文に注意。文全体の意味は，「スマートフォンがなければもはや生活できない」という意味である。　(4)　このshouldには仮定法的な意味があることから「もし，…すれば」で考えればよい。

【5】(1)　①　カ　②　エ　③　ウ　④　イ　⑤　キ

(2)　state of cognitive arousal which provokes a decision to act　(3)　その動機の程度は，達成しようと望んでいる結果を，本人がどの程度重視しているかによる。　(4)　成功を促すものとして，内発的な動機が非常に重要である。

〈解説〉(1)　①　単語の意味を考えればカまたはキが考えられるが，which以下の記述(何かを達成するために人を突き動かす)からカが適切であることがわかる。　②　空欄前にあるa newからenhancementまでは「新たな肉体のイメージは自我の育成に役立つ」という意味なので，and以下は，これと並列すると考えればよい。　③　空欄以下では「外部と内部」が話題になっているので，「差異，区別」といった意味の単語が適切である。　④　空欄の前後で例をあげている。したがって，「試験の合格」，「将来の旅行」と並列するものを考えるとよい。　⑤　第4段落のa desire以下，つまり「自分自身を気持ちよくさせようとする欲求」と並列するものを考える。enjoyment … itselfを「それ自

身を楽しむこと」と捉えるとよいだろう。　(2)　後にあるa result以下がヒントで，「人が以前に設定した目標を達成するために，持続的に知的または肉体的な努力をした結果」を踏まえて考えるとよい。
(3)　下線部のhow以下は，全体として名詞節を構成し，depend onの目的語である。to achicvcは不定詞の名詞用法であることを踏まえて考えること。　(4)　第5段落のMostで始まる文が該当する。Even以下は例示である。

【6】(1)　①　ウ　　②　ア　　④　エ　　⑨　エ　　(2)　③　are invited into the office to see where and　　⑤　Here is something quite ironic that might surprise you　　(3)　audience　　(4)　イ　　(5)　アメリカ人は，大きな集まりであれ小さな集まりであれ，改まった場で話すよう求められると，口を閉ざしてしまうことがまだまだ多いというわけです。　　(6)　・若いうちに始めて，大人になっても続ける。・恐れずにはっきりと話す。　　・遠慮せずに率直に言う。

〈解説〉(1)　①　空欄は「言葉を発する前に」という意味である。
②　空欄は「日常生活や学校生活のさまざまな側面がある」という意味である。　④　become used to …は「…に慣れるようになる」という意味であり，直後にtheir opinionがあるので，expressingが適切である。
⑨　直後の部分は「次のバラク・オバマになるための」の意味であり，第1段落でオバマ氏などは演説の名手としてあげられている。したがって，ここでは演説を行う能力のことを指している。
(2)　③　文章はいわゆる「職場見学」のことであり，to see where and howの用法が思い浮かぶかどうかがポイントである。　⑤　後で，日常生活で恐ろしいものの中に，クモ，ヘビや高所と一緒に「公式な場所でのスピーチ」があげられていることを踏まえて考えるとよい。
(3)　第5段落の最後の部分，「演説の草稿と演説の違い」に注意すればよい。両者の大きな違いは，聴衆がいるか否かである。　(4)　ア，ウ，エは，いずれもそれらの前の部分に，overcome my shynessとは矛盾する表現があるので誤りである。　(5)　clam upは「黙りこくる」という

意味で，when called uponの部分は分子構文である。Whenの後にthey areを補えばよい。　(6)　後にあるStart以下をまとめればよい。

【7】(1)　(ア)　イントネーション　(イ)　事実　(ウ)　問答
(エ)　つなぎ言葉　(オ)　スピーチ　(2)　①　働き　②　発達の段階　③　判断力　④　尊重　⑤　国際協調
〈解説〉(1)「話すこと」のねらいの一つとして，「与えられた語句や文を繰り返すことができるだけでなく，自分の考えなどを話すことができることを重視」(学習指導要領解説)をあげており，そのため指導事項に「与えられたテーマについて簡単なスピーチをすること」を新たに加えた。以上を踏まえて，学習するとよい。　(2)　まず，外国語の教科目標ではコミュニケーションや言語だけでなく，文化に対する理解についても示されていることをおさえておきたい。したがって，教材の選定について，学習指導要領解説では「広い視野から国際理解を深め，国際協調の精神を養うのに役立つもの」「生徒の興味・関心を引き出し育てることのできる」もの等が示されている。

【8】①　観点別　②　外国語表現　③　外国語理解　④　総合
⑤　コミュニケーション　⑥　思考　⑦　判断　⑧　生涯学習
⑨　自律　⑩　主体
〈解説〉「CAN-DOリスト」とは学習の到達目標を「…することができる」という形で指標化し，英語を使って具体的に何ができるようになったのかを明確にするものである。その効果として，指導方法や評価方法の工夫・改善が容易になる，地域の実態や生徒の能力に応じて具体的な目標に設定し直すことにより，すべての子どもたちの英語力の水準向上に資する等があげられている。

【9】(1)　①　three point one four　②　one billion　③　three fourths
④　twenty-four times six is one hundred forty-four　(2)　・(Why) don't you play Tennis with me ?　・(Do) you want to play tennis with me ?

・(How) about playing tennis with me ?　　(3)　　・We went to Okinawa on a school trip this April.　　・People in Okinawa were very friendly and the beautiful nature welcomed us.　　・In contrast, Okinawa, as we learn, has a sad experience.　　・The trip taught me what the most important is.

・I learned that we should not only hope but also act for the future peace.

(4)　継続…(I) have studied English for two years.　　経験…(Our ALT, Mr. Clapton) has been to China many times.　完了…(My father and sister) have just finished cleaning the room.

〈解説〉(1)　③は4分の1が3つと考えれば分かりやすい。④について，timeは数式では「×」にあたり，名詞で「倍」の意味をもつ。

(2)　いわゆる「勧誘」や「提案」の表現である。1つ目のWhy don't you …? は，「なぜ…しないのか？(ぜひ，…すべきだ)」と考えればよい。　　(3)　簡単な表現だが，どこへ行ったのか，どんな場所なのか，それに基づいた自分の意見の表明が重要である。　　(4)　継続…「2年間英語を勉強している。」の意味である。具体的な行動ならば，He has been playing baseball for two hour.(彼は2時間野球をやっている)のように進行形になる。　経験…「我々が教わっているALTのクラプトンさんは，何回もカナダへ行ったことがある」の意味である。「～に行ったことがある」という経験を表すには，have been to … が一般的だが，He has gone to Kyoto many times.の場合には「彼は京都に何回も行ったことがある」の意味になる。　完了…「私の父親と姉(妹)は丁度部屋の掃除を終えたところです。」の意味である。部屋の掃除が完了したことと同時に，その結果，部屋がきれいになっていることにも言及しているのである。

【高等学校】

【 1 】part 1　(1)　C　　(2)　D　　Part 2　(1)　B　　(2)　A　　(3)　D　　Part 3　(1)　D　　(2)　B　　(3)　C

〈解説〉スクリプトが公表されていないので，一般的な注意を述べておく。part1は写真が出ているので，説明文が読まれ，適切な状況を表してい

るものを選択する問題と考えられる。part2〜3は，英文が読まれて，適切な答を選択する内容だと類推できる。2回読まれる場合は1回目で数字や名詞などに注意して聞き，2回目でチェックをすればよい。1回しか読まれない場合には，最初から集中して聞き，聞き逃さないようにする必要がある。かなりの集中力が必要である。

【2】(1) ③　(2) ①　(3) ①　(4) ④　(5) ③　(6) ①
(7) ③　(8) ④　(9) ②　(10) ①

〈解説〉(1) 空欄は「新車は目立って展示されるだろう」という意味である。　(2) 空欄は「食事を提供する多くのホテルがある」という意味である。　(3) 空欄は「もっとも一般的な死因」という意味である。(4) 空欄は「最近の調査によれば」という意味である。　(5) 空欄は「長期的には見合う，元が取れる」という意味である。　(6) 空欄は「彼の体重は増加した」という意味である。　(7) 空欄は「集中治療を受けている」という意味である。　(8) 空欄は「特定する」という意味である。　(9) 空欄は「回転させる」という意味である。命令文＋andの用法に注意すること。　(10) 空欄は「叙述的な位置」という意味で，She is kind.の場合は，kindの位置にあたる。

【3】(3番目・6番目の順) (1) ④・③　(2) ④・⑦　(3) ③・⑦
(4) ①・⑦　(5) ②・③

〈解説〉(1) 全文は(That) depends on how soon you want to arrive it. である。(2) 全文は(Could) you have left the office lights on all night? である。第5文型でonは補語のはたらきをしている。　(3) 全文は(I) could clear my schedule to do it toward(the end of the week.) である。　(4) 全文は(We will) need to order spare parts and that will take (two weeks.)である。
(5) you以下の部分は(you) can opt to make scheduled payments every month for(a period of 10 months beginning on July 15th.)である。

【4】(1) Gracefulness means "the economy of force" — that is, the greatest possible strength with the best possible weight.　(2) A bat has wings covered with skin, and a bat's body is covered with fur. But a bird's body is covered with feathers.　(3) Without veracity and sincerity, politeness is a farce and a show. "Propriety carried beyond right bounds," says Masamune Date, "becomes a lie."

〈解説〉(1) the economy of forceは，effective use of powerまたはefficient utilization of powerでもよい。that isはin other wordsでもよいだろう。また，the greatest以下は，putting out the maximum power under most desirable physical weightのように考えてもよい。　(2) and a bat'sのa bat'sはitsでもよい。　(3) Withoutからpolitenessまでは，ひとつにまとめてCourtesy without veracity and sincerityでもよい。また，isはmay be fallen intoとすることも可能である。"Propriety carried以下の部分は，"Excessive courtesy will become a lie," says Masamune Date.でも可能である。

【5】(1) エ　　(2) ②　エ　　④　オ　　⑥　ウ　　⑦　カ
⑧　ア　　(3) reject / no　　(4) the cost is a little steep for our budget
(5) コストが高いという問題点に対する解決策を示すことで，商談を実現可能にすること。

〈解説〉(1) DIALOGUE Ⅰの後にready to turn it down(却下を決めている)という記述があるので，これを踏まえて考える。　(2) ② 空欄の後の文にあるinstead of issuing a direct rejection(直接反対することをせずに)を踏まえて考える。　④ 空欄の一つ前の文がヒントである。If it isからstraight out?までは「もしうまく行かないのなら，なぜBはAに明確に言わないのか」という意味なので，何か理由があると考えればよい。　⑥ 空欄の前文で，if there is anything you need(もし何か必要なものがあれば)と言っている。　⑦ DIALOGUE ⅠとⅡの違いを考えればよい。前者に比べると後者は「より明確な」会話といえる。
⑧ カッコの直前の不定冠詞がanなので，意味がわからなくともア以

外該当しないことがわかる。　(3)　Firstで始まる段落で，Cが「再考します」と言う言葉で計画の却下を述べている。したがって，否定を表す単語が適切である。　(4)　DIALOGUE ⅡでBはWe would like to pass this time around.(今回は計画を回避したい)と言っている。また，Cはコストが高いことを述べている。したがって，「コスト高で予算がオーバーする」という主旨のことを記述すればよい。　(5)　下線部は「不可能を可能にする」の意味である。DIALOGUE ⅡでのAの発言covering part of the costがヒントになる。

【6】(1)　①　ウ　　②　オ　　③　エ　　④　イ　　⑤　ア
(2)　⑥　オ　⑦　ア　⑧　イ　⑨　ウ　⑩　エ
〈解説〉英語科で学習指導要領関連の問題が出題される場合，出典は英語版と日本語版の2通り考えられる。試験対策としては，まず日本語版で趣旨などをおさえ，その後英語科試験対策として英語版を学習するほうが適切と思われる。原典は日本語版であり，英訳版はあくまでも仮訳であること，学習指導要領の内容については，他に教職一般問題や面接で問われることが多いが，それらは日本語版を前提としているからである。今回は英語コミュニケーションⅠと英語表現Ⅰからの出題であったが，当然，今後は他の科目が問われる可能性があるので，丁寧に学習しておく必要がある。

【7】(1)　学習者がその言語に十分に触れて，学習する動機づけをもつ場合。　(2)　②　イ　③　エ　(3)　言語項目の中には，教えられなければならないものがあり，それらは極めて明示的に教える必要があるという点。　(4)　ア　(5)　ウ　(6)　ア　T　イ　F
ウ　F　エ　T　オ　F
〈解説〉(1)　第3段落にあるifからto learnまでがヒントになる。have adequate exposureで「十分に触れる」という意味である。　(2)　第3段落4文目でmeaning-focusedとform-focusedの教授法に触れている。②の直前にbothがあるので，両者の特徴に関しての記述だとわかる。なお，

③は前にlevelがあるので，エが適切である。　(3)　次文がヒントであり，「対立している点」とはin that 以下を指しているので，ここをまとめればよい。　(4)　空欄後で「例えば」と続いているため，後ろの部分の内容に合う選択肢を選べばよい。アは習得中の言語についての状況を述べているので適切とわかる。　(5)　第5段落のAs we以下で空欄の内容を説明している。また，「教員が生徒の気づきを適切な時期に指摘する」といった記述がある。　(6)　イ　第6段目で "in the end" と "from the beginning" の両方の指導法について述べているが，どちらがよいとは記述されていない。　ウ　第6段落目のwithout以下でfocusing以下を否定している。　オ　第6段落目のdraw以下で「学習者の注意を誤りに向け，語学的に重要な点に集中させる」と述べている。

【8】(1)　イ・オ　　(2)　①　underscoring　　②　exceeding
③　erupted　④　receding　　(3)　⑤　with　　⑦　for　　⑨　In
⑩　in　　(4)　⑥　エ　　⑪　イ　　(5)　⑧　既に生活保護を受けている人々が保護から抜けたがらない。　　⑫　例えば，政府は生活保護受給者に支出の明細を明らかにすることを求めたり，仕事があれば働ける受給者の受給期間を，就労支援を前提に区切るべきだ。
(6)　ア
〈解説〉(1)　ア　第2段落1文目ではThe number of people，つまり生活保護費の「受給者数」とある。　ウ　第3段落に「日本が経済的に発展するにつれて費用は減少した」と記述されているから。　エ　第5段落に「疾病，障がい，母子などの世帯を除いて」とある。　カ　「失業給付を受けながら」とあるが，第6段落のwhoからassistanceまでで「就労支援金を受けながら職業訓練を受ける」とある。　　(2)　①は「力説する」，②は「戦後で他を圧する」，③は「2008年に勃発した危機」，④は「社会保障を受けたがらない」といった意味になるように単語をあてはめればよい。　　(3)　⑤は「手段」を表す前置詞，⑦は「…の割合を占める」といった意味にする単語を入れる。⑨は「…に照らして」といった意味のイディオム，⑩は「必要な，困窮して」といった意味

で使われている。　(4)　空欄前後の文章を読んで考えること。⑥は前に政策が，後にコストに関する文があるので「As a result(結果として)」，⑪の前の文では「現金給付は真に必要な人に限られるべきだ」，後の文では「制度はその合法性を失うだろう」とあるので，「Otherwise(そうでなければ)」が適切である。　(5)　⑧　already on welfareは「既に受給を受けている」，come off …は「…から離れる」という意味で考える。　⑫　those deemed capable of workingは「働くことが可能だと思われる人々」，on condition that …は「…という条件で」という意味で考える。　(6)　前半は「社会保障給付の約半分が健康管理に費やされている」，後半は「何らかの方法が考案されるべきだ」という意味である。

●書籍内容の訂正等について

　弊社では教員採用試験対策シリーズ（参考書，過去問，全国まるごと過去問題集），公務員試験対策シリーズ，公立幼稚園・保育士試験対策シリーズ，会社別就職試験対策シリーズについて，正誤表をホームページ（https://www.kyodo-s.jp）に掲載いたします。内容に訂正等，疑問点がございましたら，まずホームページをご確認ください。もし，正誤表に掲載されていない訂正等，疑問点がございましたら，下記項目をご記入の上，以下の送付先までお送りいただくようお願いいたします。

> ① **書籍名，都道府県（学校）名，年度**
> 　（例：教員採用試験過去問シリーズ　小学校教諭 過去問　2025 年度版）
> ② **ページ数**（書籍に記載されているページ数をご記入ください。）
> ③ **訂正等，疑問点**（内容は具体的にご記入ください。）
> 　（例：問題文では"ア～オの中から選べ"とあるが，選択肢はエまでしかない）

〔ご注意〕

○ 電話での質問や相談等につきましては，受付けておりません。ご注意ください。

○ 正誤表の更新は適宜行います。

○ いただいた疑問点につきましては，当社編集制作部で検討の上，正誤表への反映を決定させていただきます（個別回答は，原則行いませんのであしからずご了承ください）。

●情報提供のお願い

　協同教育研究会では，これから教員採用試験を受験される方々に，より正確な問題を，より多くご提供できるよう情報の収集を行っております。つきましては，教員採用試験に関する次の項目の情報を，以下の送付先までお送りいただけますと幸いでございます。お送りいただきました方には謝礼を差し上げます。

(情報量があまりに少ない場合は，謝礼をご用意できかねる場合があります)。

◆あなたの受験された面接試験，論作文試験の実施方法や質問内容

◆教員採用試験の受験体験記

- -

送付先	○電子メール：edit@kyodo-s.jp
	○FAX：03-3233-1233（協同出版株式会社　編集制作部 行）
	○郵送：〒101-0054　東京都千代田区神田錦町 2-5
	協同出版株式会社　編集制作部 行
	○HP：https://kyodo-s.jp/provision（右記の QR コードからもアクセスできます）

　※謝礼をお送りする関係から，いずれの方法でお送りいただく際にも，「お名前」「ご住所」は，必ず明記いただきますよう，よろしくお願い申し上げます。

教員採用試験「過去問」シリーズ

鳥取県の
英語科 過去問

編　集	ⒸＣ 協同教育研究会
発　行	令和5年12月10日
発行者	小貫　輝雄
発行所	協同出版株式会社
	〒101-0054　東京都千代田区神田錦町2‐5
	電話　03－3295－1341
	振替　東京00190－4－94061
印刷所	協同出版・ＰＯＤ工場

落丁・乱丁はお取り替えいたします。

2024年夏に向けて
―教員を目指すあなたを全力サポート！―

●通信講座

志望自治体別の教材とプロによる
丁寧な添削指導で合格をサポート

詳細はこちら

●公開講座 (＊1)

48のオンデマンド講座のなかから、
不得意分野のみピンポイントで学習できる！
受講料は6000円〜　＊一部対面講義もあり

詳細はこちら

●全国模試 (＊1)

業界最多の **年5回** 実施！
定期的に学習到達度を測って
レベルアップを目指そう！

詳細はこちら

●自治体別対策模試 (＊1)

的中問題がよく出る！
本試験の出題傾向・形式に合わせた
試験で実力を試そう！

詳細はこちら

　上記の講座及び試験は，すべて右記のQRコードか
らお申し込みできます。また，講座及び試験の情報は，
随時，更新していきます。

＊1・・・ 2024年対策の公開講座、全国模試、自治体別対策模試の
　　　　情報は、2023年9月頃に公開予定です。

協同出版・協同教育研究会
https://kyodo-s.jp

お問い合わせは
通話料無料の
フリーダイヤル

0120 (13) 7300
いい み　なさんおうえん

受付時間：平日 (月〜金) 9時〜18時　まで